THOMAS CORNELL
AND THE
THE CORNELL STEAMBOAT COMPANY

THOMAS CORNELL
AND THE
CORNELL STEAMBOAT COMPANY

Stuart Murray

Introduction by Roger W. Mabie

Essays by William duBarry Thomas

PURPLE MOUNTAIN PRESS
Fleischmanns, New York

THOMAS CORNELL AND THE CORNELL STEAMBOAT COMPANY

First Edition 2001

Published by
PURPLE MOUNTAIN PRESS, LTD.
1060 Main Street, P.O. Box 309
Fleischmanns, New York 12430-0309
845-254-4062, 845-254-4476 (fax)
purple@catskill.net
http://www.catskill.net/purple

Copyright © 2001 by Purple Mountain Press, Ltd.
All rights reserved under International and Pan-American Copyright Conventions.
No part of this book may be reproduced or transmitted without permission
in writing from the publisher.

Library of Congress Control Number
2001 130239

ISBN 1-930098-15-4

Front cover:
Painting of the *Pohcahontas* by Antonio Jacobson, 1894,
oil on canvas, private collection, used by permission
(image reversed and slightly modified).

Back cover:
The Rob copyright © 1999 by L. F. Tantillo,
oil on canvas, private collection, used by permission.
www.lftantillo.com

Frontispiece and title page:
Tugs at the Cornell shops in 1946, near the end of the steam era for Hudson River towing (left-right):
John D. Schoonmaker, Stirling Tomkins, Perseverance, Cornell No. 21, Geo. W. Washburn, Bear, and
J. C. Hartt; the last three would never run again and soon would be scrapped.
(Hudson River Maritime Museum Collection)

Manufactured in the United States of America
5 4 3 2 1

For C. W. (Bill) Spangenberger

Contents

	Foreword	9
	Introduction: The Cornell Steamboat Company	11
Chapter One	Cornell's Last Boat	13
Chapter Two	Canals, Coal, and Steam	17
Chapter Three	Thomas Cornell's Rise to Power	28
Chapter Four	War, The *Mary Powell*, and S. D. Coykendall	38
Chapter Five	Railroads and Towboats	49
Chapter Six	The Last Passenger Boats	60
Chapter Seven	Tugboats	73
Chapter Eight	Coykendall's Reign Begins	83
Chapter Nine	Lord of Hudson River Towing	97
Chapter Ten	Loss and Transition	111
Chapter Eleven	Dissension in Cornell	127
Chapter Twelve	From Coal to Diesel	143
Chapter Thirteen	Last Act for the Coykendalls	156
Chapter Fourteen	Recovery and Close	171
	Chapter Notes	179
Appendix A	Technology Along the Rondout Creek	183
Appendix B	The Art of Towing on the Hudson	188
Appendix C	Instructions to Captains	190
Appendix D	*Geo. W. Washburn*, "King of the Hudson"	191
Appendix E	Fleet List	194
	Acknowledgements	216
	Selected Bibliography and Sources	217
	Index of Vessels and General Index	219

Foreword

EARLY in the twentieth century, the mighty Cornell Steamboat Company was at its peak and dominated Hudson River towing. Within two decades, however, the tides of change—natural and industrial and social—overwhelmed Cornell just when bitter conflict within the family that had built the company caused it to founder. Although its executives and trustees worked gallantly to rescue Cornell, and with considerable success, by 1964, Cornell as an operating company was gone forever.

By the end of the century, the Cornell Steamboat Company was only a distant memory to the cities and communities of the Hudson River, although Cornell's beautiful passenger vessels and hard-working tugboats used to be seen every day at the waterfronts. For generations, the company's boat whistles were heard and recognized from the northern canals to New York harbor, but the names of Thomas Cornell and S. D. Coykendall have been forgotten even in Kingston, New York, the city they helped to build in the mid-Hudson Valley.

What Cornell and Coykendall achieved with such brilliance is virtually unknown to the descendants of hundreds of men and women who worked for them, competed with them, envied them—and surely admired them. Since it is impossible to mention all the Cornell employees by name in these pages, those who are included here must stand for all.

It would be gratifying if this book helps renew interest in the Cornell Steamboat Company, and in the people and boats who made Cornell one of the finest and most enduring business enterprises America has ever known.

Stuart Murray
East Chatham, New York

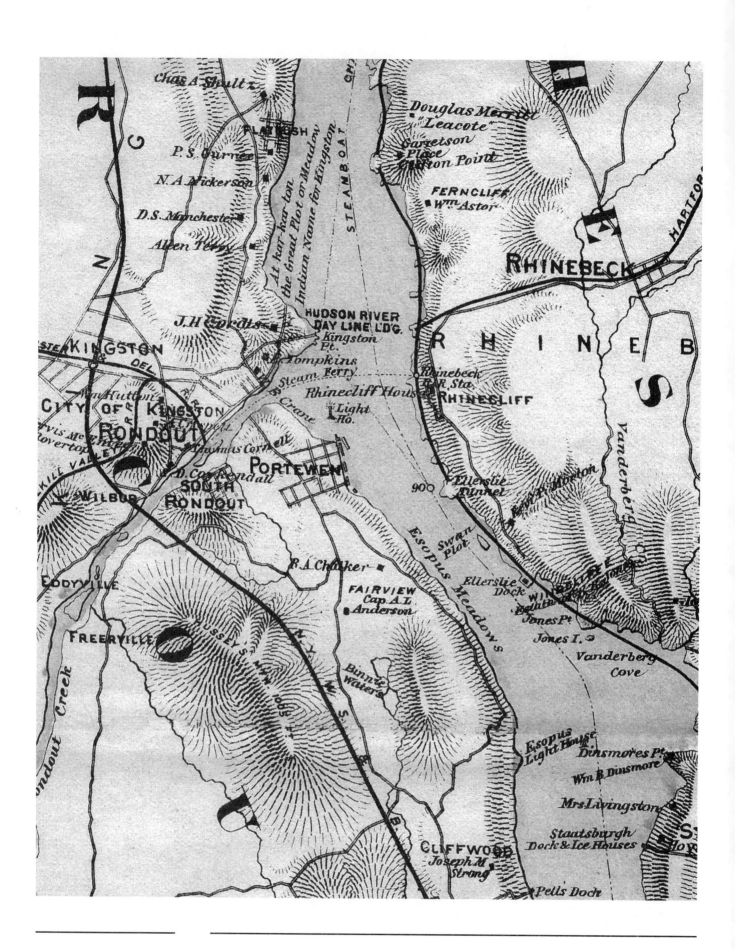

Introduction
The Cornell Steamboat Company
by Roger W. Mabie

DURING the nineteenth century, a combination of the forces of geography and economics were to make the mid-Hudson Village of Rondout (later to become part of the City of Kingston) the principal center of commercial activity between New York and Albany.

The geographic factor was a valley extending in a southwest direction from Rondout to the Delaware River at Port Jervis, through which a canal was built to bring anthracite coal from northeastern Pennsylvania to the Hudson River and a commercially attractive market. The economic factor was the exponential growth of the City of New York, at the Hudson's mouth, with its insatiable demand for the goods and services the areas bordering the Hudson could provide.

The canal, known as the Delaware and Hudson Canal, opened with the passage of the first vessel in late 1828. Less than a decade later, Thomas Cornell, age twenty-three and already the owner of a Hudson River sloop, arrived on the scene to mainly transport coal as his vessel's cargo.

By the mid-1800s, a million tons of coal annually was carried on the canal, and the surrounding region was booming. Cornell developed a strong entrepreneurial talent and now was the owner and operator of steamboats transporting freight and passengers to New York as well as operating a cross-river ferry service. By 1862, for service between Rondout and New York he had built a steamboat named *Thomas Cornell*, which was surpassed in size and appointments only by those operating from Albany.

Following the Civil War, there was great demand in the New York metropolitan area for coal from the D&H Canal, common brick from the brick yards lining the Hudson's shores, ice harvested from the river's surface north of Poughkeepsie during the preceding winter, Ulster County bluestone for sidewalks and curbing, Rosendale cement, grain from the Midwest via the Erie Canal, baled hay for the thousands of horses on the city streets, crushed stone, and agricultural products. All, except the agricultural products, which were shipped by steamboat, were moved because of their weight and bulk by barges and scows lashed together in tows pulled by steam towboats and tugs.

Towing on the Hudson River in the post-Civil War years was a highly competitive and lucrative business. Thomas Cornell and his new son-in-law, Samuel Decker Coykendall, pursued the opportunities with enterprise and vigor. The resulting Cornell Steamboat Company, in an era of unbridled free enterprise, emerged with a virtual monopoly of Hudson River towing, obtained generally by either buying out or driving out the competition. At its peak, the company owned more than sixty towing vessels and was the largest commercial organization of its kind in the nation.

The lively Hudson River port of Rondout was the terminus of the Delaware and Hudson Canal and the home of the Cornell Steamboat Company. The names of Thomas Cornell and his son-in-law S. D. Coykendall appear on this 1894 map from *The Hudson* by Wallace Bruce. The villages of Rondout and Kingston were united and incorporated as the City of Kingston on May 28, 1872.

In addition to his maritime activities, Thomas Cornell was a man of many and varied interests. He engaged in the building and operation of railroads on both sides of the Hudson, was a congressman elected to two separate terms, was a principal in the construction of one of the large Catskill Mountain hotels, and was a founding member and president of two banks in the Rondout section of Kingston—one a commercial and the other a savings bank.

The Cornell Steamboat Company had a long and colorful history. At its high point it was a dynamic force in the region's economy. Its decline and final demise was in large measure due to changing economic conditions beyond its control. Railroads made canals obsolete. Changing methods of construction virtually put an end to the demand for common brick. Almost overnight the electric refrigerator ended the demand for natural ice. Fast-curing Portland cement made Rosendale cement and Ulster County bluestone unnecessary. The Deeper Hudson project that permitted ocean-going ships to reach Albany was completed in 1930 and ended the towing of grain by barge.

All had been cargoes towed by Cornell in its heyday. At its end, since the company did not actively pursue the towing of petroleum products, almost its sole customer was New York Trap Rock Corporation, towing scows loaded with crushed stone for construction purposes.

On a personal note, when I was a boy growing up in Port Ewen in the late 1920s and early 1930s, the village was still pretty much a boatman's town. A majority of the male residents worked on the river boats or at the shipyards along Rondout Creek. It seemed almost all of the Cornell tugboats had at least one crew member who lived in Port Ewen and, when going up or down the river past the hamlet, the tug would blow a salute on its whistle. There was one series of whistle blasts that even became known as the "Port Ewen Salute."

At that point in time, almost all of the tugboats were steam powered and obviously had steam whistles. Steam whistles were all different and, sight-unseen, one could tell which tugboat it was by the sound of its whistle. Diesel horns, on the other hand, all seemed to sound alike. On a stormy night in early spring or late fall, when fog blanketed the river, somehow it was a comforting feeling to hear the tugs with a tow out in the river blowing their fog signals or "talking" to each other by their system of whistle signals while adding or taking barges to or from the tow.

Another sound that was peculiar to steam-powered vessels and is now history was what was known as "blowing off." When a tug would come into Rondout Creek for a day or two lay over—generally early on a Sunday morning— the engineer would, after docking, reduce the steam pressure on the boilers by opening the steam valves and "blowing off." The result was a thunderous roar that I am sure awoke every late sleeper within a two-mile radius of the Cornell shops.

The saga of Thomas Cornell and the company that bore his name is virtually forgotten today. It is fitting that a period of Hudson Valley history so colorful and important should be recorded and not left to fade away in the files of long-forgotten local newspapers. This book accomplishes that goal.

One night last week, the Francis Carter, a steam tug of Thomas Cornell's fleet, took fire at New York, and when all efforts to quench the flames failed, it was scuttled. The vessel is not a total loss, though it will cost $5,000 to rebuild it. It was fully insured. —*Kingston Argus*, 28 August 1861

Chapter One

Cornell's Last Boat

AS DUSK settled down over the Hudson River on a January evening in 1964, the towboat *Rockland County* of the Cornell Steamboat Company left the quarry at Clinton Point, pushing half a dozen barges loaded with crushed stone through floating ice that covered the river. The tide was ebbing, always the best time to leave for New York, seventy miles downstream, because the fall of the Hudson's powerful tide carried a boat faster on its way.

In the old days, the river would be frozen solid this time of year, but now it was seldom that ice could shut the river down, for a path was kept open by regular traffic. Large, ocean-going ships came and went, more than a match for the ice, and the powerful *Rockland County* slowly pushing its ten or twelve thousand tons of stone could hold its own on the winter river. Captain Clark Leiching was master of the towboat—a term applied to *Rockland County* though she was actually a "push-type" towboat, the first of its kind in the Northeast when built for the Cornell Company in 1960. Leiching had been with Cornell since he was a teenaged deckhand in the early 1930s, and he took pride in the large, white "C" with a red dot in the center fastened to the black smokestack of his boat. For more than a hundred years the Cornell name had been respected up and down the Hudson, and it still was, although everything had changed.

As night came on, the running lights of other vessels moved past, and lights of river communities sparkled in the distance. *Rockland County* pushed out into the main channel at four and a half miles an hour, its heavy-laden scows fastened together out in front of the boat. With the familiar feel of the river all around, and this fine towboat under his hand, Leiching could settle down at the steering lever in the pilot house and reflect on his long career as a Cornell captain.

Like his father before him, Leiching had worked most of his adult life for Cornell, starting out "boating," as the profession often was called, at the age of sixteen. He was a deckhand on the diesel-powered *Cornell No. 41* and worked his way up to earning licenses as a pilot and master. Most tugboat captains qualified in one of three main categories—for canals and the upper reaches of the Hudson, for the main length of the river, or for New York Har-

The new steamer now being built at Green Point [*sic*] by Major Thomas Cornell, of this village, will be launched at 10 o'clock A.M., on Tuesday of next week. We are requested by the Major to extend an invitation to all who may be pleased to be present on the occasion.
—*Rondout Courier*, 16 January 1863

The diesel-propelled push towboat, pioneered on the nation's western rivers by the Dravo Corporation—builder of the pictured *Rockland County*—promised to revolutionize the movement of barges on the Hudson. Compare the appearance of this third-generation towboat to those of her predecessors, the steam tugboat and, before that, the side-wheeler. Whatever *Rockland County* may have lacked in aesthetic appeal, she more than made up for that in efficiency and power. (C. W. Spangenberger Collection)

bor work. Leiching, however, was qualified in all three and could steer a boat in any inland waters, as well as two hundred miles out to sea.

Leiching knew the confines of the New York Barge Canal System of northern and western New York and was experienced in the fast-moving, changeable currents of the upper Hudson below Albany. He knew the deeper waters of the mid-Hudson Valley, where the ebb and flow of tidal streams could slow a tow of barges to a near standstill or could lift it downstream so fast that there was danger of running aground or colliding with another craft. During his younger days, Leiching had worked for a number of different towing companies, which gave him a broad range of experience, but he was always welcomed back with Cornell when he was ready for a higher position.

And he had learned secrets and skills by listening to the wisdom of long-time Hudson River boatmen like his father, who had been a Cornell chief engineer. Such knowledge had been handed down over more than three centuries of Hudson River maritime history. Accomplished boatmen had plied the Hudson River for the Cornell Steamboat Company since 1837. Generation

after generation of Hudson River families had "gone boating" for Cornell or were employed in the workshops and offices. Among them were the names Hornbeck, North, Benson, Gibbons, Tubby, Saulpaugh, Carroll, Brennan, Aliton, Parslow, Flynn, Hamilton, McCabe, Van Woert, Leiching, Mabie. . . .

In 1960, Leiching had been given charge of *Rockland County* soon after she came off the ways down in Wilmington, Delaware, built by Dravo Corporation of Pittsburgh. *Rockland County* was designed for the Hudson River, and she was not only the first push-type towboat ever to operate on the river, but she was the finest towboat on the Hudson since steam power first arrived in 1807. She might not look as impressive as the famous tugs, *Cornell* or *Perseverance*, or have the elegant lines of *Geo. W. Washburn*, but *Rockland County*'s two Kort-nozzle propellers were capable of 1,800 shaft horsepower, more than those venerable, long gone coal burners could have generated. And she could turn within her own 105-foot length—a dream to maneuver, whether in a churning, eddying river current or in a busy harbor.

Once *Rockland County* reached New York Harbor early in the morning, these stone barges would be taken by other tugs that would tow them to clients of the New York Trap Rock Corporation, the firm which now owned the Cornell Steamboat Company. In 1958, Trap Rock had bought Cornell, now a wholly owned subsidiary. Leiching and some other good boatmen and administrators had gone to Trap Rock then along with the Cornell name, but all the company's old tugboats, save one, had been sold off. They had been replaced by *Rockland County*.

Those tugs had been fairly old vessels, but still strong and able. Yet they could not match the power and maneuverability of push-type towboats that for years had been used on the Mississippi and Ohio Rivers but not on the Hudson. This kind of boat had been on drawing boards for Cornell in 1957, the year before Trap Rock announced it wanted to acquire Cornell. As Cornell's biggest customer by far, Trap Rock dictated the sale and the terms. If Cornell had refused to go along, then Trap Rock would have started its own towing organization and left Cornell to wither. Soon after the sale in March of 1958, Cornell contracted to build *Rockland County*, with contingency plans to build another two boats to serve customers in addition to hauling Trap Rock barges. It was thought in maritime circles that Trap Rock intended to build Cornell into a major towing operation once again.

Being a towing company with only one vessel was a long way from Cornell's once-dominant presence on the Hudson at the turn of the century, when its sixty-five tugboats controlled almost all the towing from Albany to New York. It had been inconceivable that there could ever come a time when only one boat remained in Cornell's fleet. *Rockland County*, too, had been inconceivable back then. She was so precisely maneuverable: instead of the traditional wheel in the pilot house, there were steering rods, designed so that their positions told the captain the exact angles of the boat's rudders—six rudders, not one or two. Her innovative slip-clutch kept *Rockland County*'s bow exactly where a helmsman wanted it to stay. The boat's living quarters were comfortable, and it had the finest navigational aids, ship-to-shore telephone, and powerful search lights.

David Relyea is tearing away at the hull of the old Mohegan, which lies on the south side of the creek, just above the ferry. We understand he has purchased her for 500 dollars, and by the time he gets the firewood and copper out of her we suppose he'll retire on an independent fortune. There is something about the breaking up of an old steamboat that leads one to thoughtfulness, and as we see the sturdy old vessel, a pioneer of our towing trade, now grown to such immense proportions, it moves us to think of the changes always taking place in animate and inanimate things, but inspires us with faith in the better future—for good as was the old Mohegan, better boats have followed her, and still better will follow them.
—*Kingston Daily Freeman*, 12 December 1874

From the pilot house, Leiching could completely control the engine speed. That had never been possible in the old tugboats, which required an engineer down below to run the engine controls in response to the commands of the captain. The *Rockland County* had the power of three old-fashioned tugs—and she could still tow from behind, if need be, such as when the waters were too rough. *Rockland County*'s sole purpose was to deliver stone barges, taking them back and forth between Trap Rock's three main Hudson River quarries and their delivery docks around New York Harbor. "Push-towing," as it was called, was the best way to do that, especially when working against the currents of the river and in heavy traffic. *Rockland County* could push more than twenty Trap Rock barges and was second to none of those splendid coal-fired steam tugs or diesels the Cornell Steamboat Company had sent with pride onto the Hudson every springtime, freshly painted and superbly maintained.

Clark Leiching's father had served on Cornell's legendary big tugs *Geo. W. Washburn* and *J. C. Hartt,* as well as on smaller boats. Three of Leiching's brothers had gone boating for Cornell, two of them diesel engineers, the third a pilot. When he was young, the family had lived at Port Ewen, just below the mouth of Rondout Creek, where Cornell had its base of operations over most of its 127 years of existence. Leiching would never forget hearing the familiar whistle of his father's boat coming in, or those occasions when he and his brothers went out on the river for trips with their father's boat.

Port Ewen had been a boatman's town since the mid-1800s, and although by 1964 there were not many active boatmen still there, there were memories, long and keen. Leiching had served on a few legendary Cornell tugs himself, had steered the helper tugs *R. G. Townsend* and *J. G. Rose,* and had been captain of the tugs, *Lion* and *Jumbo,* these last two among the first diesels on the Hudson. The other four early Cornell diesel tugs had been converted from coal-burning steamers.

For all the glory of those beloved old tugboats, they did not compare to *Rockland County,* which to Leiching was also a beautiful boat, something to be proud of as he steered her into New York Harbor. The trip had taken all night, and by mid-morning the barges had been transferred to other tugs or landed at a wharf. Leiching turned *Rockland County* in time to catch the flood tide that would get him home faster. First he picked up "light," or empty, scows or barges that were lashed together into a new tow. These would go back to Trap Rock's operations at Clinton Point or Tomkins Cove to be reloaded and again delivered down to New York Harbor.

Later on that winter's day, as Leiching brought *Rockland County* into Hudson River Shipyards in Newburgh, about thirty miles south of his home in Port Ewen, he made a routine phone call to headquarters at Trap Rock's office in Nyack. To his dismay, he was told *Rockland County* had just been sold to the Red Star Towing and Transportation Company. Leiching was to deliver the boat to them immediately. Trap Rock's directors wanted out of the towing business altogether, so Cornell was to be shut down for good.

It hit Leiching hard, but he dutifully steered *Rockland County* toward the Red Star dock, realizing this had been his last trip with the Cornell Steamboat Company, which was out of business after 127 years on the Hudson River.

We understand that a number of ship carpenters in the employ of Morgan Everson, at Sleightburgh [sic], on Monday, struck for higher wages. They were getting $2.50 a day, and demanded $3. —*Rondout Courier*, 3 March 1865

Chapter Two
Canals, Coal, and Steam

IT was coal that started it all, Pennsylvania anthracite mined near the upper Delaware River and shipped by canal boats 108 miles along the narrow Delaware and Hudson Canal to tidewater at Eddyville, three miles upstream from the mouth of Rondout Creek. From there it went by the Hudson River to the growing cities north, south, and east. Coal made the first fortune of young Thomas Cornell, founder of the Cornell Steamboat Company—coal and the appetites of the canal workers who in 1828 built the D&H. Their every need had to be shipped in by water and bought in general stores at the docks near the canal's first lock and the canal basin.

In 1822, Cornell's uncle and namesake, Thomas W. Cornell, had come to New Salem, a hamlet across and up the Rondout Creek from what a few years later would become the community of Rondout. There Thomas W. opened a general store that soon profited from the building of the D&H Canal. Patrons could buy everything there, from dry goods, glassware, crockery, and hardware to the staples of a working man's diet—pork, fish, and flour. In 1828, Thomas W. bought land close to the first lock of the canal, which had just been completed. He would later enter into the cement business as well as merchandising and freighting on the river and canal. Thomas W. Cornell's brother, Peter, arrived a few years later and bought a dock on the Creek near Eddyville, soon becoming a partner in a thriving emporium there. Peter's son, Thomas, arrived around 1837, bought a sloop, and entered the freighting business with his base at Rondout Creek.

The younger Thomas Cornell was twenty-three and in the right place at the right time for his ambitions and abilities. He learned much from his father's store, Cornell and Gedney, which provided individuals and companies with food, clothing, equipment, ship supplies and gear, and building materials. Patrons could even book passage on freight steamers heading down to New York City or up to Albany, for Cornell and Gedney were agents for the steamboat *Frank,* one of several plying between increasingly busy Rondout Creek and the outside world. Farmers, stockmen, lumbermen, tanners, quarrymen, distillers, and brickmakers all sent their goods and produce to market on steamboats whose owners used Cornell and Gedney as agents.

The steamer Manhattan that at one time belonged to Major Cornell, and which ran between this place and New York for a number of seasons was burned at the levee in New Orleans on the 13th ult. —*Rondout Courier,* 2 June 1865

Young Thomas Cornell's first river freight cargo was coal that had been transported by canal boat down the D&H, off-loaded onto a pile, then loaded by hand into his vessel's hold. Sloops always had been the most common cargo-carriers on the Hudson River, but steamboats were overtaking them in importance. That same year of 1837 was disastrous for American business because of a widespread financial panic, and commerce in the canal dropped briefly to just over 76,000 tons of freight, compared to more than 110,000 tons in 1833.

Economic uncertainty was pervasive that year, yet that was when the first lighthouse was built at the mouth of Rondout Creek to guide vessels in and out past a hazardous sandbar. A true sign of growth and prosperity for the bustling communities appearing along the Creek, the lighthouse marked the busiest harbor on the Hudson between New York and Albany, 145 miles apart. The Cornells made the most of the opportunities Rondout Creek offered.

Thomas Cornell, founder of the company that was to bear his name, was a nineteenth-century "man for all seasons," having been a sloop owner at age twenty-three, the owner and operator of steamboats, builder of short-line railroads, head of the largest marine towing company in the country, a major in the New York militia, a U.S. congressman, and founder and president of two banks. (J. Matthews Collection)

Born on January 23, 1814, Thomas Cornell was a native of White Plains, an inland village in Westchester County, about seventy miles to the south of the Creek. As a youth he had gone to New York City to work in the family business. The Cornell family came from old New England stock that had arrived from England before the Revolution. The branch of the family that led down to Peter and his son Thomas had migrated westward from the seacoast and into the Hudson Valley, continuing a tradition of steady entrepreneurial success. Peter Cornell taught his sons well. Another was Joseph, by Peter's second wife; like his half-brother Thomas, he was also intensely interested in boats and shipping. Joseph would, himself, enter the business, and with some success. Of course, the boats of the future were those driven by steam, which had fully come into their own in the thirty years since Robert Fulton's *North River Steam Boat* paddled her way up and down the Hudson (also then known as the North River).

Ambitious and ruthless adventurers such as Cornelius Vanderbilt and Daniel Drew were battling for control of steamboat business on the Hudson, for there was no faster way to travel on the river, and no more efficient way to ship most freight. The Erie Canal had opened in 1825, leading from the Hudson River above Albany westward across the state and linking the richly productive West with the burgeoning East. Daily in 1837, the Hudson River had several sidewheel passenger steamboats passing north and south, one grander than the other. They became ever faster, more opulent, and more comfortable. The steamboat usually had its forward deck and midships laden with freight, while the passengers had the run of the stern quarter and the upper decks.

Lesser steamboats that were not able to compete in speed often made a profit by towing loaded barges that were lashed firmly alongside. There were also "safety barges," which carried passengers as well as all sorts of freight, and early on they had a brief run of popularity. "Safety barges" promised to be quieter and safer than traveling as a passenger on a steamboat whose boiler might at any moment explode—which did happen infrequently—with injury to crew and passengers and sometimes with loss of life. These barges were secured to the stern of the steamboat by timbers joined like the legs of a compass and fastened to the bow of the barge.

Towing by steamboats was a coming business, and even those proud little Hudson River sailing sloops, the traditional workhorses and once-dominant vessels on the Hudson, were often towed to their destinations by steamboats. Steamboats could run later in the year than sailing vessels, and also began earlier, as they broke up river ice in a way sloops and wind-power could not do. It was apparent to men like young Thomas Cornell that with the growth of commerce on the river there was good profit to be made from a steamboat that advertised itself as a towboat as well as carrying freight and passengers.

The first steamboat to enter Rondout Creek was said to have been a towboat: in 1826, the steamer *New London* had brought the hull of an unfinished boat into the Creek for one of several boatyards being established there. Soon, canal boats were built by the hundreds in Rondout Creek to carry the coal, with at least 1,700 boatloads coming down from the Delaware in 1830. The canal boats, most about thirty tons burden at the start, were drawn by a team of horses or mules walking along the towpath. When a canal boat exited the lock at Eddyville, it was generally hauled down the Creek by a small side-wheel towboat, such as the canal company's own *Rondout*, about seventy-one feet long. The coal was unloaded near the base of the canal company's operations at the settlement of the same name as the towboat.

Established as a company town during the years of canal construction between 1825-28, Rondout stood on the north shore of the Creek and was from the start a booming, rowdy place, with more establishments selling liquor than anything else. Hardened workmen, cocky sailors, travelers, gamblers, and country laborers from farm and lumber camp crowded the muddy, narrow streets of Rondout looking to spend money or to win it gambling during their brief hours of leisure. Those hours were often determined by the sailing times of boats to and from New York or Albany. Some folk made their way up the steep hill to visit the more sedate old town of Kingston, as conservative and god-fearing as Rondout was sin-ridden and unruly.

In their emporiums a little way up Rondout Creek, the Cornells prospered at the end of the 1830s from the growth of population and industry, and by 1839, when Peter Cornell left to return downriver, son Thomas established a new partnership with Jacob B. Bidwell. Soon Cornell, Bidwell and Company did a thriving business as agents for the steamboats *General Jackson* and *Victory*, and the market barge *Saratoga*, a former passenger boat that had succumbed to age and no longer ran under her own power. *Saratoga* was towed by *Victory*. Bidwell was the company's agent at the New York City end of the line, and Thomas Cornell handled business at Rondout Creek. They also leased canal boats, whether to carry coal, other freight, or passengers back and forth. Coal, however, was by far the most important cargo on the D&H Canal, with more than 122,000 tons coming down to tidewater on the Hudson in 1839.

Few harbors of this size anywhere in America could boast of as much business as little Rondout Creek, where hundreds of schooners, sloops, and brigs arrived each year to load up on coal and sail away with it as far as the New England coast. By 1840, there were about 1,500 residents in the Rondout area and 2,500 living up the hill in Kingston. Both communities profited from the commerce passing through the port in Rondout Creek.

In 1839, bulk tonnage of freight other than coal was broken down as follows: cement, 14,760; general merchandise, 7,418; stones, hoop-poles, and lath, 1,313. Bulk shipments totaled 29,674 tons, and also included plaster, tanners' bark, leather, mill stones, glass and glassware, charcoal, lead, and stoneware. There were wood products, too, such as shingles, ship timbers, and construction lumber, most of it sent to New York City, the great marketplace and engine of growth that was thriving from the commerce of canals such as the Erie and the Delaware and Hudson.

Cornell and Bidwell, as the firm renamed itself by 1840, prospered as the "steam freighting line" agent for two of the leading steamboat companies serving Rondout Creek: the New York and Kingston Line with its steamer

General Jackson and the Steam Forwarding and Freight Line, which had the steamer *Victory* and the market barge *Saratoga*. Cornell and Bidwell also offered the services of canal boats as well as two sloops that ran between Rondout and New York. The river and canal became ever busier, the demand for coal soaring, as did Cornell and Bidwell's commissions as agent for the steamboat lines.

That same year, the now-successful Thomas Cornell married Catherine Ann Woodmansee of nearby Rosendale. Catherine was the daughter of Cornell's stepmother, Mary Catherine (Snyder) Woodmansee. Their first child, daughter Mary Augusta, was born in June 1842, but two sons would die in infancy in the next few years. Their fourth and last child would be daughter Cornelia Lucy, born in July 1854.

Competition between steamboat companies was constant and bitter. Those boats that depended upon speed to attract business competed ruthlessly, racing each other from port to port, often disregarding safety and endangering passengers and boat. Boilers burst, boats struck rocks or ran aground in bad weather when they should by rights have been left at the pier; vessels sideswiped each other in the race for entry to a landing and the passengers waiting there. More than one steamboat accident was the result of pouring on the speed in an effort to beat a competing boat in close quarters.

At times, price wars cut fares to almost nothing, but on the other end of the spectrum, passengers found themselves at risk when, instead of the steamboat stopping at a wharf to let them off, they were required to go ashore in a small boat which was connected by a line to the moving steamboat. The passing steamboat played out enough line to give disembarking passengers a moment or two to get out of the boat and onto the dock, while at the same time boarding passengers were trying to get into the small boat. All the while, baggage was being tossed up and down, from boat to wharf and vice versa. This dangerous practice was eventually prohibited by law, but steamboat travel could be as perilous as it was both efficient and enjoyable at its best on the lovely, scenic Hudson.

In 1845, one of the fastest passenger steamboats on the river was *Swallow*, built in 1836 and a regular participant in races from New York to a point south of Albany, 142 miles apart. *Swallow*'s engineer was ordered by his captain to stoke up the boiler and build up a head of steam that made the boat shudder and shake as it plowed through the waters. Nearby, moving just as fast at almost twenty miles per hour, the opposition boat, *Rochester*, would be neck-and-neck with *Swallow*. Up ahead, the Hudson narrowed, and the first boat through would take the lead for good, because passing safely was impossible in the waters just south of Albany. Sometimes *Swallow* won, sometimes the competition, and the newspapers, company employees, and passengers broadcast word of the race far and wide.

It was well known there was danger in traveling on steamboats, so to make the journey safer and more comfortable for the passengers, the companies built "safety barges" to be towed behind the vessels. "Steam towboats,"

Morgan Everson is to build an ice barge for Major Cornell, which will be 120 feet keel, 32 feet beam, and 10 feet depth of hold--after the model of the barge Wm. A. Ballantine, recently built by him. Mr. Everson has the reputation of being one of the best builders about. —*Rondout Courier*, 23 October 1868]

In a line engraving published in *Appleton's Journal* in 1869, artist Alfred R. Waud offers a dramatic, if somewhat fanciful, impression of mid-nineteenth-century river traffic in the Hudson Highlands—the glory days of steamboats and sail. The steamer *Dean Richmond* is running "hooked up" in the midst of a grand assemblage of sloops, schooners, towboats, canal boats and barges. Waud's imagination notwithstanding, river towing in those days is accurately portrayed in the two towboats on the right half of this image. (William duBarry Thomas Collection)

the barges were also called, though they had no propulsion, and their passenger cabins and lounges were elegantly appointed, with delicious cuisine served at individual tables far from the racket or perils of the steamboat's machinery. Of course a steamboat towing a safety barge or market barge was not in business to race. Profits for them came from slow but steady and stately progress on the crowded river—still far faster than traveling overland on bad roads in these days before railroads.

More secure the safety barges might be for passengers, but the thrill of a spontaneous race often was appealing, and many of the 350 passengers who boarded *Swallow* at Albany early in the evening of April 7, 1845, were prepared for the exhilaration of the impending race against time all the way to New York City. Even a "night boat" like *Swallow,* which ran through darkness, was expected trip after trip to try to make its best time.

Thirty miles below Albany, in the western channel just off Athens, the pilot in charge accidentally went off course, and in the darkness *Swallow* struck a rock at full speed. The vessel broke in two, its stern sinking in deep water as passengers and crew struggled to save themselves. Then *Swallow* caught fire, and scores of screaming people leaped into the water and drowned. Steamboats and small boats appeared out of the night to do what they could to help. Among the rescuers was the competitor, *Rochester*. More

than 200 were saved this way, and others swam to land, where local people had lit bonfires to illuminate the river banks. Church bells rang up and down the shore, calling out for more help, but by the time it was over, more than forty had died. This was one of the worst disasters in Hudson River maritime history.

The racing continued, however, although there were hazards aplenty to damage or sink a boat, and even to destroy the careers of otherwise successful steamboat owners. One of these was David P. Mapes, owner of the sidewheeler *General Jackson,* which held the lucrative contract to haul barges for the D&H Canal Company. Many a businessman coveted that contract, including the ambitious Daniel Drew, who was watching for the main chance to get it. Mapes was a tough competitor, intelligent and effective as a man of all trades and business interests.

A native of Coxsackie, on the Hudson's west shore thirty miles north of Rondout, Mapes was in his late thirties when he entered the steamboat business. He intended to continue his run of success as a lumberman, whisky distiller, and farmer. He had been a state assemblyman and also postmaster, and he soon opened a grocery store in Rondout, where he became a civic leader.

The Rondout Freeman says that Michael Mooney, first pilot of the boat S. E. Brown, was drowned on Monday evening. He had been drinking quite freely with some companions and was partially intoxicated. —*Newburgh Daily Journal*, 9 July 1870

In 1838, Mapes invested much of his funds in *General Jackson*, joining the fray for passenger and freight competition between Rondout and New York. He also set out to establish a connecting stage line in the mountains beyond Kingston. Using his considerable political connections, he arranged for a mail route to be opened on his stage line, which was advertised as coming and going at Rondout in time for through travelers to catch his steamboat.

After 1839, Thomas Cornell's agency represented the industrious Mapes, who had struck a deal with the D&H Canal to have him manage its steamboat, *Victory*, at the same time contracting with him to tow the company's coal barges to market. Mapes was the shining example of the Hudson River entrepreneur, and on his way to a fortune as a merchant prince. Though he was financially overextended, his prospects were great, and by 1842 he confidently renamed his New York and Kingston Line, calling it the D. P. Mapes Steam Freight and Passage Line. Mapes even took charge of funding and building a Baptist Church in Rondout, to which businessman Thomas Cornell took his own young family.

One of the more noteworthy initiatives undertaken by Mapes during this time was to arrange for the sidewheeler *Norwich* to join his fleet on the Rondout-New York runs. *Norwich* had been built in 1836 for service on Long Island Sound, and her owners brought her into the Hudson River just before Mapes arranged with them—either by charter or some other financial terms—to have her run in tandem with *Victory*, one going down while the other was coming back. Unlike *Norwich*, *Victory* carried no passengers, only freight, and also towed barges, which *Norwich* did not. This relationship soon dissolved, and by the next year, 1843, Mapes was concentrating on his profitable towing business with only the *Victory*, while *Norwich* continued operating under other ownership as a passenger boat. Then *Norwich* was purchased by a former Rondout blacksmith named William B. Dodge, who, like Mapes, was determined to broaden his horizons. Dodge named himself captain of the vessel, which did not necessarily mean he knew how to handle her, but that he was in charge and would be responsible for getting his customers a good price for their freight when he brought it to New York. Cornell and Bidwell became *Norwich* agents at the New York end of the line.

When it came to public admiration and appreciation of steamboats, *Norwich* fully earned it by her unique ability to battle river ice, even to break up packed ice that no other steamboat could break through. She was known as one of the most "staunch and powerful boats," nicknamed the "Ice King" because she was so effective. The method employed by her captain was to run her bow up on the ice as far as possible and let the weight of the vessel break through. Then *Norwich* would back up half a mile and charge forward to repeat the sally, breaking up another few dozen yards of ice.

It meant much to the people of the river and Rondout Creek to have *Norwich* do this work, for it was a melancholy moment every winter when the last boat sailed away and the community was effectively shut off from the outside world for months. *Norwich* was generally the last boat to depart, fighting ice as she went and carrying a heavy and extremely profitable final load bound for the New York market. In the early spring, as folk watched for the first plumes of black smoke to appear downriver, it was inevitably *Norwich* that arrived first. To read the newspaper announcements of "Steamboat in Sight!" was as joyous and exciting a moment for Rondout and Kingston as the last boat out was a sad one.

The association of David Mapes with *Norwich* was brief, but it came at the height—and the end—of his New York State career.

Mapes and his Rondout associates, such as Cornell and Dodge, weathered a virtual blockade of their port in 1843 when false reports of yellow fever forced the place to be quarantined. The port shut down for months. Yet progress continued, as the canal was deepened, permitting much larger boats to pass through and further increasing the volume of coal, which in 1842 had been more than 200,000 tons. Until now, Mapes had been successful as no other single individual had been operating out of Rondout Creek, but his luck ran out in late spring of 1844, when his steamboat *Victory* unexpectedly began to leak heavily while on a return trip from New York.

No one knew what had caused the leak—whether the boat had struck a fisherman's set pole in the water or there had been an unreported collision in the harbor while Mapes was ashore—but there was no way to save her. *Victory* sank in shallow water during an attempt to run her aground to prevent a total loss. She was eventually raised, but was too badly damaged to be repaired. Mapes tried to charter another boat for the D&H Canal coal-hauling contract, but the only vessel available on short notice was owned by Daniel Drew, who set a price too high for Mapes to meet it. Instead, Drew took over the contract himself. Mapes was unable to continue the lucrative towing business that had brought in the cash to finance his far-flung business enterprises. Defeated, he ran away from his debts and obligations, absconding, heading west.

Watching from close by, young Thomas Cornell was learning from the likes of Mapes and Drew, and he could see how the towing business was a means of acquiring quick cash that could be used to finance other ventures or to leverage loans. As Mapes slipped away, bankrupt, owing so many creditors that the sheriff was close behind him, Cornell positioned himself to take over the opportunities Mapes had missed.

Daniel Drew handled the D&H Canal towing Mapes had lost, but Drew's heart was more in great passenger boats that plied the river day and night. Thomas Cornell, however, was interested in the towing business.

By 1847, Cornell had become part owner of the steamer *Telegraph*, with a dock at nearby Eddyville, the entrance to the Delaware and Hudson Canal. Cornell now was in partnership with his uncle, Thomas W. Cornell, eleven years older than his nephew and owner of an Eddyville dock. Their firm was named Thomas W. Cornell and Company. The other partners in ownership of *Telegraph* were local men, Asa Easton, H. E. Barber, and Henry Wilbur.

Telegraph, built in 1836, had been operating on the lower Hudson. She was purchased by the Cornells and their partners to run three times a week to New York and back. The main competition was Captain Dodge's *Norwich* and another steamer, *Mohegan*, which were operating at considerable profit on the

The Kingston Gazette says [quite erroneously] that Thomas Cornell has in course of construction a new and very large steamboat to have two tiers of staterooms.
—*Newburgh Daily Journal,*
12 July 1870

route between Rondout Creek and New York. There was also a night boat, *Santa Claus,* owned by E. Fitch and Company, of Wilbur, a community farther up Rondout Creek. Also, the steamboat *Emerald* was running twice a week to New York from the Creek. Soon, *Santa Claus* was taken off the Rondout run and transferred to the New York-Albany route as a night boat.

Competition remained stiff, with at least five steamboats operating out of Rondout Creek; by summertime, *Telegraph* was put on a run from Newburgh to Albany and Troy, stopping at Rondout on the way. A year later, in 1848, competition became even worse, as Anderson, Romer and Company's Barge and Steamboat Line was established by experienced boatmen who had solid ties to finance and business in the Village of Kingston.

Still, Thomas W. Cornell and Company forged ahead. When Captain Dodge decided he wanted out of the passenger business, he sold *Norwich* to them. The Cornells hired Captain J. Steward Barber to be master of *Norwich*, which sailed to New York from Rondout at 7:00 P.M. Her first trip for the new line of Thomas W. Cornell and Company was on August 28, 1848. By now, *Norwich* was considered quite elderly as steamers went, but she had been well maintained, and her remarkable ability to buck the ice made her a valuable possession, especially on those trips early or late in the year, when cargoes were heavy and rates were high.

Little Rondout was steadily growing, with its original Hudson Valley Dutch residents outnumbered by the arrival of Irish and German immigrants who had landed at New York for the most part and were looking for work on the canals or in the quarries, cement works, mines, lumber mills, and factories developing in the Rondout-Kingston region. Brick yards were springing up along the Hudson River's shores, and the newfound ice industry was employing hundreds of men through the wintertime. Ice was cut and stored in the winter for shipment by boat to metropolitan areas in the warm months.

In 1848, three local militia companies were combined and officially designated the 20th New York Militia, nicknamed "The Ulster Guard." All three companies had been founded largely by the efforts of Rondout businessman George F. von Beck, an emigré from Germany who had arrived in Ulster County in 1834 and through enterprise and good fortune became a wealthy man. Von Beck was a leading landowner on both sides of Rondout Creek, and he was proud of his status as a captain and founder of the militia companies, which were supported by prominent figures such as Thomas Cornell, who would become an honorary major.

In 1850, to gain a slice of the business of shipping raw materials and carrying passengers up and down the Hudson, Thomas Cornell and partner David Abbey Jr. bought the sidewheel steamer *James Madison,* which had been built to run from Newburgh to New York. Abbey was *James Madison's* captain, and the boat became an excursion steamer around New York, making trips to the new amusement park at Coney Island, and later operating on the Hudson River. Competition on the river would be too much, however, as the passenger steamboats were being built more palatially than ever. *James*

> Tug boat excursions, while those busy little craft are engaged in towing vessels, are very popular with many young ladies of the eastern district of the city—and the tug boat captains as well.
> —*Kingston Daily Freeman,* 6 August 1872

Madison was to become a towing steamer for the Cornell Line, and would serve profitably—and in one case as a lifesaver for scores of people.

As Thomas Cornell had hoped, his ambitions would be financed by the profitable river freight and passenger business. He had seen David Mapes come and go, and with the steady, deliberate hand of his uncle Thomas W. to assist him, Cornell forged ahead in the risky arena of steamboating. He had other ideas, too, for he saw that the Hudson River Railroad was being built and coming ever closer. That year the railroad, laying track from New York, reached New Hamburg, ten miles south of Poughkeepsie. Already, an enterprising steamboat owner was running into Rondout Creek and offering passengers and shippers connections with landings near the new railroad.

It was apparent that railroads, not steamboats, would be the key to travel and shipping in the future. Just how distant, or how near, was that future? An enterprising businessman like Thomas Cornell, strategically positioned as he was at the outlet of the booming Delaware and Hudson Canal, would never let that future pass him by, no matter how profitable steamboats might be at present.

Chapter Three
Thomas Cornell's Rise to Power

RONDOUT was incorporated as a village in 1849, proof it was here to stay. The Delaware and Hudson Canal was deepened in 1850 to accommodate canal boats of 136 tons, and the towing business picked up even more. Now there was no need to laboriously transfer the coal from these boats, which instead were lashed to the sides of a steamboat and towed directly from the canal to their destinations. The D&H Canal was carrying more than a million tons of coal a year, and during this same time the Erie Railroad built a terminal at Newburgh, where coal was also brought to be transferred to barges and towed downriver.

During this year, William Dodge lost the lucrative contract for D&H Canal Company towing to Thomas Cornell. Dodge conceded defeat by selling Cornell the steamboat *Mohegan*, used nowadays mostly for towing. In 1851, Thomas W. Cornell withdrew from the business, as had his brother Peter before him. Thomas W. retired, and moved back downriver. The business was now all Thomas's, who was among the most prominent citizens of Rondout and Kingston and referred to himself as "Major," the honorary rank in the militia regiment. Good and bad economies had come and gone, the false fear of yellow fever back in 1843, and the very real cholera outbreak that struck Rondout in 1849. Boatmen came and went, businesses boomed and went bust, and Cornell had one especially solid opponent: Anderson, Romer and Company. The competitors came to terms, however, and while Cornell's nightboat *Norwich* ran south to New York on Monday, Wednesday, and Friday, returning on the alternate days, the other company operated its popular sidewheel steamer *Highlander* on the same route on Tuesday, Thursday, and Saturday.

That truce did not last long. As Thomas Cornell saw new prospects for expansion and kept an eye on railroad development, he found that Anderson, Romer and Company were no longer interested in their cozy relationship of sharing the New York to Rondout route. Anderson, Romer and Company had arranged to bring a running mate to *Highlander* into service—the handsome *North America*, one of the first large steamboats to burn coal exclusively instead of wood, the usual fuel. Cornell now had direct competition, but at first he could do little more than expand *Norwich*'s run to include the community of Wilbur, farther up Rondout Creek.

The La Vergne [sic] of Cornell's line, which broke down on her trial trip after receiving an extensive overhauling, did not have the work done at McEntee & Dillon's foundry, though she laid at their dock. Mr. Cornell's machinists did the work. —*Kingston Daily Freeman*, 6 September 1873

Then the owners of *North America*—Poughkeepsie associates of Captain Dodge, who had owned her briefly himself before selling out to them—sent her elsewhere for a time, and Anderson, Romer and Company found themselves in need of another steamboat. They arranged for the *Emerald* to enter their service and continue in opposition to Cornell. To make *Emerald* more appealing to the public, which was acquiring a taste for only opulent steamboats, her passenger accommodations were renovated.

When *North America* returned (after having been sunk by hitting a rock off New Jersey, then raised and repaired) *Emerald* was withdrawn. Other boats came into the Creek to compete with both Cornell and Anderson. That fall, Cornell became the agent for an old steamer named *Norfolk*, which ran from Rondout in opposition to *Highlander*. By now, there were at least ten steamboats operating out of Rondout, battling for freight and passengers and towing, and still more were trying to break in.

Cornell turned *Mohegan* and *James Madison* into full-time towboats, and with other partners purchased the small sidewheeler, *John F. Rodman*, to tow in Rondout Creek. The Creek had not only the canal lock disgorging coal boats, but there were a number of boat-building enterprises that regularly needed the services of a towboat. On the Creek, too, was the newly established Island Dock, an insular coal-storage area adjoining Rondout, where coal boats unloaded and larger barges and sloops were loaded for the outward-bound journey.

Thomas Cornell was alert for every chance to profit, including chartering *Rodman* as an excursion boat for locals to take moonlight trips with music and dancing late into the night.

By now, William Dodge had moved to New York, but he continued to keep a hand in Hudson River steamboating, ultimately to the advantage of Thomas Cornell. Dodge found that an associate who owned the grand *North America* was hopelessly in debt, and Dodge decided to buy him out. In 1851, himself in need of ready cash, Dodge sold *North America* to Thomas Cornell—a man who always used his cash to great advantage. At about this time, Dodge bought out this same hard-pressed associate's controlling interest in the steamer *Emerald*, which, a year later, he sold to Cornell.

Dodge was suffering financially, and soon withdrew completely from the Hudson River scene. Thanks to Dodge's departure, Thomas Cornell's star was rising ever higher. In *North America*, he now possessed a finer, newer boat to pit directly against Anderson, Romer and Company's *Highlander*. The arrival of *North America* in Cornell's growing fleet meant the aging *Norwich* was taken out of service as a passenger boat and put exclusively to towing. *Norwich* was also used for icebreaking, at which she was the best vessel on the river. Her paddle wheels were made of live oak and iron, and her bottom was sheathed in protective copper. Jacob Dubois, one of her captains of long-standing, remarked that she "could run through a stoneyard without damaging herself."

The Baltic, of Cornell's Line, has had her new gallows frame in, and it fits snugly as paper on a wall. —*Kingston Daily Freeman*, **4 December 1874**

The towboat *Norwich*, built for passenger and freight service on Long Island Sound, came to the Hudson River in the 1840s and was later purchased by Thomas Cornell, who converted her to a towboat in 1851; during the Hudson-Fulton celebration of 1909, *Norwich* played an important role, and on her paddle wheel housing was painted "The oldest steamboat in the world. Built in 1836." (Roger W. Mabie Collection)

Norwich was predictably the first boat to appear rounding the Rondout lighthouse at the end of winter, and in 1851 she arrived on February 28, to the cheers of welcoming crowds on the Creek's wharfs. She was always kept in top shape, repainted and refitted every year. Thomas Cornell was fastidious in this sort of care, and his boats won high repute for their outstanding condition—just as his masters, pilots, and crews were highly regarded by other boatmen up and down the river.

Norwich was a special favorite of Rondout and Kingston, where stories were told about her battles with the ice. Early in 1851, she had what was considered her sternest ordeal. While running through Long Island Sound, she spotted the steamboat *New Haven* caught in the ice. This could mean disaster, for passengers could freeze or starve, or the boat might be overturned by the force of shifting ice floes. The "Ice King" approached the *New Haven* to break away the ice that buckled around her, and mounted so high that the trapped boat could not be seen even from up in the pilot house of *Norwich*. Gallantly driving again and again against the packed ice, *Norwich* at last broke open a path for *New Haven*, which escaped.

That was not the only time *Norwich* had performed heroically, but by the 1850s it was apparent that her career as a passenger boat had been eclipsed by new vessels much finer and faster than she. Naturally, it was thought that the beloved old *Norwich* soon would be made a towboat, which she would remain for a few years before being scrapped.

The steamboat *Manhattan*, purchased by Thomas Cornell in 1855 for overnight freight and passenger service between Rondout and New York, continued in this service until replaced by the new steamer *Thomas Cornell* in 1863. (Roger W. Mabie Collection)

In 1852, Thomas Cornell decided he wanted out of the freight and passenger business, and he sold *North America* and its route franchise to a relation of the Anderson family of Anderson, Romer and Company. Although that firm and its associates had firm control of the Rondout to New York route, the astute Cornell had his own plans, which mostly included towing, but at the same time he took control of the ferry line that crossed the Hudson from Rhinecliff to Kingston Point on the northern shore of Rondout Creek's mouth.

Cornell bought an interest in the steam-powered sidewheel ferryboat *Rhine* and immediately established a second ferry route from Rhinecliff into Rondout Creek and Rondout itself. This offered a more direct road up to Kingston than did the original ferry terminal at Kingston Point, sometimes also called Columbia Point. The next year Cornell discontinued altogether the crossing to Kingston Point.

It might have been suspected that Cornell was positioning himself to take advantage of the Hudson River Railroad line, which was almost completed on the east shore of the Hudson. The railroad linked New York City to Greenbush, across the river from Albany. With control of the Kingston-Rhinecliff ferry, Cornell had a distinct advantage when it came to moving people and freight over the river to and from the railroad stations across at Rhinecliff.

That same year, 1852, *James Madison* became involved in another riverboat tragedy as she was towing canal boats under the command of Captain A. Matson.

The steamboat *Henry Clay*, just a year old, was built for speed and already had proven to be among the fastest boats on the river. At 198 feet in length, *Henry Clay* was not large for a Hudson River steamboat, some of which were far longer, such as her well-known contemporaries, *Alida* (265 feet), *Manhattan* (256 feet), and *Francis Skiddy* (312 feet). *Armenia* (181 feet, but later lengthened by thirty more) was about the same size as *Henry Clay*, and in 1852 was her main competitor. Like *Henry Clay*, *Armenia* was built for speed.

Henry Clay ran against *Armenia* in the New York to Albany route. They often left within a few minutes of each other, pouring on the steam all the way up or down the river in quest of victory and bragging rights, which brought more passengers and freight and resultant profit. Getting first into a harbor or alongside a wharf usually meant the other boat was locked out, and the spoils belonged to the first boat in. So it went from landing to landing, and more than once there were close calls and near-collisions between them. The race during their southbound journey on July 28, was typical of the sort of extremes to which rival steamboat captains sometimes took matters.

Henry Clay and *Armenia* had raced without letup as soon as they left Albany, finding themselves neck-and-neck above Kingston. There, they sideswiped, with *Armenia* suffering the worst, almost grounded, and forced to slow down. *Henry Clay* steamed triumphantly off toward other landings to pick up approximately 400 more passengers and try for a record-setting time to New York.

Late that afternoon off Riverdale, *James Madison*'s Captain Matson was among the first to see the *Henry Clay*, beached, ablaze from stem to stern, the water full of struggling passengers. Matson immediately cut loose his tow and rushed toward the disaster, managing to save many people, but more than one hundred lives were lost. This was the worst Hudson River catastrophe to that day, and the ensuing public uproar ultimately brought about new federal regulations and steamboat inspections as well as safety rules that, among other things, banned boats from racing each other while in service.

> On Monday a somewhat elderly gentleman from Troy, who is the proprietor of a line of towing steamers between that city and this, and whose advancing years cause him to be not quite as erect as formerly, was in town, and the agent of his towing lines here wanted him to remain here until today, but he insisted on going home. "Home?" said the agent, "What do you want to go home for?" "I don't feel well," was the answer, "I guess I'll go home and have a hog-frame put in me." —*Kingston Daily Freeman*, 8 December 1874

In March 1853, Thomas Cornell became partners with Peter Dubois in a brand new towing steamer built in Hoboken, New Jersey. She was named *Walter B. Crane*, honoring a longtime superintendent of the D&H Canal Company. Naming boats after important clients would become a common way for towboat companies to get on the good side of their best customers. *Crane* was one of the first vessels on the Hudson built specifically as a towboat. Then, in 1853-54, Thomas Cornell moved back into the passenger steamboat business by purchasing the aging *Santa Claus*, which belonged to E. Fitch and Company and had once been a fine passenger steamboat.

Santa Claus, with attractive paintings of Saint Nick himself on the paddleboxes, had been used by Fitch mainly as a towing steamer, but in new public advertisements that called her a "splendid steamboat" in "perfect order," Cornell announced plans to start up again with passengers. That August, while promoting *Santa Claus*, he did his community a service by taking the three Rondout militia companies out on the sidewheeler for an excursion to Albany; the next month he carried the fire companies of Rondout and Kingston on an excursion to Hudson.

At this time, although some combinations of boat owners collapsed or dissolved, the competition in steamboating out of Rondout Creek was still tough, with the Freight and Passage Line, the Daily Steam Line, and Masten's Line all operating from Wilbur. In Rondout, however, the competitors came to terms as Romer, Tremper and Gillette bought out the Sleight Line—owners of *North America* and *Highlander*—and then Romer sold *Highlander* to Cornell.

The well-known *Highlander* was converted into a towing vessel, with her main duties being to take coal boats from the Pennsylvania Coal Company's newly developed depot and docks at Port Ewen, a riverfront community in the Town of Esopus south of Rondout Creek. Just coming to life after being established in the spring of 1852, Port Ewen eventually became the home of generations of boatmen and canalmen, and it produced some of the best-known personalities in the towing business. The Pennsylvania Coal Company, which employed many of the Port Ewen men, soon would surpass the D&H Canal Company in tonnage of coal delivered to tidewater.

Rondout, with almost 6,000 residents, was by now larger than the older community of Kingston, which had about 4,000. Rondout was the river port, rowdy and bustling at the mouth of a busy creek where water traffic was heavy and getting heavier. Kingston, up on the hill, was more staid, although it had a share of laborers who worked at the Newark Lime and Cement Company, which owned much of the high ground above the Creek and was building mills, offices, and warehouses down to the waterfront. In the heart of Rondout, the imposing Mansion House hotel was being built, and there was no lack of public houses, dances, and shows where hard-working folk could spend their few leisure hours. Public stagecoaches, or "omnibuses," linked Rondout to Kingston, helping to mingle these very different populations, and the Cornell-controlled ferry to Rhinecliff was a key link for both communities to the outside world.

In 1854, resident John Horton wrote his vivid "Rondout in the Fifties," published in one of the several local newspapers:

> Rondout, on the pretty Rondout Creek,
> Will be a city very quick.
> It has one bank and lots of stores
> Besides the hardware store of More's.
>
> Lots of steamboats have we here
> That bring up freight and take down beer;
> They bring up merchants' eggs for "Pass,"
> The North America and Santa Claus.
>
> At Cornell's dock the Santa's moored,
> For freight and passage, apply on board.
> At Romer's & Gillette's, down below,
> The North America's colors blow.
>
> The Mansion House is going up,
> And there the lager beer we'll sup.
> We go to Metzger's on the hill.
> We get our boots of William Still.
>
> Winter, he keeps a fancy store;
> Elting & Decker are next door.
> Canfield and Roosa across the street,
> And 'tween them 'Deusen's drug store, neat.
>
> Suydam's on the corner, and Davis below,
> 'Twixt the post and law office, you know.

From Smith's tailor shop, Deyo's can be seen,
With Sherer's big saloon between.

The next you find is Brother Dunn,
Stebbins & Staples, too, are some.
Welch, he keeps a tailor shop,
Schoonmaker & Wood sell ginger pop.

McElroy, he keeps the Hotel Exchange,
And Kerry's below is just the range;
The ferryboat Rhine, which there is nigh,
From Rondout does to Rhinebeck ply.

Good horses Davis keeps to please,
As doth our worthy Major Keys.
Omnibuses here have taken root,
Or we'd have to go to Kingston afoot.

The Clinton is kept by Mr. Hartt,
And Clinton Hall is of it a part;
'Tis here we have all kinds of shows,
Balls and dances and fandangoes.

There likely were many more such verses written by Horton and not published, but these capture the liveliness and community pride of Rondout, which had a bright future as an inland harbor, with no sign of letup in development. Thomas Cornell was considered the ideal local businessman, and around this time an editor of the Rondout *Courier* wished him many more years in the community, hoping that "the smoke of his multiplying boats become so dense as to completely becloud Rondout and the Hudson."

The side-wheel towboat *Pittston*, built in 1850, shown at South Rondout near the end of her career, was used almost exclusively for towing canal boats and coal barges in and around Rondout Creek, first for the Pennsylvania Coal Company, and then for Cornell from 1868 until dismantled in 1909. (William duBarry Thomas Collection)

Cornell's overhauled *Santa Claus* was to have David Abbey Jr. as captain and counted among its crew Cornell's cousin William, son of his uncle Thomas W. Cornell.

Ever able to produce ready cash, Thomas Cornell bought *Washington* from the Daily Line and turned her into a towing steamer, effectively putting the Daily temporarily out of business. Legal conflicts between owners of Masten and the Freight and Passage Line hampered their business, and all the while Cornell grew stronger—although mainly in towing, not passenger service. Now, Cornell ran the towing steamers *Norwich, James Madison, Mohegan, Highlander,* and *Emerald;* and he was partners with his brother-in-law, Coe F. Young of Honesdale, as owners and operators of a fleet of twenty canal boats. In 1854, Cornell took an important step in steamboat fuel development by experimenting with anthracite coal "screenings," small particles of coal considered too small to be used commercially. He tried the screenings out in *James Madison,* and by the end of the season this otherwise useless coal was clearly usable as boiler fuel. And it was cheaper than regular coal.

At the close of 1855, the *Santa Claus* was fated to end her passenger-carrying career and become another of those faded "belles of the Hudson," those once modern, elegant passenger steamboats converted to become hard-working towboats. To replace *Santa Claus* in passenger service, Cornell bought the ten-year-old sidewheeler *Manhattan*, which was newer and at more than 256 feet was even larger than *North America*. *Manhattan* was the largest vessel thus far to operate out of the Creek. Captain Abbey transferred to her from *Santa Claus,* and so did William Cornell, the clerk.

The competition for passenger service from Rondout was varied, with Romer and Tremper succeeding the reorganized Romer, Tremper and Gillette, and running the steamers *North America, Rip Van Winkle,* and *Mazeppa.* Although strong competition faced Cornell's steamboat line plans, his ambitions were expansive, as indicated by the magnificent home he built on Wurts Street, overlooking Rondout and the Creek. Cornell's dreams went beyond steamboats, for he had seen how the Hudson River Railroad was such a success, as it already carried more than a million passengers a year.

Many of those passengers were riding the trains on their way to and from vacations in the Catskill Mountains. The morning train from New York took less than four hours to reach the station across from Catskill, while the same steamboat trip was seven or eight hours. Granted, the steamboat was far more comfortable than the train, even opulent, and the Hudson River scenery was lovely to look at, while the train noisily rattled and banged its way along, smoke and cinders bedeviling the passengers. There was a constant risk of derailments, too, which caused injuries and even deaths. In spite of the railroad's shortcomings, it left the steamboats far behind when it came to speed and convenience. Further, cold weather seldom stopped the trains, while Hudson River steamboats and their ports of call were frozen solid for many weeks during the winter.

The very real dangers to steamboating, too, persisted for passengers and for crew. One minor but spectacular incident happened in the fall of 1857, when the small towboat *Thorn* burst into flames near the wooden lighthouse at the mouth of Rondout Creek. The blazing boat drifted onto the flats just above the lighthouse, threatening to set it on fire. The young family of widow Catherine Parsell Perkins, the lightkeeper, watched helplessly as the fiery blaze drifted closer and closer. George Murdock, Mrs. Perkins's four-year-old son by her late first husband, felt the very windowpane was too hot to touch. From the passing towboat *James Madison,* George's uncle, Abe Parsell, stood helplessly on deck, thinking the lighthouse itself was burning. It would have burned, indeed, had the strong wind and rainstorm not fortunately pushed *Thorn* farther down the river and drenched the blaze.

From his vantage point of years living in the lighthouse and in a career as a boatman, George Murdock saw more than one steamboat catch fire, run aground, and burn to the waterline. Still, shipping by water was the least expensive way, especially for bulk products, most of which were transported on the Erie Canal and the Hudson River. Already, however, there were rail lines laid all the way from Albany to Buffalo. Thomas Cornell knew the great costs of railroad construction were far beyond his personal means, but he had influence, had made a name for himself as a man who "jumped at a conclusion" while others were half asleep. And the profits of towing and passenger lines could be put to good use in railroad development, in which he would be a pioneer.

By 1859, as Rondout prospered, Cornell bought more warehouse space there and donated a new building site on the corner of Wurts and Spring Streets for his First Baptist Church. He was a leading member of the congregation of the new church, which was right next to his home.

This year was notable for Thomas Cornell, who announced he would build a steamboat that, at 260 feet, would be the largest to run from Rondout to New York. Cornell's towboats began to work regularly in New York Harbor, towing the D&H Canal's coal boats from the railroad terminus at Weehawken, New Jersey; and 1859 was the year an enterprising young man named Samuel Decker Coykendall arrived in Rondout to manage a branch of a Newburgh dry goods store.

Born in Wantage Township at the northwestern corner of New Jersey, the twenty-two-year-old Samuel Coykendall had worked as a boy in nearby Port Jervis in a general store. Coykendall later moved to Newburgh, gaining experience in the dry goods business, until he was asked to establish the branch in Rondout. The Coykendall name harked back to one of the oldest Dutch families in Ulster County and Kingston, so he had roots in the region that went far deeper than did Thomas Cornell's. By 1862, young Coykendall was working as a clerk on the Cornell passenger steamboat *Manhattan,* taking the position formerly held by William Cornell.

As the assistant to the captain, the position of clerk on a steamboat was one of considerable responsibility and authority and was no mere clerical position. In some cases, the clerk might be second in command.

It is likely that at this time Thomas Cornell's seventeen-year-old daughter, Mary Augusta, and Samuel Coykendall were falling in love. First, however, came the Civil War.

Great events were reaching a head, and Thomas Cornell wanted to lead them rather than simply be caught up in them, for he had the wealth, influence, and popularity to believe he could win a seat as an Abraham Lincoln Republican in the United States Congress.

Samuel Decker Coykendall was the son-in-law of Thomas Cornell and generally referred to as "S. D." He is pictured as a young man, about the time of the Civil war. (C. W. Spangenberger Collection)

Chapter Four
War, The *Mary Powell,* and S. D. Coykendall

IN 1860, Thomas Cornell purchased a D&H coal barge that was all that remained of one of the first steamboats operated by inventor Robert Fulton and his partner, the Hudson Valley land baron Chancellor Livingston. *James Kent* had been built with great expectations in 1823, but she would be the last boat in the Fulton Livingston line. The company went out of business just two years later, in 1825, when a Supreme Court decision took away its monopoly, granted by New York State, to control all steamboating on the Hudson River. As soon as freedom of the steamboat operations on the river was granted, competition overwhelmed the Fulton-Livingston combination.

By the time Cornell bought *James Kent* in 1860, the venerable old sidewheeler had been stripped down to little more than a hull, undergoing what awaited every steamboat that outlived its ability to ply the waters with passengers, freight, or tows. It had been a fine craft in its day, but was too slow and was shunned by passengers and shippers. By mid-century, all the passenger steamboats abandoned the common practice of towing barges, which slowed them down, and instead went in for fast travel times and the grandest style and comfort on board.

James Kent had been dismantled, and what was usable was cannibalized for other boats, while her hull, with its 400-ton carrying capacity, was employed by the D&H Company as a coal barge carrying anthracite out of Rondout Creek. What Thomas Cornell needed in 1860 was not another coal barge, but a stationary "stake boat" to support his expanding operations in New York Harbor. Stake boats were floating moorings anchored permanently in the harbor as a place where empty barges could be assembled. The barges were then organized by the captain of the stake boat according to how they were to be towed northward and dropped off. When the tow was ready, a towboat would take it back upriver, dropping off the boats at their various destinations. For another twenty-five years of humble service as a stake boat, the remarkably well-constructed *James Kent* would remain a legacy to the first days of steamboat enterprise in America.

The tug Sammy Cornell went out of the creek this morning with a merry excursion party. —*Kingston Daily Freeman,* **19 July 1876**

In 1860, however, memories were not as important as expectations and demands. The country was hurrying toward war, fervent patriotism surged in almost everyone's blood, whether out of loyalty to an individual state or to the United States, and militias were drilling all across America. At forty-six, Thomas Cornell was too old to enlist as an active militiaman, but his duty was to help elect Abraham Lincoln, the Republican candidate for president. At the same time, Cornell was still in contention with the prominent Anderson family, which like the Cornells had started its rise by managing a store on the Rondout Creek waterfront and had served as shipping agents.

The Andersons had bought and sold interests in steamboats and wharfage, establishing lines they controlled, and by 1860 the son, Absalom L. Anderson, was respected as a top captain on the river. Much of their early fortune came from part ownership in the profitable market barge *Ulster County*, launched in 1847, and a boat that Ulster County farmers and growers were pleased to patronize with their produce and as passengers. By 1848, the Anderson family was investing in steamboats sailing from Rondout Creek, including *Highlander* and later *North America*. Absalom Anderson was captain of *Highlander*, where he earned his reputation for punctuality and for taking care of his boat and passengers. He set a tone of decorum on his boat so that families felt welcome, and rowdy troublemakers were inevitably put ashore at the next landing.

When Thomas Cornell briefly withdrew from the passenger business in 1850, the Anderson family—Absalom's brother Charles was also a fine master of steamboats—was firmly in control of steamboat trips from Rondout to New York. When Cornell returned to the fray in 1853, the contest for passengers and freight resumed, although by 1860, Cornell was more involved in towing and working for the election of Abraham Lincoln, while the Andersons were primarily in the passenger business. In this year, Cornell moved his New York terminal to Jay Street, where the Andersons, and the other competitors, Romer and Tremper, already had piers for passengers for Rondout to congregate.

Romer and Tremper's steamer *North America* was growing old by now, in need of an expensive overhaul that still might not give her an edge over the boats of Cornell or Anderson. Absalom Anderson was owner and master of *Thomas Powell*, one of the superior steamboats on the river, although for a few years before the Andersons bought her she had been used by her owners only as a towing steamer. *Thomas Powell* was aging, and Anderson announced that soon he and his partners would have another boat built that would be the fastest ever seen on the river. His declaration was soon followed by Thomas Cornell's promise to build a steamboat of 260 feet, with a hull and engine that would make her the equal of any on the river. Cornell's new boat was to run in direct opposition to Anderson's *Thomas Powell*.

Anderson negotiated with the ship builder to insert a contractual clause that if his new steamboat did not outperform the *Thomas Powell* by a speed of at least one mile in twelve, then there would be a financial penalty to the builders. The new Anderson boat—he had a majority interest—would be named *Mary Powell*, in honor of Mary Ludlow Powell, widow of the late

The only place in the city that "looks like business" is the machine shop of Cornell & Co., which is running at its full capacity and is doing a great deal of work. Four or five steamboats and propellars are being refitted and repaired. —*Kingston Daily Freeman*, 23 September 1876

A nineteenth-century woodcut of the steamboat *Mary Powell* passing a tow of canal boats and an armada of sloops and schooners in the northern entrance of the Hudson Highlands, south of Cornwall.

Newburgh businessman for whom *Highlander* originally had been built and after whom Anderson's fast steamer had been named. The Powell and Ludlow names were highly respected in the Newburgh-Kingston region, and that brought passenger and shipper loyalty for Anderson, whose own success had been made largely with *Thomas Powell*.

Because of the great cost, no new passenger boats had been built for the Rondout-New York run in the past fifteen years. In order to attract passengers, the larger steamboat companies operating from New York to Albany were, for the first time in eight years, building new boats. The companies gambled fortunes to make sure their vessels were grander and more palatial than ever, and like the new *Daniel Drew*, they were faster than ever. They had to be if they wanted business.

Much was at stake for Absalom Anderson, with the cost of *Mary Powell* at more than $80,000. There was much to win. Quick cash profits could be made on a good trip carrying as many as 1,500 passengers aboard *Mary Powell*. The business was there for steamboats, but who would get it and keep it? The potential profits from the passenger business were enormous, but the boats were costly to run and maintain. On one trip *Thomas Powell* suffered serious damage to her engine, and after being laid up for an unproductive three weeks she cost $6,000 to repair. Anderson was required to charter another steamboat, but she was too slow, and unfortunately not as appealing to many customers, whom he lost. That same year, before the breakdown, Anderson won acclaim by bringing *Thomas Powell* from New York to Rondout in the record time of four hours and thirty-nine minutes. Where the businessman "Major" Cornell was becoming financially powerful, with a cash reserve for future investment, the dashing Absalom Anderson was earning acclaim as being "born for the office" of captain, and it was said that "courtesy, decision, control, promptitude, are all native to him."

In 1860, as Anderson's *Mary Powell* was being built in Jersey City, Peter Cornell, Thomas's father, died.

Cornell decided to delay the construction of his own great steamer, largely because of the uncertainty of the approach of war, which broke upon the country on April 12, 1861, with South Carolina's bombardment of Fort Sumter in Charleston Harbor. Troops were urgently needed to defend Lincoln's government and Washington, D.C., which was virtually surrounded by pro-secessionist sympathizers in Maryland, Delaware, and Virginia. For the most part, only militia regiments were available, including the 20th New York State Militia, the "Ulster Guard," formed by combining the local companies from Rondout and raising more companies from the Kingston area.

Within days of the fall of Fort Sumter, Rondout and Kingston turned out to cheer the men of the 20th NYS Militia as they boarded Cornell's steamer, *Manhattan*, and a barge that would be towed along with it. Cornell had written to the governor offering to transport Ulster County soldiers "to New York by Steamboat, without Charge to the State or United States," adding, "May God prosper the American army." The volunteers were lacking full uniforms and adequate equipment, but they were eager to fight for the Union. They and the crowds on wharves and housetops cheered and waved to each other

as the bell of *Manhattan* began to ring, and the vessel steamed away with the militia, which was prepared for three months' duty protecting Washington, D.C.

Those three mostly idle months of threat and counter-threat between Federals and Confederates were only the beginning, and many more regiments would be needed, properly trained and equipped, and enlisted for three years. The 20th regiment came back to Rondout that August, again on the *Manhattan* and the barge, soon to be reorganized and officially mustered in as the 80th New York Volunteers. In October of 1861, the 80th departed on the *Manhattan* and the newly purchased Cornell steamer *John Marshall*, a former passenger sidewheeler converted to towing steamer and now carrying the regiment's gear. *John Marshall* had been named after the famous United States Supreme Court chief justice, who in 1825 had heard the case that broke the Fulton-Livingston steamboat monopoly.

In November, another regiment was mustered in at Kingston. Nicknamed "The Mountain Legion," the 156th New York Volunteer regiment was sent to federally occupied New Orleans for basic training. Like the 80th, the 156th would serve gallantly throughout the war. In August 1862, the hard-working *Manhattan* also carried away the 120th NYV, the "Washington Guard," also made up of men from Ulster and Greene Counties. In another year, *Manhattan* would join some of those troops in southern waters, but she would never return to the Hudson River.

With the 156th NYV on the journey south went twenty-five-year-old Samuel Coykendall, who had resigned his position as a clerk on *Manhattan*. Coykendall now was a first lieutenant and regimental quartermaster, respon-

Mary Powell, the "Queen of the Hudson," was twice owned by Thomas Cornell—from 1865 to 1869, and again from 1883 to 1885. This view of the handsome steamboat in Haverstraw Bay illustrates what made her a remarkable example of naval architecture at its very best. She is running at speed, yet there is only the slightest suggestion of a bow wave. Full credit to Michael Allison, her builder in 1861, for building an almost perfect hull, but it was only after *Mary Powell* was lengthened in 1862 that she became a true flier and a Hudson River legend. (Roger W. Mabie Collection)

sible for organizing supplies and equipment for the 156th. He would rise to become a member of the headquarters staff of General Nathaniel Banks in the Mississippi and Red River campaigns of 1863 and 1864, serving out a full three-year term, until May 1865.

In 1862, Thomas Cornell ran for Congress as a representative from New York and a Republican ally to President Lincoln, but he was defeated. He still had plenty to do, of course, adding to the fleet of towboats by acquiring the twenty-year-old passenger boat *Herald* and converting her. Cornell's coal barge towing business was growing, stimulated by the bottomless demands of the war effort, so *Herald* was needed to tow barges and scows between Rondout and New York.

Two impressive new steamers now were operating out of Rondout: Romer and Tremper's, one of the fastest on the river, and Anderson's new *Mary Powell*, first launched in August 1861. *Mary Powell* was 275 feet in length and said to be the most beautiful steamboat on the Hudson. A New York newspaper called her the "Queen of the Hudson," but she apparently was not as fast as Anderson had hoped her to be. At the same time, Cornell had ordered the construction of a grand steamboat of his own, and it was being built on the East River at Elisha S. Whitlock's shipyard at Greenpoint, Long Island. This vessel would be longer than either *James W. Baldwin* or *Mary Powell*, and would have a cylinder diameter ten inches greater than the *Mary Powell*'s, meaning it ought to be potentially faster.

She would be named *Thomas Cornell*.

There was a great need for steamboats to carry troops, supplies, and equipment to support the Union war effort, so Cornell profitably sold *Manhattan* to a Delaware River company that was contracting with the military. She would

The passenger and freight steamboat *Thomas Cornell* ran between Rondout and New York from late 1863 until March 27, 1882, when she came to grief after running upon Danskammer Point above Newburgh. She is shown here at her wharf in the Rondout Creek, probably about 1872. Built at Greenpoint, New York (now part of the Borough of Brooklyn), *Thomas Cornell* was propelled by a vertical beam engine having a cylinder 72 inches in diameter with a piston stroke of 12 feet. (Hudson River Maritime Museum Collection)

stay in government service throughout the war, even making a long coastal trip to New Orleans. *Highlander*, too, was sold, to be a towboat on the Delaware River.

In 1863, to replace *Manhattan*, Cornell chartered *Knickerbocker*, a steamboat that had endured a number of serious mishaps since being built in 1843. *Knickerbocker* had struck a rock and sunk in 1856, fortunately with no loss of life. Raised and put back in service, she had, in 1859, run down a sloop at nighttime, killing the entire crew. For all her misfortune, *Knickerbocker* had been considered an especially lovely vessel when in the fleet of Daniel Drew's People's Line. She would run for Cornell until *Thomas Cornell* was built.

At this time, Hudson River boatmen were experimenting with using "screw" propellers rather than paddle wheels, but were having only mixed success. Some British tugboats were operating with propellers, and in 1853 the Newark Lime and Cement Company's boat, *Cement Rock*, built with a propeller, was able to carry as many as 1,200 barrels of cement. Propeller boats were sometimes referred to as "kickers." In 1858, the large steamboat, *Charlotte Vanderbilt*, had been built with propellers, but had proved unsuccessful, far too slow to compete with even the likes of the aging *Thomas Powell*. The disappointing *Charlotte Vanderbilt* had been withdrawn from passenger service and refitted as a sidewheeler.

The magnificent new *Thomas Cornell* would be a traditional sidewheeler, with all the power, speed, and opulence that assured her a loyal following despite the popular appeal of *Mary Powell*. Cornell's pride and joy would be 286 feet long, ten feet more than *Mary Powell*. He had not, however, accounted for Absalom Anderson's quest for the perfect hull to match the perfect engine, for by the end of the 1862 sailing season, *Mary Powell* was cut in half, and another twenty-one feet added. Speed, too, was added, just as Anderson and his partners had hoped. In fact, *Mary Powell* soon was the fastest steamboat on the Hudson River.

Thomas Cornell—publicly said to have been named by the builder, not the owner—was launched on January 20, 1863. There were to be months more of finishing work and delays in construction. By now, *Thomas Powell* had been sold and sold again, with the new owner being Thomas Cornell's brother Joseph, operating out of Catskill and running to New York. The splendid *James W. Baldwin* of Romer and Tremper was running in tandem with Cornell's *Knickerbocker*, so even without his new steamboat then under construction, the "Major" had much to say about the operations of the passenger business out of Rondout.

In June 1863, *Mary Powell* made a record-setting trip from New York, reaching the Rondout lighthouse in four and a half hours, which included making eight landings along the way.

On September 15, *Thomas Cornell* passed her trials at New York, and a week later arrived at Rondout in the creditable time of five hours, sailing against a northwest wind and making four landings. It was considered that *Thomas Cornell*, *James W. Baldwin*, and *Mary Powell*, all serving Rondout Creek, constituted the finest fleet of steamboats operating from any port on the Hudson River with the exception of Albany.

Already, Thomas Cornell was considering how to take control of his arch-competitor, *Mary Powell*.

Under the supervision of Boss Houghtaling, the Thomas Cornell's outside spring dress is nearly completed and she shines like a new silk hat. —*Kingston Daily Freeman,* 12 February 1877

The Civil War seemed never ending by mid-1864, although the industrial power of the North and its far greater population were combining with improved military leadership to bring the South to its knees. Naval power and seaport blockades as well as fleets of fast steamboats on the rivers played a great part in the emerging triumph of the North. Yet one modern technology rose above all the rest in defeating the South: railroads. Thousands of miles of new track had been laid in the North, engines and cars constructed to carry armies swiftly into battle, and the western states of Ohio, Indiana, and Illinois were turning to railroads rather than steamboats to carry on their vast commerce with the East.

Thomas Cornell anticipated the same growth for railroads in New York's Hudson Valley, the great route of America, beginning and arriving in New York, with its burgeoning population, great seaport, financial institutions, merchants, and world traders—all of which needed raw materials and manufactured goods, both for this growing country and for markets overseas. Railroads coming from the West would terminate at the Hudson River, where barges towed by steamboats would carry their cargoes across while passengers crossed on ferries.

Cornell had increasing control over the towing business on the Hudson River and already owned the ferry crossing from Rhinecliff to Rondout. Now he wanted to own railroads, for if he also controlled the railroad lines terminating at both sides of the Hudson, then he would have a monopoly on the region's commerce. He saw the passes through the Catskill Mountains as potential arteries of that commerce once railroads were built through them. He also saw the importance of an eastward-running rail line from Rhinebeck, on the east side of the Hudson. That rail line would follow a traditional route between the Hudson River and New England, linking with the railroad south to the mid-Atlantic states or north to Canada, as well as with Cornell's ferry and towboat operations at Rondout.

On June 8, 1864, another steamboat disaster occurred on the Hudson, when the newly built *Berkshire* caught fire just off Hyde Park, between Rondout and Poughkeepsie. *James W. Baldwin* was the first steamboat to the rescue, setting out small boats to pluck survivors from the water. Most of *Berkshire*'s 130 passengers had embarked from the riverfront towns of Hudson and Catskill, and by the time the horror was over, forty had drowned or been killed by the fire.

Fear of such steamboat accidents certainly contributed to the early rise of railroads, although the magnificent passenger steamers of the Hudson River Day Line and the Night Line attracted folk who found the beauty and tranquility of the voyage irresistible.

In April 1865, the Rondout-Kingston community keenly felt the national tragedy that occurred when President Lincoln was assassinated in Washington. Lincoln's body was brought to New York City to lie in state at City Hall, and on Monday, April 24, many people boarded *Thomas Cornell* to journey to the city and pay their respects. The next evening, the president's body was carried by a bunting-draped train up the east side of the Hudson River on its way back to Springfield, Illinois. Hundreds of mourners crossed by ferry to Rhinecliff, where the funeral train passed by slowly, lit up in the darkness. Cannons were fired in salute up and down the river as church bells tolled. The German Band of Rondout assembled at Rhinecliff station to play a mournful dirge as the train rumbled through and away into the night.

Many folk surely remembered standing at these tracks in 1861, cheering as newly elected President Lincoln passed by on his journey to take office in Washington.

In May 1865, the war veterans who had served their three-year enlistments were discharged and returned home, among them S. D. Coykendall. He brought with him considerable experience at organization and supply, since he had been quartermaster of the 156th, and was an officer on Banks's headquarters staff.

Later in 1865, Coykendall married Mary Augusta Cornell. As the son-in-law, he became a partner in the firm, ready to work in combination with Cornell—a combination that would not only establish the steamboat company as the most powerful towing operation on the Hudson River, but which would open the way to a railroad empire.

In the summer of 1865, there were rumors that Absalom Anderson and his partners were interested in selling *Mary Powell*. Anderson wanted to retire from steamboating. By October, at the end of the sailing season, Cornell bought the much-prized vessel for $200,000, also purchasing the lucrative day-line route between Rondout and New York. Ever mindful of the need for cash, he soon sold a half interest in *Mary Powell* to tycoon Daniel Drew for $100,000. In 1867, Cornell bought Daniel Drew out and became sole owner of *Mary Powell*.

The prospective railroad business was much trickier than operating side-wheel passenger steamboats and towing freight. In terms of the high investment costs and the tremendous effort and unrelenting commitment required to construct and maintain track, bridges, stations, and tunnels, creating railroads was a costly undertaking, not recommended for the fainthearted.

Both Cornell and Coykendall took to railroads with enthusiasm and energy, as they set out to develop the enterprise they named the Rondout and Oswego Railroad. The company came to life in April 1866, when it was chartered by New York State, with Cornell as president. He personally bought $25,000 worth of stock and worked to sell shares for the company. The plan was to sell stock in the amount of $1.5 million and build the railroad to con-

The Oswego, the star towboat of Cornell & Company's fleet, with Captain Jacob Dubois in command, having been thoroughly overhauled under the supervision of Chief Engineer Andrew Barrett during the past winter, is again in the line looking as straight as the day she was launched and as handsome as a yacht. —*Kingston Daily Freeman*, 9 April 1877

nect with the Albany and Susquehanna then under construction in the valley west of the Catskill Mountains. There was no real intent to build the more than 200 miles of track required to reach Oswego on Lake Ontario. Actually, Cornell and his investors—which included the Village of Kingston, a subscriber for $600,000 in stock—wanted to open the route to rich farmlands beyond the Catskills and also to promote summer tourism to the mountain hotels that were becoming even more popular with New York metropolitan area residents. Other towns along the way invested in the railroad, anticipating great benefits for themselves.

Steamboating was not being neglected, although the face of that business was changing, with towing coming more into its own. The Cornell Towing Company, as it was known, had added towing steamers: *Ceres*, one of those few vessels built to be towboats; *Sarah E. Brown*; *Pittston*; and the propeller towboat *Poppy* (immediately renamed *Isaac M. North*, after a leading Rondout figure, who would become a superintendent of operations for the Cornell company). The vessels *Ceres*, *Sarah E. Brown*, and *Poppy* all were purchased from the military fleet that was being deactivated, and they came to Rondout Creek in their war color: black. By now, the career of the towboat *Mohegan* was finished, and she was converted into a coal barge.

The George A. Hoyt, of the Cornell Steamboat Company, took the milk to New York in place of the William Cook, the latter steamer lying up to permit the boilers to cool and be cleaned, after having had steam on them for several weeks. —Kingston Daily Freeman, 6 May 1878

In 1866, before much happened in the way of railroad construction, Thomas Cornell was elected on the Republican ticket to serve in the Fortieth Congress, 1867-68. During this time, S. D. Coykendall assumed much of the management responsibilities. In December 1866, his wife Mary gave birth to their first child, son Thomas Cornell Coykendall. It was an era of great promise and mounting success for the Cornell Company.

Around this time, the Rondout lighthouse managed by George Murdock's family was damaged, rammed by the bowsprit of a sailing ship caught in one of the freshets—spring floods—that swept down Rondout Creek. Freshets were roaring walls of water released by the sudden breakup of an ice dam upstream. Water thundered down in a torrent, taking boats in the crowded Creek by surprise, lifting them, breaking their moorings, and sometimes capsizing them or piling them onto the shore.

In 1867, to replace the lighthouse that had been damaged, a new lighthouse was built of stone close to the original site on the south shore of the Creek mouth. This new lighthouse seemed a perfect symbol of prosperity for the port of Rondout, for Kingston, and also for the Cornell and Coykendall families.

Chapter Five
Railroads and Towboats

RAILROADS were very much on Thomas Cornell's mind in the spring of 1868, as the Rondout and Oswego finally commenced construction, with the first track being laid out of Rondout in a steeply graded letter "S," and leading up to Kingston. In Rondout were Cornell's steamboat repair shops and offices, and now the railroad shops would also be there, making an already busy industrial community even busier.

The mid-Hudson region was roaring in 1868, with brickyards along the west shore from Haverstraw Bay north to Coxsackie. In a couple of decades, there would be approximately 140 of them, annually providing millions of common brick to builders in the New York City region. Combined with the traditional mid-Hudson Valley industries of leather tanning, lumber, farm produce, and quarrying, a vital ice-cutting industry approached maturity, as did boat-building, especially of canal boats. The D&H Canal had as many as a thousand working canal boats using the channel each year, with three million tons of coal shipped in one year.

Bluestone was being quarried and brought down to the water's edge near Rondout, where it was dressed and then shipped off to become sidewalks and curbstones in places like New York City and Troy. The quarrying operation and cement works of the Newark Lime and Cement Manufacturing Company were prospering; the company had warehouses, wharfs, and sheds at the base of the steep hill called Vlightberg. The waterfront area of Rondout Village, known as The Strand, had a number of impressive brick buildings as tall as four stories. Cornell's offices and shops were among the largest. Smoke from the cement works and the steamboats, and now from a railroad locomotive, was thick in the air, and it spoke of employment, profit, and growth for the communities of Rondout, Kingston, and Wilbur, as well as for those south of the Creek: Sleightsburgh, South Rondout, and Port Ewen.

In Rondout, too, stood the handsome First National Bank of Rondout, founded by Thomas Cornell in 1863 when money was flowing, thanks to the war economy. In March of 1868, Cornell established another: the Rondout Savings Bank. He also became a member of the board of directors of the D&H Canal Company, which meant he had all the inside news about the company's plans, especially those that might have an impact on his own designs as a railroad magnate. Cornell's towing business was producing capital for him, whether for establishing a bank or building a railroad.

The crews of the Sammy Cornell, the Mills and other boats were entertained on board the Columbia this morning with lemonade—simply this and nothing more. —*Kingston Daily Freeman*, 14 July 1880

Rondout Village now was the largest community in Ulster County, with more than 10,000 residents, while Kingston had about 6,300, and the entire county had a population of approximately 84,000. Rondout's people had aspirations of being a city one day, but so did Kingston.

There had been occasional labor unrests in Rondout over the past twenty years, with limestone workers and canal boatmen both striking briefly in 1853, and laborers on the canal striking the following year. The canallers had demanded a raise from $1 to $1.10 per ton of coal they transported, and the laborers had asked for $1 rather than seventy-five cents a day—a ten-hour-day at that—but these strikes were not very successful. The canallers did not get their increase, and the laborers got only a very gradual increase to a dollar, while their workday was not shortened.

Brief strikes followed now and again, and the glimmer of workers' associations could be seen but, for the most part, labor unrest was insubstantial. This was a result of the vigorous post-war economy and the subsequent business boom's general prosperity that dissuaded workers from organized unrest.

The employees of the Cornell Towing Company were proud of their positions, aware they and the company were highly regarded in the industry. Many a fellow working as a deckhand or fireman on the boats fully intended to work up to captain or pilot or engineer. In years to come, most of the leading boatmen on the Hudson River, whether in passenger steamers or towboats, would have begun their careers as Cornell men. The shop workers and office staff, too, had high regard for their own company and were generally well contented with their jobs. A majority of the company's boatmen came from on or near Rondout Creek, and "Rondout, N.Y." was proudly painted on the sterns of all Cornell vessels as their home port.

These days, successful young Rondout businessmen like S. D. Coykendall were building mansions on newly developed West Chestnut Street, high on the hill overlooking Rondout Creek. Coykendall's was a spectacular pile of red stone in keeping with the grand homes of other industrial barons of the period, which was to be known as the "Gilded Age." His neighbors included cigar magnates, tanners, politicians, store owners, and brick manufacturers, many of whom were clients of Cornell Towing Company.

Another Coykendall son, Harry Shepard, was born to Samuel and Mary Coykendall in June of 1868.

Thomas Cornell owned the two leading steamboats operating out of Rondout: *Thomas Cornell* and *Mary Powell,* but he had long-range plans to become the number-one towing business on the Hudson. Cornell was convinced that railroads were the future for moving passengers, but much of the bulk-commerce would still go by water, and that would mean barges moved by towboats.

In the winter of 1868-69, he had the aged steamer *Santa Claus* totally rebuilt into the towboat *A. B. Valentine,* named after his company's longtime

New York City superintendent. *A. B. Valentine* was placed on the route between Rondout and New York. Cornell was on the lookout for more towboats, even if it meant buying out the opposition to do it, even if it meant selling some of his own valuable steamboat properties. The speedy and beautiful *Mary Powell* appealed to anyone in the business and would bring a top price if Cornell were to part with her. He had run the "Queen of the Hudson" from Rondout to New York, and in the fall of 1868 he made the most of her popularity by carrying passengers of any political party up from New York City for free so they could come home to vote in the election that year.

Cornell himself was up for re-election, but the publicity was not enough to win him a return to Congress, for he lost.

The first large sidewheel steamer built exclusively for service as a towboat on the Hudson River was *Oswego*, in 1848, for "Commodore" Alfred Van Santvoord. The commodore was well known for his extensive towing business, but better known for the excellent steamboats of his New York-Albany Day Line. Van Santvoord operated *Daniel Drew, Armenia, Chauncey Vibbard*, and *Alida*, to name a few of the popular boats of his Day Line. In early 1869, his fleet of towing steamers, known as the Hudson River Steamboat Company, was of prime interest to Thomas Cornell, and the feeling was mutual when it came to how Van Santvoord felt about *Mary Powell*.

A deal was struck in February of that year, and Cornell sold *Mary Powell* to Van Santvoord and a partner for $180,000, and at the same time bought from them three towing steamers for $80,000: *Oswego; Anna,* and *Cayuga*.

The crew members of the handsome little tug *Sammy Cornell* pose on their vessel in the Rondout Creek, probably during the early 1880s. It can be surmised that they were, forward to aft, the deckhand, captain, cook, fireman, and engineer. In the background is the spidery bridge that originally carried the tracks of the West Shore Railroad across the Creek, later replaced with the more substantial structure which remains in use today. (Roger W. Mabie Collection)

Railroads and Towboats

These were three of only seven large sidewheelers ever originally built as towboats on the Hudson. Van Santvoord, whose towing company had been losing money anyway, now was effectively out of the towing business, eliminating a formidable competitor for Cornell. In short order, Cornell traded towboats with Samuel Schuyler, owner of the Schuyler Line Towboat Association, giving *Cayuga* and *Anna* in return for the converted passenger steamer *Baltic*—which Schuyler had used on the Albany-Rondout towing route—and the towboat *New York,* also a converted passenger steamer. *Cayuga* would be employed by Schuyler on the Albany-New York route, leaving Rondout towing to Cornell.

Samuel Schuyler had been one of the true innovators in the towboat business, having developed the method of towing on hawsers rather than having the barges lashed directly to the towboat. This made maneuvering much easier for the towboat. Each barge had its own captain, who lived—sometimes with an entire family—on the boat, in a small deckhouse. The captain steered the barge with a tiller as the towboat pulled it along. Schuyler also built the *America* in 1852, one of those seven large sidewheel towboats built for the Hudson River.

Of prime advantage to Cornell from the sale of *Mary Powell* and trade for the towboats was that the Rondout-Albany towing route now was virtually under his control.

It is estimated that the commerce of the Hudson River amounts to $500,000,000 a year. This is more than half of the total exports of the whole republic. —*Kingston Daily Freeman,* **4 june 1880**

In 1870, Cornell and Coykendall turned themselves more intently toward railroading, as they established the Rhinebeck and Connecticut Railroad across the Hudson and the Delhi and Middletown Railroad for the Catskills. This year saw the first regularly scheduled Rondout and Oswego Railroad runs on about twenty-four miles of track that had been completed from Rondout to Mount Pleasant Station.

As with boats, locomotives were given names in these days, and Cornell's was called the "Pennsylvania." Two more locomotives were acquired along with rolling stock, and freight service was established to Shandaken, with bluestone being the main commodity. Since the communities along the projected line of railroad had invested heavily in the Rondout and Oswego, they had some reason for concern when Cornell turned more of his attention to the Rhinebeck and Connecticut and the Delhi and Middletown Railroads, especially because construction of their track was behind schedule.

In September 1870, Cornell found himself pressured by stockholders to resign as president of the Rondout and Oswego, and even though he held $500,000 in company bonds, he angrily resolved to take no further interest in its development. The Delhi line did not develop, but the Rhinebeck and Connecticut would be uppermost in Cornell's railroad efforts for the next five years.

There was also much in the way of the boat business to keep Cornell busy, but S. D. Coykendall was an excellent manager of the diverse aspects of his father-in-law's businesses, and his responsibilities increased.

There were setbacks and crises, of course, as when old boats sank at the dock and had to be raised and repaired. The towboat *Sarah E. Brown* sank in the Creek in 1869 and, after she was raised Cornell decided to rebuild her completely, renaming her *Sandy*. Other difficulties came with the spring freshets, as in the March 1870 flood that swept down Rondout Creek early in the morning, driving the steam-powered ferryboat *John P. Sleight* away from her moorings at Sleightsburgh. The unmanned ferryboat swirled along in the torrent, striking against the old, abandoned lighthouse, then drifting out into the river, leaking dangerously.

Typical of how boatmen helped each other in times of difficulty, Cornell's *Norwich* was sent to catch up with *John P. Sleight*, and did so near Esopus Island. The ferryboat was towed back to Port Ewen and beached, but she sank, and when raised for repairs, it was found her hull was too far gone. Another freshet had claimed another vessel, and these spring floods would continue to bedevil boats and boatmen in Rondout Creek.

Ice, of course, was the bane of steamboating, sometimes unexpectedly cutting short operations, freezing the canals that often held laden boats that would have to wait until spring to reach tidewater, and arbitrarily determining when the next shipping season would begin. It was the old towing steamer *Norwich*, that still so often broke up the ice each year, battling her way from New York to Rondout at the first sign of warmer weather. The "Ice King," she had been called, but now sometimes was the "Old Ice King," because she had been built back in 1836. *Norwich* still could drive up onto the ice, with her reinforced hull momentarily resting there, and then break through with her weight. Of course, her remarkable accomplishments as an ice breaker and rescuer of ice-bound boats led to stories that went the rounds, and even to tall tales, such as one that was published in the *Nautical Gazette* under the title "Sparks from a Paddle Wheel."

> There were five of them—all steamboat pilots. They sat around the Towing Office, in Rondout, spinning yarns about the wonderful 'doings' of the towboat *Norwich*. . . . Finally, one of the pilots, a grizzled veteran, after taking a huge quid of plug tobacco from his mouth, said: "I don't egzactly remember, but kalkerirate it was around about the middle of winter of '57. We was boun' from N' York to Rondout, with the *Norwich*. We encountered heavy ice all the way ter Perkeepsie, but managed to git through. You all know what the 'Old Ice King' can do when she gets her back up, don't you? After passin' Perkeepsie the ice began to git thicker and tougher. Pritty soon we run inter sixteen-inch ice. I thinks to myself, now we will have to put back to Perkeepsie and stop there the rest of the winter. We made slow headway for a leetle ways, and then stopped altogether.
>
> "The Cap'n was bound to go to Rondout with the boat, and when he got his dander up, he meant business. He gave orders to back up about a quarter of a mile, and then go ahead on a full head of steam. I expected to see the old craft shivered from stem to stern when she struck the ice, but I'll be gosh darned if she didn't raise herself up, like, and jump clean on top of the ice, her paddle wheels goin' round like a windmill. The ice held her, and as she sailed

Edward Meeker, chief engineer of the steamer Norwich, fell into the Rondout Creek on Saturday afternoon. He was walking along the dock and a piece of the string piece gave way and he plunged into the water. The accident was witnessed by several persons who immediately went to his assistance. —*Kingston Daily Leader*, 11 November 1901

along all right, the Cap'n gin orders to the engineer and firemen to keep things hummin'. Every time the wheels made a revolution, sparks of fire could be seen flyin' in every direction. She come inter Rondout skytin', I tell you, and made the distance, nigh outer 14 mile, in less than an hour and a quarter. The pilot, who steered her, said she minded her rudder beautifully.

"But I must hurry home now, fur I've got to git ready to 'tend prayer meetin' to night."

The *Nautical Gazette* remarked that it had no complaints about the old pilot's story, except for one slight exaggeration: it was well known that *Norwich* was not capable of going fourteen miles in an hour and a quarter.

Ice had another side to it than just harrying boats and boatmen. Cutting and storing it in winter for shipment to cities in the warm months became a major industry for the mid-Hudson Valley. Boatmen whose vessels were laid up for the winter usually found work at the many huge ice houses along the river—even the horses that pulled the ice-delivery wagons in the cities were employed upriver in the winter. They were brought up from New York on night boats and used to pull scrapers over the snow on the ice and also equipment that scored the ice for cutting. Horses also pulled blocks of ice to the conveyor belts that carried it to the ice houses, cavernous buildings where the ice was stored, each layer covered with straw as insulation to keep it cold.

Cornell towboats were busy in the summer hauling hundreds of barges laden with ice. One of the largest local ice boat owners was Cleary Brothers Barge Company, which was formed to carry ice and eventually had more than one hundred barges. Rapidly growing New York City was the great market for Hudson Valley ice, as it was for bluestone, farm produce, cement, lumber, crushed stone, brick, and coal. Since 1869, Rosendale cement, quarried and manufactured locally and shipped on barges towed by Cornell boats, had been used to construct the Brooklyn Bridge. This cement had remarkable strength and hardness, and although it was relatively slow to set, it even hardened under water. A number of Rosendale cement manufacturers and many others in the industry would belong to Cornell before long.

The Cornell Towing Company hauled great quantities of these bulk commodities, but the largest towing fleet on the river was still Schuyler's, based in Albany. Others included the Robinson and Betts Troy Towing Line, the Albany Towing Line, and the Beverwyck Towing Company of Albany. Thomas Cornell's towing business was growing rapidly and was firmly established, but his railroads needed financial muscle and political influence to be developed. He had both.

In Cornell's arsenal was his ownership of the Rondout *Daily Freeman*, which he used as his mouthpiece when it suited him, and which served him in attacks against the principals who replaced him in the Rondout and Oswego Railroad. In 1871, Cornell's local influence led to the appointment of S. D. Coykendall as Ulster County treasurer, replacing John C. Brodhead, who had come under scorching editorial attack from the *Freeman*, which accused him of misappropriation of county funds. It was no coincidence that Brodhead was the man who had been elected president of the Rondout and Oswego Railroad to replace Cornell and was considered an arch enemy.

In April 1871, Coykendall's third son, Edward, was born.

The next year, Cornell became president of the Wallkill Valley Railroad, then building its way toward Kingston from the southwest. His relationship with the struggling Rondout and Oswego, which changed its name to the more practical New York, Kingston and Syracuse, continued to spark controversy. In 1872, the railroad found itself being foreclosed upon by the Farmer's Loan and Trust of New York, the leading bondholders, who claimed the interest had not been paid on time. The next significant development in what became a lengthy legal struggle took place that summer when officers of the railroad sued former managers Cornell and Coykendall for malfeasance, misappropriation of bonds, and theft of money from the company treasury during their time running the railroad. Cornell angrily denied the charges, saying the suit was laid because the railroad's officers wanted to pressure him into influencing the Farmer's Loan and Trust to stop their foreclosure proceedings. Cornell and Coykendall threatened a countersuit for libel, and the standoff was eventually settled in their favor.

Now creditors were obtaining judgments against the New York, Kingston and Syracuse Railroad, which went into receivership in 1875. The railroad was bought at auction by the Farmer's Loan and Trust, which reorganized the

Isaac M. North is here shown in the Rondout Creek at an unknown date, probably in the 1870s or 1880s. The paddle box of the side-wheeler *Oswego* is visible over *North*'s stern, and a least three other towboats and tugs can be discerned on the opposite side of the Creek. *Isaac M. North*, built in Philadelphia in 1862 as *Addie Douglas*, was acquired by Thomas Cornell in 1866 after her Civil War service as USS *Poppy*. (Roger Mabie Collection)

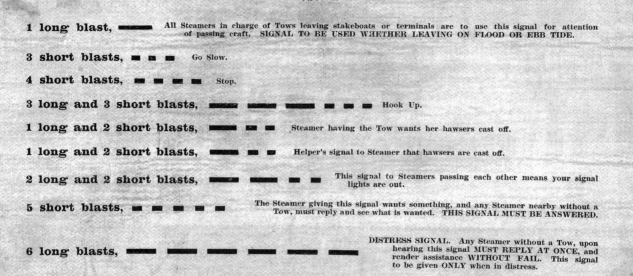

An 1870s placard displaying the whistle signals of the Cornell Steamboat Company. During the late nineteenth century, the proliferation of tugs and other harbor craft around New York made company whistle signals necessary. Eventually, however, these signals came into question in the harbor when their use was deemed to interfere or at least cause confusion with the warning signals recognized by the maritime rules of the road. (C. W. Spangenberger Collection)

railroad as the Ulster and Delaware, working closely with Cornell, who became the new president, and Coykendall, vice president. George Coykendall, brother of Samuel, was named superintendent of the U&D, which by now had seventy-five miles of track laid through the mountains and was in need of a complete overhaul, including new track, bridge construction, more rolling stock and locomotives, as well as a total reorganization of employees' duties. There was also a pressing need for freight and passengers to pay the bills.

Meanwhile, Cornell was closely involved with directing the Wallkill Valley Railroad, and he was completing construction of the Rhinebeck and Connecticut to Boston Corners. He also had to contend with labor unrest among his U&D employees, for when he laid off a number of men from the Rondout railroad shops in 1876, the result was an arson fire that completely destroyed the shops. This incident was followed by an arsonist burning the wooden trestle over Esopus Creek, but this incident was said to have been the work of striking employees at the bluestone quarry near West Hurley who wanted to stop the railroad handling stone from there.

All this time, the Cornell Towing Company was on its way to becoming the leading towing firm on the river. While Cornell's railroad and financial machinations spun out their course, the steamers plied the river under the hand of masterful captains—many of whom had taken to wearing high beaver hats and fashionable clothes these days.

Local identity of the Rondout Creek population was affected drastically in 1872, when Kingston pulled political strings and was incorporated as a city, beating Rondout to it. Rondout's population was double that of Kingston, but the state chose to ignore Rondout's petitions for status as a city. The City of Kingston included both Rondout and Wilbur in its boundaries.

Although there no longer was an official municipality of "Rondout, N.Y.," the Cornell boats kept that name on their sterns as hailing port.

In November 1872, a fourth son, Frederick, was born to Mary and Samuel Coykendall.

The towing company launched *George A. Hoyt* in 1873, the last of the seven sidewheel steamers built exclusively as towboats for the Hudson River.

Vessels came into the company and others went, such as the towing steamer, *Baltic*, under Captain Jeremiah Patterson, which caught fire five miles below Albany in July 1876, burning to the waterline and sinking. Considered one of the best towboats in the company, *Baltic* had been in first-class condition after being rebuilt two years earlier at a reported cost of $20,000. Her place was taken by *George A. Hoyt*, which operated in company with *Herald* on

The mighty *A. B. Valentine*, named for Thomas Cornell's agent at New York, was constructed in 1869 from the hull of the 1845-built passenger steamboat *Santa Claus* and lasted until 1901. The hog frame, a heavy timber truss which provided strength to the hull of a slim, shallow wooden steamboat, dominates this image. The sidewheel towboat was an elegant engineering solution to the problem of moving barges in the river in the nineteenth century, and the 205-ft *A. B. Valentine* was a classic example of the type. (Roger W. Mabie Collection)

the upper Hudson River. *Hoyt*'s engine originally came from the old steamboat *James Madison*, scrapped in 1871. The engine was rebuilt in the versatile Cornell shops at Rondout before being installed in *Hoyt*. In fact, as was common practice for the day, parts of several scrapped steamers were recycled for the *Hoyt*, including the walking beam from Cornell's *Mohegan*.

Another once-grand steamboat that came into the Cornell fleet at this time was the *Alida*, a dayboat that had been a favorite with travelers when she had made fast passages between Albany and New York back in 1848. In the mid sixties, she had been converted to a towboat, her upper decks and passenger facilities removed, and she ran for Robinson and Betts before Cornell bought her when that company sold out in 1874. *Alida* made only one trip for Cornell Towing Company, and that was in December of the year she joined the fleet. There had been hope that her engine could be rebuilt and installed in another vessel, but that did not work out, and she was towed to Port Ewen to await being broken up in 1880.

In 1875, *New York* was deemed of no more use as a towing steamer and was beached on the flats south of Kingston Point, broken up, and scrapped.

Cornell's competition in the towing business was further diminished in 1876 when the Jeremiah Austin towing line, the Albany and Canal Towing Company, went into receivership. By 1878, Cornell had acquired three of that company's sidewheel towboats, including *Silas O. Pierce*, well known for her military exploits in the Civil War, and *General McDonald*. The third was *Austin*, which had been built in 1853 as a sidewheel towboat, and at 197 feet was one of the three largest vessels of its kind on the river. Cornell's talented shopmen partly rebuilt her and, as a modernized towboat, *Austin* was always an impressive sight running from Rondout to New York.

A rare, undated, view of the towboat *George A. Hoyt* alongside a barge at Rondout. Built for Thomas Cornell in 1873 at New Baltimore, New York, *George A. Hoyt* was the seventh—and last—vessel built on the Hudson River as a sidewheel towboat. (Roger W. Mabie Collection)

Two more Coykendall children were born in these years: Catherine, in November 1874, and Frank, in October 1876.

In 1877, Cornell daughter Cornelia Lucy married Robert M. Bayard of New York City and went there with him to live. They would have no children.

During this same year, Thomas Cornell became president of the Wallkill Valley Railroad. At the same time, his U&D had been completely overhauled and was becoming successful. An example of the relationship of various components in his empire could be seen in the growing commerce in milk from the Catskills. It was brought down to Rondout by a Cornell train, then shipped to New York on his old sidewheel steamer *William Cook*, nicknamed the "Milkmaid." The city came to depend on this milk, which was a profitable commodity for Cornell's railroads as they made their way into otherwise undeveloped mountains. The development of commercial dairying in the Catskills was in large part stimulated by S. D. Coykendall, who with remarkable foresight financed the first creamery, which was built at Roxbury.

The railroads themselves were not profitable yet, but they did have the advantage of Cornell Towing Company connections, as evident when locomotives from the Rhinebeck and Connecticut were routinely brought over the river by Cornell barges and towboats for repair in the Rondout shops.

The towing company now had about 450 employees; sixty coal-burning towing vessels; extensive repair and boiler shops at the Rondout Strand, including a brick building one hundred yards long, fifty wide, and forty high. Cornell shops could fabricate or repair any part of a vessel.

In addition to having "Rondout, N.Y." as the hailing port on their sterns, Cornell towboats generally had a gilded eagle on their pilothouses, and by this time most of the boats were painted in standard company colors: deckhouses Indian red with chrome yellow decorative panels; smoke stacks black down to the height of the pilot house, below which the paint was yellow or buff. The hulls of most towboats were black, with red below the water line. Through the black of the hull ran a narrow yellow stripe.

It was said that one could always pick out the house of a Cornell boatman because it was invariably painted in company colors—with company paint that had found its way there.

On March 29, 1878, the towing company formally incorporated as the Cornell Steamboat Company, with directors Thomas Cornell, who was also president, S. D. Coykendall, George Coykendall, R. G. Townsend, and A. B. Valentine.

In July of that same year, the sixth son and last child of the Coykendalls was born, named Robert Bayard. It must have seemed that seven Coykendall children guaranteed future executives who would continue to run the various Cornell companies. Would any of them turn out like their father?

Samuel D. Coykendall was proving to be everything Thomas Cornell could ask for in a son-in-law.

Chapter Six
The Last Passenger Boats

BY 1879, Cornell's steamboat business was thriving, but the railroads were demanding much capital and time from him and Coykendall, and with uncertain results.

As a result of accidents and damage claims that sapped the resources of the Wallkill Valley Railroad, Cornell and his fellow bondholders were obliged to buy it at auction and reorganize it in 1877 under his presidency. More accidents, the need to lay new rail, and the demands of developing safer operating rules all kept Cornell's mind on his railroads during this time, but by 1880 his determination and an investment of $300,000 over five years began to bring the U&D, at least, into solvency. During this year, the U&D had a $12,000 surplus, with bond interest paid on time, and Cornell could fairly dream of linking with the Delaware and Hudson Railway at Oneonta, opening his short line, and Kingston, to the West.

Annual U&D passenger traffic rose from 83,000 in 1875 to 111,000 in 1880, with freight tonnage also climbing steadily to more than 100,000 tons per annum. Cornell had achieved all this with the minimum of new rolling stock, and his success was typified by the milk shipments over the U&D, which continued to rise in volume and would approach 30,000 tons of milk by 1900.

In this time, Thomas Cornell heard of plans of major financiers to extend the West Shore Railroad up the Hudson River and through Kingston to Albany. He knew his Wallkill Valley Railroad would find itself up against stiff competition, with prospects of a fare war that would cut into its already weak income. To counter the West Shore plans, Cornell immediately announced his intention to extend the Wallkill Valley north to Albany, which meant laying track parallel to that of the West Shore route. He actually started surveying his projected route and ordered new steel track to be delivered to Kingston.

It likely was just a bluff to make the West Shore tycoons think twice about pushing ahead with their plans, but the days of the Wallkill Valley remaining under Cornell's control were numbered. He was losing money every year by having to pay the bond interest that income from operations could not cover, amounting to $5,000 annually in its first years under his control.

In 1880, twelve years after being defeated for his second term in Congress, Cornell ran again, once more winning a seat. The triumph was in large part thanks to the concerted efforts of S. D. Coykendall, who wrote many letters on his father-in-law's behalf and solicited everyone he could to help. While

The Sammy Cornell, having her pilot house and smokestack removed, was sent up the [D&H] canal with a cement boat for Rock Locks. She will return with this boat and another loaded.
—*Kingston Daily Freeman*, 24 November 1880

Cornell was away in Washington, the family empire would be in the able hands of S. D. Coykendall, named president of the railroads; and he would be aided by Cornell's excellent managers of the steamboating, railroading, banking, quarrying, and ferry businesses. Family interests in various other industries included cement, hotels, and ice.

In 1881, the year Thomas Cornell again set off for Washington, he sold the Wallkill Valley Railroad to the North River Construction Company, which was contracted to build the West Shore Railroad toward Albany. It was a profitable transaction, as Cornell earned several hundred thousand dollars that made it possible for him to provide the financing for the builder of the Grand Hotel, above Pine Hill, a beautiful vacation spot on Highmount in the Catskills. The builder of the Grand Hotel, which was reached by the main line of the U&D, soon ran into trouble, and Cornell took possession. During this year, Cornell and Coykendall also built the short-line, narrow-gauge Stony Clove and Catskill Mountain Railroad north from Phoenicia to carry clientele up to such hotels as the Laurel House and Hotel Kaaterskill.

In 1882, Cornell sold the Rhinebeck and Connecticut Railroad at another good profit and began construction of the narrow-gauge Kaaterskill Railroad to serve Greene County's large hotels such as the Catskill Mountain House near Haines Falls. Until now, vacationers had to get up there by a bumpy stage ride over rough and sometimes dizzyingly twisting roads. In 1884, next on Cornell's agenda would be the construction of the Hobart Branch Railroad, which he immediately leased to the U&D.

The U&D, which was steadily growing westward, profited by the building of the north-south West Shore Railroad into Kingston, where they connected. The U&D's passenger and freight traffic increased, especially into the Catskill Mountain resort areas. Cornell was able, as a result, to pay off U&D bonds and thus reduce his interest expense. The development of the railroads was going so well that they seemed about to fulfill the immense promise they had, for three decades, so teasingly held out to Thomas Cornell.

On January 23, 1882—Cornell's birthday—a tragedy cost the lives of several boatmen. An explosion destroyed the tugboat *H. P. Farrington*. The blast killed the second engineer, a fireman, and cook, and injured the captain and the rest of the crew. *Farrington* had been lying off Haverstraw while awaiting brick barges to be made up for the tow to New York.

Despite the company's best efforts, the boat was not raised until two months later, and it was only then that the body of Albert Hennion, second engineer, was recovered and returned to his family at Kingston for interment. The cause of the *Farrington* explosion was never officially determined.

That year the regular towing season began fairly early, with Cornell's ice breaker *Norwich* scarcely needed because the weather was almost balmy. As soon as March 3, the Hudson River was open for navigation from the mouth of Rondout Creek southward, and freshly painted Cornell tugs were at work, including *Dr. David Kennedy* and *Sammy Cornell*, which towed ice barges and vessels to Barrytown, above Rhinebeck. *Norwich* towed barges as far north as

There is a rush of work at the boiler shop of the Cornell Steamboat Company, and a chance for some good workmen to find employment there at remunerative wages.
—*Kingston Daily Freeman*, 6 January 1881

The steamer *Thomas Cornell*, shown after she was wrecked on Danskammer Point on the foggy night of March 27, 1882. The name of this noted Hudson landmark on the west shore of the river about five miles above Newburgh, was derived from the Dutch, *De Duivels Danskamer*—"The Devil's Dance Chamber." (Hudson River Maritime Museum Collection)

Saugerties on March 7, and the towboat *Cayuga* set off for Albany with a tow of canal boats on March 9, usually a bitterly cold time in the mid-Hudson Valley. The magnificent steamboat *Thomas Cornell* also finished her test runs for the new season.

Then came another major disaster. On March 27, *Thomas Cornell* ran aground at Danskammer Point. She had just left Marlborough and was on her way to New York in a heavy fog, cautiously proceeding at half speed in waters above Newburgh. Obviously the pilot misjudged the strength and set of the tide and, instead of rounding Danskammer Point and entering the broad expanses of Newburgh Bay, the steamer ran right onto the Point with the stern sinking in deep water. The passengers rushed toward the bow, clambering over it and down to dry land, where they waited to be rescued, building fires to stay warm in the mist and chilling drizzle.

No one died in the accident that night, but *Thomas Cornell* was finished. Her hog-frame—the reinforcement that ran the length of the ship—was broken.

News of *Thomas Cornell*'s grounding flashed by telegraph to Rondout, where newspaper reporters rushed out to get a story from company spokes-

The steamer *City of Kingston*, built to replace the Thomas Cornell—wrecked in 1882 on Danskammer Point—First appeared on the Hudson River in 1884 and was a distinct departure from her predecessors, having an iron hull and being propelled by a single screw propeller at the stern. She was also the first Hudson River steamboat to be equipped with electric lights. Later sold to interests on Puget Sound, *City of Kingston* steamed under her own power around South America (this was prior to the Panama Canal) to reach her new area of operation. (J. Matthews Collection)

men. It was said that they heard S. D. Coykendall himself was at that time coming up by train from New York. When he arrived in Kingston, Coykendall was met by an excited reporter who asked whether he had seen the grounded *Thomas Cornell* from the train carriage, and what did he think about it. Exhibiting no sign of the shock and grief that must have surged through him at that moment—likely he had heard of the situation long before he reached Rondout—Coykendall brushed off the reporter, casually saying he had been sitting on the opposite side of the train, reading the newspaper, so he had not been looking out the window. That report got into the papers, amazing and delighting readers, who marveled at Coykendall's coolness under the circumstances.

The broken *Thomas Cornell* was laboriously raised, made temporarily watertight, and was towed back to Rondout Creek, yet it was clear the pride of the Cornell Steamboat Company would have to be scrapped. There was nothing to be done to save her, but it was decided to take her engine out at J. McCausland's shipyard for use in another vessel. In so doing that October, a crane accident further damaged the steamboat. A detailed description ran in the *Freeman* under the title, "A Thrilling Accident," with the subtitle, "A

Derrick Breaks Under a Heavy Weight and Seriously Damages the Thomas Cornell." The article gave some sense of the great size of the steamboat's inner mechanics, and of the sort of difficulties and risks that faced boatyard workers in those days.

> A very serious mishap occurred at the foundry dock about 11:30 this morning. The remnants of the steamer Thomas Cornell have been lying at the dock, in order to have the gallows frame and cranks and shaft taken out. The frame has been lifted out successfully, and this morning the task of lifting out the shafts and cranks was commenced. The shafts are two wrought iron rods, each about 20 ft. in length and 18 inches in diameter. To one end of each shaft is attached a crank which is turned by the walking beam, and to the other three heavy flanges, each weighing several hundred pounds, which form the hub of the paddle wheels.
>
> Each shaft with cranks and flanges attached weighs 20 tons. To lift this great weight, the powerful steam derrick located on the dock, and which is perhaps the largest on the Hudson, was used. The mast of the derrick is 72 feet high, and the gaff is about 85 feet long. Heavy chains were attached to the shaft on the port side of the boat, the engine was started and the great piece of machinery was slowly raised upward and swung over the stern of the boat, upon which it was designed to lower it. The derrick was used some weeks ago to take out the heavy engine, and performed the work easily, and it was thought that the derrick was strong enough to lift the shaft, even though its weight was so much greater.
>
> Everything went well till the ropes were slacked off to lower the shaft upon the deck. At that time it was suspended at height not exceeding ten feet. "Lower away easily," was Mr. McCausland's order. The blocks creaked as the ropes ran through them, and then suddenly, there was a loud cracking report, like musketry; the mast of the derrick broke in two like a pipe stem, and with a tremendous crash the great shaft descended upon the deck of the boat. The workmen ran for their lives, and fortunately, none of them was hurt, although there were several narrow escapes.
>
> The breaking of the derrick and the fall of the shaft made sad havoc on board of the steamboat. Three great holes yawned through the deck and heavy timbers had been snapped like straws. The mast of the derrick in its descent struck a part of the gallows frame—a timber measuring two feet thick—which was lying upon the deck, and drove it through the deck and down into the hold of the boat, breaking off stout timbers as though they were egg shells. If the fall of the mast had not been impeded by the gallows frame, it would have forced itself not only through the deck, but also through the bottom of the boat.

The snapping of the derrick's guy rope put a sudden strain on the derrick and seemed the cause of the accident, which resulted in *Thomas Cornell* being brought back to Port Ewen to await repairs to the boatyard's derrick and a resumption of the work. It had been hoped the steamer at least could have been made into a barge, but now there was too much damage for even that. In time, her hull would be cut in two and converted into a pair of coal boats. The engine was taken by the salvagers at Port Ewen, but it was never used again and eventually had to be scrapped.

Thus did one of the best-known Rondout passenger steamboats prematurely meet a rather dismal end. But *Thomas Cornell* would not be forgotten

---

Alderman Isaac M. North, of this city, has again been chosen one of the vice presidents of the Albany Boatman's Relief Association.
—*Kingston Daily Freeman*, 12 January 1881

by those who had seen her daily in Rondout Creek or had traveled on her, and certainly never forgotten by the men who had served on her.
During this same year of 1882, a devastating fire struck the Cornell Steamboat Company's offices in Rondout, destroying almost all the company's records to that date.

To replace the *Thomas Cornell* as the night boat running on the Rondout-to-New York route with Romer and Tremper's night boat, *James W. Baldwin*, the company chartered the almost-new steamboat, *City of Catskill*. *City of Catskill* had been built in 1880 for the Catskill-to-New York line that served the great hotels of the mountains behind the village of Catskill. At 250 feet in length, and with the finest of furnishings and passenger accommodations, she was the largest and most elegant steamboat built for that route thus far.

At this time, Cornell ordered another great steamboat built in place of the *Thomas Cornell*. To be named the *City of Kingston*, she would be propeller-driven.

With all his railroad and tugboat involvement, Thomas Cornell apparently still had a soft spot for *Mary Powell*, for late in 1882 he learned that Captain Absalom Anderson was sickly and was compelled to sell her. It was rumored that Anderson believed the coming of the West Shore Railroad would completely doom the passenger steamboat business, and this was another incentive to part with the cherished boat he had built and captained over most of the past twenty years.

That November, Cornell acquired *Mary Powell* for the second time, and he kept her as a day boat on the Rondout-to-New York line, for which she was so well known and patronized. His cousin, William H. Cornell, who had been master of *Thomas Cornell* when she struck Danskammer Point, would be *Mary Powell*'s next captain.

News of the comings and goings of boats and of incidents and accidents affecting vessels and crews, and reports of the number of boats in a tow, the fortunes of steamboat companies, their building, buying, and selling of boats—even job offers that were turned down when a man stayed with Cornell instead of leaving—were a staple of local papers such as the *Rondout Courier* and Kingston *Daily Freeman*.

Of course, family and friends had a keen interest in the welfare of the men on board, but there was also a certain civic pride in seeing Rondout Creek busy with boats as the industries along the shore resounded with hammer blows and throbbed with the sound of engines and machines. The term "tugboat" rather than towing steamer or towboat had lately come into vogue when, on September 6, the Kingston *Daily Freeman* published a typical report on boats docked in the Creek, on the movements of passenger boats, and on tugs sighted out on the river with tows.

> The tug [George] W. Pratt is now lying on the south shore of the creek.

The tug C. D. Mills has been launched from the dry dock of Andy McMullen, of Sleightburgh [sic] and again glides smoothly and silently about the Rondout Creek.
—*Kingston Daily Freeman*, 23 May 1881

The Vanderbilt passed south Tuesday with a large tow of canal boats for Albany.

The I. M. North came in the creek this morning with nineteen boats from Newburgh.

The tugs Camelia and P. C. Schultz passed north last night with a large tow of ice barges.

The Valentine left this port on Monday with thirty canal boats in tow for Albany and Hudson.

The Marshall left this port on Monday night with fifteen canal boats and one schooner for New York.

On Monday night the creek presented a business like appearance from the foundry dock to the lighthouse. The Valentine, Oswego, Marshall, Metamora, City of Catskill, W. B. Crane, Transport, Sammy Cornell, Pittston, and the I. M. North were all going out of the creek at the same time, the majority of them with tows.

The side-wheel towboat W. B. Crane, Captain James Dubois, Engineer D. B. Eighmey, is laid off half a day today for repairs. This is the first time in the last three months that the Crane has been without steam on her boilers. —Kingston Daily Freeman, 7 June 1881

And the majority of those boats mentioned belonged to the Cornell fleet or were chartered to it.

Reporters were candid with their assessment of a boat's condition when it was brought to the Creek to be repaired or perhaps for inspection by state officials who by law annually checked the boilers and pipes of steamers. No one in this boatman's community could deny a vessel's obvious shortcomings, hull condition, or mechanical problems without being considered uninformed about important local news. A reporter's stroll through town and past the waterfront brought bits of information and news that was published the next day, and it was not unusual for the reporter's personal opinions to be put in print, such as a comment that a boat being caulked in dry dock "was showing her age."

Yet another Cornell tugboat sinking that eventful year of 1882 ended with the crew barely escaping. At four in the morning on October 10, the tugboat *F. Lavergne* was lying in the slip between Harrison and Jay Streets at the North River docks in New York when the men were awakened by the sound of snapping cables that made the boat fast to the wharf. They sprang out of bed to discover the tugboat was sinking, and they barely managed to escape through windows before she went under.

Lavergne sank because its firemen had gone to sleep the night before without turning off the water being taken on to fill the boilers. The overflow filled the hold of the boat, and she began to settle to the muddy bottom, with only the top of the pilot house left showing. As was often the procedure in such sinkings at the dock—which was not an infrequent occurrence with old or leaky boats—the *Lavergne* was raised that afternoon and found to have little damage.

The embarrassment to the firemen and officers, however, was lasting.

The following year, 1883, started with yet another disaster, as *City of Catskill* caught fire on February 11, while berthed at her winter quarters in Rondout Creek. The cause of the blaze was mysterious, and it is disputed as to whether it started on the dock and spread to the boat, or vice versa. She was only three years old, but was a total loss, burning down to the ice that held her fast and kept her from sinking.

For that season, Cornell Steamboat Company chartered *City of Springfield* in the interim, until the new *City of Kingston* came off the ways in 1884. Thomas Cornell's passenger steamboat business prospered along with the tugboats, the U&D Railroad, the Grand Hotel, and his financial interests in the many businesses that were essential to the well-being of the mid-Hudson Valley.

In the handsome *City of Kingston,* he would have a propeller-driven steamboat with the most modern of attributes, including 300 electric lights! New York City had just undergone electrification at the direction of inventor Thomas Edison, and so it was remarkable that any vessel would have its own generator and lighting. As did *Thomas Cornell, City of Kingston* would run as a night boat, opposite *James W. Baldwin*. Electric lights made *City of Kingston* outstanding, the more so when added to the fact that she was capable of speeds up to nineteen miles per hour. It would, however, take some time for her pilots to learn to handle propellers at the stern instead of the usual paddle wheels amidships. Some men could not do it and called her a "cranky" boat. Veteran pilot William H. Mabie of Port Ewen proved *City of Kingston* was not "cranky," and that it was a matter of taking into account the torque of the screw propeller, which, if the pilot was not ready for it, caused the stern to swing to port when the boat was backing. Another difference with screw propeller-driven boats was that they did not stop as fast as paddle wheelers could, and that also had to be accounted for.

There were those who still favored sidewheel paddles, of course, but others knew screw propellers were the future for steamboats. Tugboats, in particular, were more compact and maneuverable with propellers instead of sidewheel paddles.

In 1884, seventy-year-old Thomas Cornell was busy attending the Republican national convention, and S. D. Coykendall was president of the towing company as well as in charge of most other Cornell enterprises, including the Consolidated Rosendale Cement Company, which now had the completed Brooklyn Bridge as a monument to its success. The Catskill railroads were still being built, the ferry business was doing well, and the Cornell Steamboat Company was renowned as the largest towing enterprise in the United States.

Early this year, Cornell grew yet again by buying out the Washburn Steamboat Company, based in Saugerties, thus acquiring the tugs *John H. Cordts, Wm. S. Earl, H. T. Caswell, Ira M. Hedges, Edwin Terry,* and *Hercules,* and the combination tug and lighter *Alicia A. Washburn.*

In March 1884, with *City of Kingston* soon to be launched, Thomas Cornell sold his interest in *Mary Powell* to a group of partners calling themselves the Mary Powell Steamboat Company. One-eighth of their stock was owned by A. Eltinge Anderson, son of Absalom, and the man who would become *Mary Powell*'s next master.

The Sammy Cornell has about the deepest toned whistle of any steamboat on the Hudson. She fairly makes the ground shake when she blows it while lying at the wharves.
—*Kingston Daily Freeman,*
20 June 1881

The Last Passenger Boats

In the following years, the railroads were the most demanding aspects of Thomas Cornell's business empire.

The battle for the wealthy tourist's dollar was on in the Catskill Mountains, as rail lines and hotels were built to accommodate the ever-increasing traffic to and from the hotels. The Grand Hotel, Cornell's stately creation thirty-nine miles from Kingston, accommodated 450, usually socially prominent, guests. Thriving along with most of the other fine hotels, the Grand was served by the U&D Railroad, while others, such as the Laurel House, Kaaterskill Hotel, and the long-lived Catskill Mountain House all could be reached by the independent Stony Clove and Catskill Mountain Railroad, established with Cornell's backing and controlled by him.

On June 25, 1883, the very first through train on the Stony Clove and Catskill Mountain was a special, carrying Thomas Cornell, S. D. Coykendall, and several of the Cornell grandsons. The eldest, Thomas Cornell Coykendall was proving to be a mechanical genius with a love of machines. Like his brothers, the sixteen-year-old Thomas would attend Columbia College in New York City. He would earn a degree in civil engineering. The second son, Harry Shepard Coykendall, would attend Columbia, but not graduate; this celebration on the through train was also his fifteenth birthday. The third Coykendall son, Edward, who was twelve, would become a Columbia graduate, also in civil engineering, and would have the strongest hand in leading many Cornell companies. Frederick, the fourth son, was nine years old; he, too, was destined to graduate from Columbia and earn his civil engineering degree. Fifth son, Frank, who was six years old in 1883, would do the same, but brother Robert, who was only four in this year, would attend but not graduate from Columbia.

For the inauguration of their new narrow-gauge railroad, the Cornells and Coykendalls enjoyed a lovely summer's day in the Catskills, with the midday meal at the Laurel House, followed by a visit to the Hotel Kaaterskill before returning that evening to Rondout. The railroad business seemed ideal on such a fine occasion, but there was little industry or population in the mountains or even to the immediate west. Other than some agricultural products, the railroad depended mostly on tourists for fares. For now, tourists of the highest social status were flocking by steamboat and railroad into the Catskills, but this was a fickle market, and the trains, just like passenger steamboats, also needed to move freight to be profitable.

Tugboats, on the other hand, did not need passengers, just commercial clients who had to get their bulk materials to market. Such clients there were aplenty in the Hudson Valley of the mid-1880s, and the Cornell Steamboat Company had more than enough tugs to service them.

An Accident Befalls *City of Kingston*

The short career on the Hudson of the steam propeller *City of Kingston*—from 1884 to 1889—was marred by two unfortunate accidents. Of serious consequence was that one which occured on the night of June 23, 1886, when the steamer ran down and sank the small schooner *Mary Atwater* shortly after leaving Cranston's Landing. The schooner, bound from Rondout to New York with a cargo of 550 barrels of cement, was struck in the stern by the steamboat while she was opposite the Grasselli chemical works at Manitou, just north of where the Bear Mountain Bridge now crosses the river.

The night was dark and a bit stormy, but it was stated that lights on passing steamboats could be readily seen. As *City of Kingston* proceeded down the river with Captain W. S. Van Keuren and two pilots keeping a careful lookout, a dim light was noticed about 150 feet ahead of the steamboat. An immediate "full astern" bell was rung to the engine room, but the vessel could not be stopped in time because of the ebbing tide, and *Mary Atwater* was struck on the stern. A minute and a half after the impact, the schooner had sunk. The captain was rescued from the water, but two crew members drowned.

At that time, sailing vessels usually displayed what was called a "flash light" astern to attract attention. A blinking light or one of variable intensity was deemed sufficient to warn an overtaking vessel. After the accident, *Mary Atwater*'s captain, James Black Jr., said he was reluctant to display a stern light because he could not see to steer. He stated during the subsequent coroner's inquest that on the night of the sinking he had placed a kerosene lamp in the vessel's cabin when he saw *City of Kingston* astern, about a quater-mile away, and walked back and forth of the open cabin door several times as the steamboat approached to produce the "flash" effect. Alas, it was too little and too late.

Mary Atwater, built in 1849 at Huntington, New York, and owned in Cold Spring by Captain Black, was a 50-ton vessel about 60 feet in length. She was uninsured. Her loss and that of the two men (one of whom was Black's father) illustrates one of the hazards of nighttime navigation in those days before the advent of electric navigation lights.

William duBarry Thomas

A panoramic photograph, circa 1880, overlooking Rondout Creek, shows, in the foreground, part of the repair shops of the Cornell Steamboat Company; on the far side is the hamlet of Sleightsburgh, and at the upper left is a huge fleet of Delaware & Hudson Canal boats, stored on the Sleightsburgh flats. (Delaware & Hudson Canal Museum Collection)

The Cornell Steamboat Company office building on Ferry Street, at the foot of Broadway in Kingston, housed the administrative functions of all the varied Cornell interests; on the former site of a Cornell office and warehouse destroyed by fire in 1883, this building was demolished during the Urban Renewal program of the 1970s. (J. Matthews Collection)

Chapter Seven
Tugboats

THE HUDSON RIVER below the Troy dam is not just a river, but an estuary more than 150 miles long, which means tides strongly influence the river almost all the way north to Troy, where the water daily rises and falls as much as three feet. Added to the flow of fresh water heading for the sea, the tidal currents make the Hudson a challenge to boatmen. For tugs in the 1880s, towing as much as 16,000 tons in dozens of boats stretching a hundred yards or more behind them, there was no room for error.

In all the years of Cornell Steamboat Company's existence, there were surprisingly few serious accidents with the tugs. Although there was a steady flow of claims and litigation from customers whose barges or docks were inadvertently damaged, that was part of the cost of doing business. Cornell continued operating efficiently, and by now famously, as its reputation for excellence grew in stature along with its fleet's size. S. D. Coykendall and the men he hired to manage the Cornell Steamboat Company had excellent personal and professional reputations.

The company's reputation rested not only on its men, but on the quality of its boats and equipment. Vessels were maintained so well that a steam tug forty or fifty years old would have been rebuilt and reconditioned many times over, so that even late in its career could seem almost new. Since most of the company's vessels operated mainly in fresh water, there was less deterioration than that suffered by sea-going tugs running in salt water; this reduced corrosion was especially noticeable on tugs with steel hulls.

Tugs were used to pull anything from canal boats and barges carrying coal, stone, livestock, or even live eels, to steamboats that had lost power or needed a trip to a dry dock, to sailing vessels loaded with freight or pleasure yachts on their way home. Most towing work was with barges, which had holds, or scows, which were decked vessels that had their freight piled on them. Canal boats generally were one of these two types. Bricks and lumber and cut slabs of bluestone usually went on the deck of a scow, while bulk raw materials such as crushed stone, anthracite, and baled hay were shipped in barges.

A "market boat" was a barge that lay at the starting dock until filled with locally produced edibles and goods to be sold in New York City. Once it was ready, the market boat was towed to New York, but when it got there might not be immediately unloaded, because the boat's captain or the captain of the towing steamer would try to get the best possible price before he made the sale. He usually received a commission as well as the fee for shipping the goods, so it was to his advantage to wait for the best return for his clients.

The propeller Rob left here at 1 o'clock and the Cornell at 2 o'clock today for the boat races at Poughkeepsie. Both tugs were gaily decorated with flags and college colors and each had a private party aboard. —*Kingston Daily Freeman,* **27 June 1908**

Until the middle of the twentieth century, each barge or scow also had its own captain, who lived in the tiny deckhouse at the stern, often with his wife and family and family dog. In the early years, the captain stood at the tiller to help in the steering of his boat when it was being towed. Later, with the boats lashed together, it was the towboat alone that steered the tow. The duties of the barge or scow captain included caring for the boat, cooperating with the tugboat captain as required to make fast and cast off, and guarding the boat when it was in port. Even the New York Harbor stakeboats had a captain and family living full-time on board, there in the middle of the broad river, just a mile or two from the seething heart of downtown.

When the method of towing with hawsers—thick cables—was developed around the Civil War period, it became possible for a tug to take as many as forty or more boats in tow. These were lashed together, usually three across and seven rows or more deep.

While the "big tug"—sometimes called a towing steamer or line steamer—pulled the tow, a smaller, or "helper," tug worked in collaboration with it. On a typical downtow from Albany during the 1930s, a Cornell tugboat permanently based in the upper reaches of the river—usually a large towing steamer—pulled the tow downriver, and the helper fetched barges or scows from the shore as the tow moved. Deckhands and boat captains lashed the new vessels to the sides or back of the tow, which became steadily larger and heavier. As the location of a customer's boat was reached, the main tow would slow down, and the helper tug would enter the cove or creek or dock belonging to the port, stone quarry, or brickyard where it was waiting to be taken out.

This process continued until the tow reached the section of river above Kingston, where it would be met by a larger line steamer from Rondout with the additional power needed to handle the tow, which continued to get larger. Here, the upriver tugs would return to their home base, sometimes taking over an uptow from the larger tug, and the downtow would continue. If the downtow was large enough to require it, there might be two smaller helpers along. Especially in the Poughkeepsie region and past Rockland County, the tow picked up heavily laden barges full of crushed stone that was extensively quarried on both sides of the shoreline.

Once the tow reached New York Harbor, it was brought close to "The Market," the main docking place for Cornell and other towing companies. Before any boats were brought in, however, the tow would wait out in the river while even smaller tugs, called harbor or terminal tugs, would appear on schedule to take off and distribute boats that already had been consigned to other docks and companies, whether over in New Jersey or around Manhattan Island and to Long Island. Harbor tugs often worked for Cornell under contract under prearranged schedules, and the coordination of boat delivery—as it was with the original pickup of boats for the tow—was a process demanding considerable organization on the part of company superintendents and managers at Albany, Rondout, and New York.

Tasty, figured ornaments for the wheelhouses of the towing steamer Oswego are now being made at the Cornell Steamboat Company's carpenter shop. —*Kingston Daily Freeman,* 29 June 1881

Even if these administrators were first-class, as Cornell's usually were, there was always the threat of bad weather, fog, rough waters, ice, other boats on the river, and spring freshets to make the best boatman's life a difficult one at times. The tidal current alone had to be accounted for as a tow came or went on the river. Downstream on the ebb tide, this was a three-knot current that could help a boatman make good time on his way to New York, and a strong flow went upriver with the flood tide, slowing downtows but speeding uptows on their way home.

In the 1880s, boats operated blindly in fogs, especially at night, with only the blast of a whistle to warn other vessels of where they were. At times, a tow had to come to a dead halt in such weather and hope for the best, but that was something a captain or pilot did not want to do, for the loss of time cost the company money, and a late delivery or pickup meant a disgruntled customer.

Ice and snow made fog even worse. Expert pilots knew the river and the shoreline so well that while in a fog they often could sound the steam whistle and listen for its echo, which would tell how near they were to shore or to a well-known mountainside. A code of whistle signals reproduced below from a printed card entitled "WHISTLE SIGNALS of the Cornell Steamboat Company" was known to every master, pilot, and virtually every crewman who had aspirations of being an officer (see page 56):

> 1 long blast: All Steamers in charge of Tows leaving stake boats or terminals are to use this signal for attention of passing craft. SIGNAL TO BE USED WHETHER LEAVING ON FLOOD OR EBB TIDE.
>
> 3 short blasts: Go Slow.
>
> 4 short blasts: Stop.
>
> 3 long and 3 short blasts: Hook Up.
>
> 1 long and 2 short blasts: Steamer having the Tow wants her hawsers cast off.
>
> 1 long and 2 short blasts: Helper's signal to Steamer that hawsers are cast off.
>
> 2 long and 2 short blasts: This signal to Steamers passing each other means your signal lights are out.
>
> 5 short blasts: The Steamer giving this signal wants something, and any Steamer nearby without a Tow must reply and see what is wanted. THIS SIGNAL MUST BE ANSWERED.
>
> 6 long blasts: DISTRESS SIGNAL. Any Steamer without a Tow, upon hearing this signal MUST REPLY AT ONCE, and render assistance WITHOUT FAIL. This signal to be given ONLY when in distress.

Boatmen always had new stories to exchange with their families and friends at home in Rondout or Port Ewen. One, told in later years, was about an eager young and green decky, who well knew that the Cornell signal of one long and two short blasts meant the tugboat wanted its hawsers cast off—meaning releasing the tow to the charge of the helper tug. What the deckhand apparently did not know was that the one long and two short was also the Nautical Rules of the Road signal that meant a tug with a tow was underway in a fog.

There was a lively race out of the creek this afternoon between the Transport, Preston and Sammy Cornell. They all reached the end of the dyke together. —*Kingston Daily Freeman*, 1 August 1882

One night, as fog set in off Hyde Park, a Cornell tug was alone with an uptow, the helper having already gone on ahead to Kingston. The tug captain blew the Rules of the Road signal, as required, while he drew nearer to Kingston and Rondout Creek. After a while he realized his vessel was moving ahead unusually fast. At that moment the young deckhand entered the pilot house and cheerfully said, "All right, Cap, all gone."

The captain asked what he meant by that.

"I threw the hawsers off. You blew to, didn't you?"

It was the captain who blew just then. The tow was drifting free somewhere out in the night fog, and he had to turn around immediately and find it before another boat collided with it, or it went aground somewhere downriver. Not only did they have to find the tow, but they had to recover the hawsers, which had drifted under the tow after being cast off.

Similar remarkable boatmanship was needed every day by Cornell men, but it took everything the captain and crew had that night to find the tow, recover the hawsers, and then round the boats up securely. By now, all this maneuvering had left the captain with no idea where he was on the river. He carefully inched ahead until the tow was firmly under control, and all night long his tugboat bucked the tide until morning came and the fog cleared, and he could head into the Creek.

Fog was worst in fall and spring, but when March arrived the men grew impatient if they had not yet started the boating season, never mind the fog. In general, the river traditionally opened for navigation on March 17, which was also St. Patrick's Day, and a double reason for celebration at Port Ewen in particular, where the "Boatmen's Ball" was held in one hall or another.

Lower Port Ewen, nearer to the Hudson, or "below the hill," was for the most part where the Irish Catholic boatmen lived; and "top of the hill" were the Protestants of mainly English, Irish, German, and Scottish descent. These were nicknamed "Binnewaters" for the nearby four lakes at Rosendale where many spent their time. The Boatmen's Ball was always a festivity, and often also a donnybrook before it was done.

In March 1888, nature interfered with the annual Boatmen's Ball, as the most savage blizzard in memory struck on the 11th. Trains were stopped for three days, and no milk got to the city for at least four. Once the brutal storm was past, boats were able to move again, but the rest of the Hudson Valley and the Catskills were snowed in for days. The weather had been almost summery the day before the blizzard struck with winds up to sixty miles per hour and the temperature below zero, and the day after it warmed up again.

Work was not long suspended at industrial Rondout, however, where the employees all lived within walking distance of the Cornell railroad yards, sheds, and shops, which shared the waterfront with Cornell steamboat docks, warehouses, shops, boatyards, and coaling pockets. There, too was Cornell's ferryboat slip and terminal, and the dock for *City of Kingston*. The nerve center of the Cornell and Coykendall business empire was at 22 Ferry Street, facing the waterfront. This impressive, four-story building was the headquarters

The tug *Wm. S. Earl*, for most of her life a member of the Cornell fleet, was used as a Rondout harbor tug. She was originally built in 1859 and acquired by the Cornell company in 1884. When abandoned in 1949, at the age of 90, she had seen service as a tugboat for a longer period than any vessel under Cornell ownership. (Roger W. Mabie Collection)

The *John H. Cordts* was one of Cornell's largest towing tugboats during the peak years of the company's existence; seen in the left rear is the large Cornell tugboat *J. C. Hartt*, coming up to join the project. (Roger W. Mabie Collection)

Facing page:
J. C. Hartt is at T. S. Marvel and Company's shipyard in Newburgh to repair a bruised stem resulting from a collision with the Old Colony Line's *City of Brockton* on September 29, 1887, while on their way to yacht races off Sandy hook. (William duBarry Thomas Collection)

Left:
The venerable iron-hulled *Edwin Terry* at the Rondout shops during the 1950s. Built in 1883 by John H. Dialogue at Camden, New Jersey, *Terry* came to Cornell in 1884 with her sister, *Ira M. Hedges*, and several other tugs, when the business of the Washburn Steamboat Company of Saugerties, was acquired. *Hedges* was dismantled in the 1920s. (Photograph by William duBarry Thomas)

for Thomas Cornell and S. D. Coykendall, where they and as many as a hundred office staff, mainly management, clerks, and accounting personnel, ran most of the Cornell businesses.

By now, *City of Kingston* was a minor, though proud, contributor to the treasury of the Cornell Steamboat Company. As an elegant and fast passenger steamer, she symbolized the old-time glory of Thomas Cornell's rise to prominence back in the days when towboats were almost an afterthought of boat builders, although now powerful tugs were foremost in the minds of designers and builders in the Hudson Valley. Most of the company's sidewheel passenger steamers, even those that had become useful towboats, were gone by now. *Manhattan* had been scrapped in 1869; *Telegraph* had sunk in 1870, following a collision; *James Madison* had been dismantled in 1872; *William Cook,* affectionately known as the "Milkmaid," was sold and scrapped in 1881, and *Alida* was broken up at Port Ewen in 1885.

Some of the sidewheel towboats built for heavy duty had expired recently, including *Ceres,* one of the Civil War-vintage sidewheelers. In 1887, the wooden-hulled *Ceres* had been judged to be in poor repair and not worth rebuilding, so she was dismantled at Rondout and turned into a coal boat. That year the towboat *Cayuga* went the same route, and the sixteen-year-old *George A. Hoyt* was on its last legs. The venerable *Herald*, built in 1842, had been scrapped in 1885, as was the comparably aged *Mount Washington,* both of them converted passenger boats. In 1887, *Walter B. Crane* sank at Port Ewen and was abandoned.

One of the sidewheelers of the period survived: *Santa Claus* had been rebuilt during the winter of 1868-69 and renamed *A. B. Valentine;* she remained in the company's service until 1901.

Although vessel after Cornell vessel had outlived its usefulness, there was one that remarkably had outlasted them all: *Norwich*. Still going strong, the "Ice King" was consistently the first boat to arrive out of the ice-strewn river in the spring, and the last to go downriver in the late fall. *Norwich* was loved in Rondout Creek, much like *Mary Powell*, still the unchallenged "Queen of the Hudson" and running regularly for Captain A. Eltinge Anderson, the son of her original builder. *Mary Powell* was as famous and as fast as ever, having

It is difficult to believe that these two tugs are one and the same. *R. G. Townsend*, constructed in 1883, appears in her original guise in the upper view, taken in 1931. An extensive rebuild in the 1930s resulted in *Townsend* looking like a modern tug in the lower image, in which she is shown in the North River at New York in 1939. (Photographs by Donald C. Ringwald. Roger W. Mabie Collection)

carried Russian dukes, American and English literati such as Oscar Wilde, Walt Whitman, and John Burroughs, as well as American politicians and celebrities like Elizabeth Custer, the wife of the massacred George Armstrong Custer. Foreign visitors and American travelers, too, could not say they had seen the country until they had travelled by steamboat on the Hudson River, and here as well as abroad the most famous steamboat of all was *Mary Powell*. For all her beauty and grace, *Mary Powell* was twenty-five years younger than the senior lady *Norwich*, and had not been built to do the icebreaking that once opened the outside world to Rondout in the days before railroads.

Norwich held a special place in the hearts of the Kingston-Rondout community, for few could remember her not being there, faithfully towing for Cornell, with a master and crew ever ready to risk their necks as she battled ice or went to the rescue of boats that had run aground or needed to be towed. Yet, there came a time when folk wondered why the old sidewheeler was still towing when that duty was turning increasingly to the propeller-driven tugboats. It was rumored that Mary Cornell Coykendall, S. D.'s wife, considered *Norwich* her favorite because it was one of the first steamboats her father ever owned.

City of Kingston did not have such enduring sentimental value, however, even though owning a great passenger steamer was a status symbol for any Hudson River steamboat entrepreneur.

By September 1889, *City of Kingston* had been sold to the Puget Sound and Alaska Steamship Company, whose principal owner came to Thomas Cornell that summer on the hunt for a propeller steamboat that would fit his service. It is said that the price was so high that Cornell, who seldom could resist making a profit, was persuaded to sell. The people of Rondout and Kingston were already enamored of the boat named after their home city and were proud of her elegant looks, plush fixtures, red carpeting, and electric lights, so a large crowd of sentimentalists waved goodbye at 6:00 P.M. on the evening of September 30, 1899, as *City of Kingston* drew away from the Rondout wharf.

The steamboat had been prepared for the sea journey, which would take her into the Caribbean, around the tip of South America—there was no Panama Canal as yet—and up the west coast of the Americas. Her furniture was all carefully stored, even the red carpeting taken up and put away. Her guards were reinforced with iron braces and wooden slats against the waves, her open bow enclosed, and windows and doorways made watertight. In case they were required in an emergency, two masts were stepped and rigged for sails.

City of Kingston departed from New York City on November 18, and arrived safely at Puget Sound at the end of February. Her service began almost immediately, running mainly between Tacoma, Seattle, and Victoria, British Columbia, and sometimes she made runs to Alaska. She would remain in this service until April 1899, when rammed amidships in a fog by a British freighter and cut in two. Although everyone was rescued, she sank within three minutes.

The departure of the *City of Kingston* ended the passenger steamer business for Thomas Cornell, who also sold the franchise outright to Romer and Tremper. Whether he had thoughts of ever resuming the passenger business someday and building yet another great vessel was never to be known, for early in 1890, Cornell fell ill, contracted pneumonia, and died at home on March 30, at the age of 77.

Rondout and Kingston's most prominent citizen, Ulster County's most powerful figure, and one of the leading businessmen in the United States, Thomas Cornell was deeply mourned by family, friends, and employees. The companies he founded and led with brilliance, courage, and foresight would continue, and for some decades would be as strong as ever. He had an able successor in son-in-law Samuel D. Coykendall, however, and surely some of his six grandsons would rise to the management of the far-flung family business empire Thomas Cornell had built from one modest sloop.

Whatever lay in the future, Cornell would be missed for a long time to come by the people of the mid-Hudson Valley. On the day of his funeral, it was a testimony to the community's affection for him that gleaming locomotives slowly pulled handsome coaches draped with black crepe through town, and carriages decorated with flowers in the form of a steamboat and a locomotive followed the funeral procession. For this day, all business along industrious Rondout Creek came to a complete stop.

The six sons and one daughter of S. D. Coykendall and Mary Augusta Cornell Coykendall, photographed about 1885; (left to right) at rear are Frederick, Edward, Harry S., and Thomas C.; in front are Frank, Catherine, and Robert B. (C. W. Spangenberger Collection)

S. D. Coykendall became the second president of the Cornell Steamboat Company upon the death of Thomas Cornell in 1890. His tenure was marked by a significant expansion of the company's activities. (J. Matthews Collection)

Chapter Eight
Coykendall's Reign Begins

THE PASSING of Thomas Cornell in 1890 left his heirs a personal estate said to have been worth $3-4 million. Most of the $2 million in bonds were liquidated to be distributed to the Coykendall family, Cornell's only direct heirs other than his wife, Catherine Ann. The estate of Thomas Cornell, which provided for the widow, was designed as a trust so that S. D. Coykendall and his wife—Cornell's daughter, Mary Augusta—and their children would receive regular cash payments all of their lives.

There would be considerable litigation over aspects of the Cornell estate for four or five years, especially regarding corporate liabilities and obligations, and particularly issues regarding the various railroads. S. D. Coykendall sailed through this period, keeping the empire intact, and then building onto it by expanding the railroad properties and adding more tugboats to the towing line. In 1890, for example, the new steam tug *Geo. W. Washburn* was built. With the sale of the *City of Kingston*, however, Cornell Steamboat Company ended its passenger business altogether and focused on the lucrative towing business.

Once the estate was settled, Coykendall named his older sons and family to positions of authority and management in the Cornell empire, with the U&D Railroad coming under the directorship of Cornell or Coykendall relations for the most part. Third son Edward was especially interested in managing railroads, as was Harry, the second son, while Coykendall's eldest son, Thomas, was masterful at working with machines. Truly gifted as a mechanic, he was a budding inventor, especially interested in steam power and the new internal combustion engine. Frederick, who was still in Columbia studying civil engineering, was most interested in the steamboats.

The Coykendall youngsters were well known in their hometown, growing up in grand style at the family mansion at 90 West Chestnut Street, alongside the children of other self-made millionaires. The sons all were groomed to attend Columbia College, and although they always lived in style with parents who had impeccable taste and high character, the Coykendall children were not pampered. Wealthy as they were, no Coykendall boy could lord it over anyone doing his job, as young Edward Coykendall well knew the night the pilot of the Rondout Creek steam-chain ferry told him the last trip was at 10:30 P.M., and he had better be on time if he wanted to get home that night.

Young Edward and a male friend were on their way with two girlfriends to make a visit at Port Ewen, all of them dapperly dressed. They crossed over

The tugboats A. C. Cheney and the Terror, which were condemned, are being broken up. —*Kingston Daily Freeman*, 10 December 1910

No fewer than fourteen tugs and towboats are depicted in the river off the mouth of Rondout Creek in the aftermath of the freshet of March 1893. A freshet might occur in the spring, when a head of water from rains and melting snow built up behind the winter's ice. Eventually, the entire mass would break up, sending water and ice down the creek, taking with it anything that floats. The two stacks in the right center belong to the side-wheel towboat *General McDonald*. (Roger W. Mabie Collection)

The side-wheel towboat *Syracuse* of 1857 evokes admiration for the skills of the mid-nineteenth century shipbuilder and marine engineer. Working with wood and cast iron, and employing little in the way of mechanical aids to construction, they were able to produce artifacts which combined, in perfect proportion, the best of contemporary art and engineering. One can only marvel at the perfection that was *Syracuse*, the sixth— and next to last—large sidewheeler built expressly for Hudson River towing. (Roger W. Mabie Collection)

from Rondout on the ferry, called *Riverside*, but sometimes nicknamed the "Other Side," because it always seemed to be over there when you wanted it. The youngsters were almost an hour late returning for the ferry, which was long gone. Desperate to get the girls home on time, Edward and his friend searched for a rowboat to take them over, which was not easy, for the tide was low, making the banks steep and muddy. They managed at last to get a boat and row across, but the opposite bank was too steep, mucky, and slick for easy climbing without ruining the girls' dresses. So the boys stuck the oars one after the other into the bank to make it easier for the girls to climb.

Years later, Edward told a Poughkeepsie newspaper reporter that "everything was going well, until an oar broke, and a young lady fell into the creek."

S. D. Coykendall became the leading citizen of Ulster County, taking up where Thomas Cornell had left off. Coykendall would serve as president of the First National Bank of Rondout and vice president of the Rondout Savings Bank; he would continue developing the railroads in the Catskills, pushing the U&D ever farther west to make that connection with a main line; he owned and operated the Grand Hotel, and he built and operated the Kingston City Street Railway and the Colonial Trolley Line. Coykendall heavily invested in Rosendale cement and had deep interests and ownership in the ice industry and in bluestone. He also was a partner with his brother, John, in a Minneapolis dry goods business that was said to be the largest of its kind west of Chicago. In 1890, well known for his quiet but generous philanthropy, Coykendall became a trustee at Vassar College for Women, across the Hudson

Coykendall's Reign Begins

in Poughkeepsie. He would serve as a Vassar trustee, with much influence and importance, for the rest of his life.

Isaac M. North, one of the leading Cornell Steamboat Company administrators and a man who had been close to Thomas Cornell, left the scene at this time. In 1891, the longtime superintendent retired from the company, and as a token of appreciation from the American Association of Masters and Pilots, North was presented with a gold-headed cane made from a section of the white oak keel of the 1823 sidewheeler *James Kent*. Scrapped recently after twenty-five years as a stake boat for Cornell in New York Harbor, *James Kent* had been so well made and cared for that it was said her keel was as sound as the day it was first laid, almost seventy years earlier.

In August of 1891, a serious nighttime collision occurred near West Point, with the northbound Cornell tug *S. L. Crosby* running into the southbound propeller steamboat *W. C. Redfield* and staving in the hull so that the steamboat was in danger of sinking. *Redfield* was run ashore a mile and a half below West Point, and the passengers were in time to catch the West Shore train for New York. *S. L. Crosby* sank but was raised a few days later.

A new derrick is being erected for Cornell's foundry dock. The mast is 73 feet high and 26 inches in diameter. The gaff is 84 feet long. It is about the same size as the old one. —*Kingston Daily Freeman,* 26 October 1882

One of the leading competitors in the towing business departed in 1892, as Samuel Schuyler's cash-strapped Albany-to-New York towing line sold out at an auction run by a U.S. marshal. Schuyler's towboats were sold mainly to Beverwyck Towing Company, and although most were in dire need of maintenance and had not recently been in regular service, that they were still worth anything at their advanced ages indicates how well they had been built and maintained over the years.

Beverwyck Towing Company's prizes included: the 1857 *Syracuse*, $11,000; the 1852 *America*, $10,100; and the 1844 *Niagara*, for $6,000. Beverwyck also acquired the 1872 helper towboat *Jacob Leonard* for $5,000.

Another buyer of Schuyler boats was the little-known towing company operator Michael Moran, who with his partner Captain Peter Cahill bought the towboat *Belle* for $7,000. Moran was a former Port Ewen-area man who once had heaved coal at Island Dock.

The Newburgh *Gazette* followed the transactions closely, observing later in the summer that the sidewheelers *Niagara*, *America*, and *Syracuse* "are being overhauled and will go into commission this week. They are to be managed by the Beverwyck Towing Company. The balance of the fleet will also be repaired and put into commission. It will look like old times to see them running again."

In August, Beverwyck began towing on the Albany route, with its management situated in Rondout. It was a direct competitor to Cornell.

The Cornell Steamboat Company was still informally known as the "Cornell Towing Company." It kept on growing, in April 1892 purchasing the fleet and business of the Hudson River Towing Line, owned by A. C. Cheney and sometimes called the Cheney Towing Line.

The Cheney Line had been successful on the river by towing the Knickerbocker Ice Company's many barges as well as the scows of the brickyards thriving along the west bank of the river. Acquiring Cheney gave Cornell a virtual monopoly on ice-barge towing and further inroads into the brick-towing business. Now there were only two large towing companies left, the Ronan Company and Cornell.

With the purchase of Cheney, Cornell acquired the tugboats *A. C. Cheney, Christiana, Camelia, Conqueror, Terror, Honeysuckle, Saxon, Adriatic, Prometheus, Ambition,* and the towboat *P. C. Schultz.* As was common practice with Cornell, most of the tugs were immediately overhauled, but if not worth the expense and effort, they would be laid up at Rondout or New York. If still sound in the hull, but not usable as a tugboat, the vessel might wind up being dismantled and anchored out in the harbor as a stake boat, as was the fate of Cheney's *Prometheus.* Cornell usually maintained a stake boat at Rensselaer, and three more in New York Harbor, one each at Spuyten Duyvil, the Hudson River off East 59th Street, and the Upper Bay.

George W. Murdock, the son of the Rondout lightkeeper, was two days away from his fortieth birthday on March 13, 1893, when he witnessed one of the most ferocious spring freshets ever to rage out of Rondout Creek. Murdock was in charge of several yachts owned by a man from Brooklyn. Murdock had been living in Brooklyn for ten years and was visiting Ponckhockie when he saw the freshet, which years later he described in his memoirs.

> The Cornell fleet was swept out of the Rondout Creek—the ice in the creek broke up and thousands of tons pushed on by a raging torrent, raised havoc with shipping—two score of boats were torn from their fastenings and rushed madly down the stream, stopping only when solid ice was encountered.
> It was a scene that never will be forgotten by those who witnessed the outgoing of the vessels as they jammed against one another and against the docks. The noise of the parting lines and the creaking of the timbers of the vessels could be heard blocks away. The shouts of the men on the boats, who worked furiously hauling in the lines and endeavoring to make the boats fast, and the cries of warning from the people on the docks to the boatmen, added to the excitement...

The water came from an enormous ice jam above Wilbur, where the rising Wallkill had been held back so that the community of Eddyville near the first lock of the D&H Canal was under water. This condition was a potential danger every spring, and old-timers had warned it was going to happen soon. When, at four in the afternoon, the ice jam broke, the immense torrent rushed down the Rondout Creek

> bearing everything before it, breaking loose the ice in the lower creek and crushing and sinking several ice barges moored along the docks at Wilbur. When the foaming water and grinding ice reached the upper end of the Island Dock of the Delaware and Hudson Coal Company, the great mass parted and

"Captain" Johnny Schoonmaker of Cornell's office is a favorite among the boatmen, and saves Mr. North a great many steps. —*Kingston Daily Freeman,* 28 October 1882

Coykendall's Reign Begins

swept with a rush through the slips where many steamboats of the Cornell fleet and a large number of canal boats were moored.

Norwich, captained by veteran Jacob Dubois, was busy breaking ice in the Creek at the time, near Island Dock, and Dubois could only hold on for dear life to avoid being capsized.

When the big side-wheelers and propellers were struck by the rushing ice and flood their hawsers snapped like threads and they started drifting helplessly down the creek. The *Austin, Oswego, McDonald, A. B. Valentine, Pittston,* and *S. O. Pierce* were the sidewheel steamboats, while the *Adriatic, J. C. Hartt, F. Lavergne, Dr. David Kennedy, J. D. Schoonmaker, H. T. Caswell, Harry, Columbia, Isaac M. North,* and *William S. Earl,* and several others, were the propeller vessels caught in the ice. Further down the creek the *John H. Cordts* and other smaller craft were struck by the onrushing torrent and swept out to the mouth of the Rondout where they were jammed in a solid mass of ice near the lighthouse.

The Cornell steamer *J. C. Hartt* was the first to get fired up and go to the rescue. By the next day, the Cornell fleet had been disentangled boat by boat and moved to where they could be examined. Most had some damage, and one, *Sandy*—formerly *Sarah E. Brown*, which had been rebuilt and renamed—had sunk at the dock near the Cornell towing office. She was beyond repair.

The 1893 freshet was one of worst ever in Rondout Creek but would not be the last.

The towboat *Oswego*, built in 1848, was the first large side-wheel steamboat to be built exclusively for towing on the Hudson River. Acquired by Thomas Cornell in 1869, *Oswego* was in service for the company until September 1918, when she was also the last of the towboat side-wheelers in use on the Hudson. (William duBarry Thomas Collection)

The new, steel-hulled tugboat *Geo. W. Washburn* is seen shortly after her initial arrival at her home port on Rondout Creek. Built in Newburgh in 1890, she originally had one large, single smokestack. Nearly two and a half decades later, she was equipped with new boilers and thereafter appeared with fore-and-aft smokestacks as shown on page 150. (Roger W. Mabie Collection)

That July, the Coykendall family had reason to be proud of their oldest son, Thomas, who was awarded a patent on a device he had invented to distribute water in the boilers of steam vessels. The device was tested in the newly built Cornell tug, *Thomas P. Fowler,* captained by Charles Warner of New York, who had served the company for twenty-three years and was particularly experienced at breaking in new tugs—which he had done with both *Coe F. Young* and *W. E. Street.*

The distribution device controlled the heating of water in the pipes coiled around the furnace. Often, these pipes became too hot in the top sections, causing expansion and resulting in leaks. More than 400 other patents had been registered to solve this same problem, but none were successful until Thomas Coykendall's was invented. It was "a thing which can be used in every steamboat afloat," said the Kingston *Daily Freeman*.

In the fall of the same year, this newspaper applauded another remarkable accomplishment by a Cornell Steamboat Company man, this time by draftsman Ivar Jungquist "a man of phenomenal strength and in lifting can easily outclass any man in the steamboat Company's employ." The twenty-five-year-old Swede was the only man known to have been able to lift an iron column twenty-eight inches long and ten in diameter, weighing 625 pounds. For "a long time" many others attempted this feat "in vain," but Jungquist "lifted [it] with ease."

Jungquist went on to become a Cornell superintendent of operations.

A year later, in August 1894, S. D. Coykendall arranged the purchase of Beverwyck Towing Company's sidewheel towboats, the vessels Beverwyck had purchased just two years previously from the defunct Schuyler line. At this time, Coykendall's brother, George, was vice president of Cornell, with R. G. Townsend as treasurer.

Beverwyck had used its own tugboats working in the northern and western canals that led to Albany and had also chartered the tugs *E. L. Levy* and *E. C. Baker* from the New York and Lake Champlain Towing Company, which dominated towing in the north country above Albany. The Newburgh *Daily Journal* reported on August 10:

> This action is regarded by canal boatmen as meaning that the Cornell line proposes to control the Hudson River towing business, and if possible to crush the Ronan Line, which with the Beverwyck Line has heretofore controlled the towing business of the Erie and Champlain Canals. It is rumored that the New York and Lake Champlain Towing Company will establish a rival line. This would mean a war in canal towing rates and a marked reduction in the cost of hauling boats from the upper Hudson to New York City.

The next day, the Newburgh paper published an expanded story under the headline "A Big Fleet," with the subhead "The Recent Purchases by Mr. Samuel Coykendall—Practically in Control of All River Towing—Forty-two Boats in the Line."

> The Kingston Freeman, in referring to the matter, says that by this acquisition to its fleet the Cornell line now practically controls the Hudson River towing business. . .
> In the past the Cornell Steamboat Company has not handled any of the business from the canals into the upper waters of the Hudson. The only opposition they will have in this business now is the Ronan line and the New York & Lake Champlain Company.

The Cornell Company had acquired eleven steamers in the past few years, and it had built several more, so that with forty-two boats in service, Cornell's towing fleet was believed to be the largest of any in the country.

A couple of days later, the Newburgh *Daily News* quoted the Albany *Argus* newspaper, which "says that from 1850 to 1875 a great deal of money was made by the towing lines on the river, but since the latter date opposition has cut the heart out of the profits and the recent owners of the Beverwyck let the line go as the small margin was not a favorable return for the capital involved."

The article continues, saying the Ronan and Beverwyck lines were prime antagonists, and it was only a matter of time before one or the other went under. The competition that also put Schuyler out of business included a rate war while at the same time captains were being paid costly bonuses to serve one line or another. The most successful "speculator" in steamboats, said the article, was S. D. Coykendall.

"He is said to have broken up more lines than any man in the business, by getting control of their boats and business."

The crew of the Norwich this morning had considerable amusement by having a green hand engaged with emery paper and sand scouring the anchor chain. [*Kingston Daily Freeman*, 6 July 1883]

The fleet during this time included sidewheel steamers *P. C. Schultz, General McDonald, Oswego, Austin, A. B. Valentine, Norwich, Pittston, America, Niagara, Syracuse, Vanderbilt,* and *Jacob Leonard;* also, the screw-propeller tugs *Terror, John H. Cordts, J. C. Hartt, Geo. W. Washburn, Christiana, C. D. Mills, Harry, John D. Schoonmaker, H. T. Caswell, Wm. S. Earl, Edwin Terry, Coe F. Young, Thomas Dickson, George W. Pratt, Hercules, Thomas P. Fowler, Honeysuckle,* and *Edwin H. Mead.*

The newspaper said, "Among these tugs are some of the finest and most powerful in their class afloat." An outstanding vessel was *Edwin Terry*, built in 1883 and one of the first iron-hulled tugboats of the era, Another was *Geo. W. Washburn*, built in 1890, also iron-hulled, and one of the fastest tugs on the Hudson.

Twenty years earlier there had been at least five major towing companies besides Cornell operating on the river: Samuel Schuyler; Robinson and Betts; Jerry Austin; Blanchard and Farnham, and the Cheney Towing Line. Added to this list were towing operations belonging to the D&H Coal Company; Coleman, Field and Horton of Newburgh; Captain Newby Barritt's bluestone company, and many individually owned boats.

The newspapers conjectured what Coykendall would do next, saying his purchase was intended to "protect" the business of his line, because Beverwyck had been making inroads into it. Some thought the purchase was not necessarily to consolidate Beverwyck and Cornell in order to battle directly with Ronan. The Newburgh *Gazette* observed that there was "the best of feeling between the Ronan and Cornell Lines," even a willingness to cooperate in dividing up territory and business between them,

> assuming that the Ronan line would be willing to agree not to interfere with the Hudson River towing business, except that which comes from or goes to the canals [Erie and Champlain], the Cornell line would have a free hand in all other Hudson River towing, for which the latter might be willing to either give the Ronan line all of the canal towing, or, perhaps, by chartering the boats of the Beverwyck line to the Ronan line, insure the latter a monopoly of the canal towing.

While admitting these were just speculations, the writer—who signed himself as "Canal Defender, New York"—warned that the New York and Lake Champlain Company had several excellent boats in dire need of work. He said that if this company came south to establish a third towing company on the Hudson River, "things might be, and probably would be, made very lively for all concerned."

He added, "It is worth remembering that Mr. Coykendall has the reputation of being one of the shrewdest business men of this city, and as a long-headed financier he ranks high." Presumably the Newburgh newspaper was claiming the celebrated S. D. Coykendall for its own, since he had once lived in the city, and his ancestors originally had come from the region.

The tug Dr. Kennedy is having a new stern put on her at the boatyard of the Cornell Steamboat Company. She has had her boiler painted, and her engine shows careful attention on the part of her engineer and is as bright as a new button. —Kingston Daily Freeman, 11 July 1883

One of the new enterprises afforded by the purchase of Beverwyck was the beginning of large-scale grain boat towing from Waterford, just above Albany, the eastern terminus for the canal boats from the granaries of the Midwest.

> Thomas Cornell, the wealthy steamboatman, has given $1,000 for erecting a monument, at Kingston, New York, to the memory of Lieut. Chipp, one of the gallant Jeannette artic heroes. —*The Nautical Gazette*, 13 March 1884

The Cornell Company did not have to wait long to see what sort of competition might shape up now that the towing companies had dwindled to two on the Hudson. In October, the Kingston *Daily Freeman* reported that the fledgling Moran Company, with only three small tugs—*F. W. Vosburgh*, *Moran*, and *George L. Garlick*—and the sidewheeler *Belle* was "making an effort to get some of the New York towing business on the Hudson now controlled by the Cornell and Ronan Lines." Called an "opposition line" in the tradition of the upstart passenger steamboat companies of the past, Moran's tugs started downriver with a tow of seven boats, and at the same time owner Michael Moran announced that he intended to compete with the other two lines.

Retired Cornell superintendent I. M. North "laughed at the idea" that so small a line could injure the other companies. "Any tug can go to Albany and pick up a tow," he said, "but the competition doesn't amount to anything."

On February 25, 1895, Catherine Ann Woodmansee Cornell at the mansion on Wurts Street, sadly bade farewell to Jennette Gillespie, who passed away in her sixty-eighth year, having been in the employ of the family for more than fifty of those years.

There had never been a good landing at Kingston for the large day liners and night boats that plied the river above Kingston, so passengers to and from Kingston and Rondout had to meet the boats over at Rhinecliff. They crossed the river via the Cornell-controlled ferryboat *Transport* to Rondout, and from there through passengers could take the Cornell-owned U&D Railroad into the Catskills or beyond. Many customers thought it too tedious and wanted to see a passenger steamboat dock on the Kingston side of the river, where travelers could more easily reach the city or catch a train that would take them into the mountains.

Kingston Point was an extreme tip of land at the river's edge, three miles from Kingston, and had been the very first ferry crossing. S. D. Coykendall had purchased the land in 1893, and it was there he was resolved to create his passenger boat wharf, and at the same time he would extend the trolley line out there to make it convenient for travelers. He had an even better idea, and that was to build an amusement park on the point, a scenic location with views of the Hudson River and Rondout Creek. Once the city streetcars were running there, prospects for a successful amusement park were bright. The Catskills were ever-increasing in popularity, and thousands of tourists passing through the new Kingston landing as well as the amusement park would surely spend time and money before departing for their destinations. The park would also attract patrons from Albany, who could sail downriver on a steamboat, enjoy the day at the park, and sail back at night.

In December 1895, after most of the railroad litigation related to the Thomas Cornell estate had been resolved, the board of the U&D elected S. D. Coykendall president. The Coykendall family owed most of the U&D stock, and so S. D. Coykendall named his sons and close allies as officers: son Thomas Cornell Coykendall was vice president, son Harry S. Coykendall was treasurer, son Frederick and brother George became directors. Son Edward became the superintendent of the U&D, a responsibility that included running much of the day-to-day operations.

It was at this U&D annual meeting that the Kingston Point landing was approved by the board.

The Kingston Point landing opened for business in 1896, as a stop for the Hudson River Day Line, which ran from Albany to New York. The Rhinecliff landing was virtually put out of business as a Day Line stop, but anyone on the west shore who wanted to catch a train over in Rhinecliff still had to cross on the *Transport*. This ferryboat had been in service since 1881, when she had been purchased by Thomas Cornell from a New Jersey railroad.

A year later, S. D. Coykendall's amusement park came into being, set in a landscaped park that had pretty lagoons and winding brick paths alongside extensive flower gardens. The amusement park had a ferris wheel, bandstand, a dance hall, penny arcade, merry-go-round, and a shooting gallery. The park was reached by the Colonial Trolley Line, which was controlled by the Cornell Company. It was an instant success, especially on summer nights, when folk took the trolley down to the end of the line at the park, a feature common to many American cities at the time, and which would be for decades to come.

During these years, electrification of the Cornell and U&D workshops at Rondout was carried out, with generators installed to create power for lights and equipment.

On May 15, 1898, Catherine Ann Woodmansee Cornell passed away in her seventy-sixth year.

In 1901, the Cornell Steamboat Company bought out C. W. Morse's Consolidated Towing Line, the successor to the Ronan Towing Line, its last major competitor on the Hudson River. This was the completion of a rise to the near pinnacle of the towing business, which Thomas Cornell had entered almost incidentally, as a way to generate some quick cash while he schemed to build a great passenger steamboat line, and later a railroad empire.

The tugboats acquired in the Consolidated purchase included the *Pocahontas* and the *Osceola*, both built in 1884; *Ellen M. Ronan*, 1883; *Victoria*, 1878; and *Mabel*, 1892 from the Ronan Towing Line; also included were two modern tugs, *E. L. Levy* and *E. C. Baker*, which had come from the New York and Lake Champlain Towing Company.

These tugs would become a familiar sight in Rondout Creek, where residents would recognize them, know their masters, pilots, and crews, and likely their families, too. The Creek's waterfront, whether industrial and roaring

Since the elephant has been removed from the wheelhouse of the steamer Norwich, that vessel is considerably lightened up as regards displacement of water to the square inch. —*Kingston Daily Freeman*, 27 March 1884

at Rondout or elegant at Kingston Point, would not have been the same without the comings and goings of the Cornell tugboat fleet, their whistles sounding in salute or in signal to their folks at home. These boats would have been well known to poet Henry Abbey, who was born and raised in Rondout.

A friend to other gifted writers and to some of the established landscape painters of the day, Abbey worked for a while in New York City as a journalist, returning at the end of the Civil War to his hometown to become a merchant. He sometimes wrote verse about his beloved Hudson River, and in 1894, when in his early fifties, he published "By Hudson's Tide." The words could have been understood by many an aging person wandering near Kingston Point in those days.

> What pleasant dreams, what memories rise,
> When filled with care, or priced in pride,
> I wander down in solitude
> And reach the beach by Hudson's tide!
> I wandered on the pebble beach,
> And think of boyhood's careless hours. . .

The youthful years of Kingston and Rondout were fast passing. The twentieth century approached, with electricity and oil the future, even though the hard-working steam tugboats were just approaching the very height of their glory.

The towboat *Sandy*, originally named *Sarah E. Brown*, lying sunk in the Rondout Creek after the March 1893 freshet. She was named for Captain "Sandy" Forsyth, an old-time Cornell employee, who was also the vessel's captain. The damage wrought by the freshet put an end to this colorful little towboat's long career. (Roger W. Mabie Collection)

Genesis of the Albany Towing Company

Around the turn of the last century, the small harbor tugs at Albany, which did most of the shifting of canal boats around that city's busy harbor, were owned by individuals. Their services were contracted for by their owner-captains on a one-to-one basis. It was a rough-and-tumble life, and there is little doubt that many of these owners made only a meager living but, like the owner-drivers of eighteen-wheelers who came to dominate much of the nation's trucking industry, it was free enterprise at work.

Owning a tugboat at Albany had its perils. Although wooden tugs were always susceptible to loss by fire, fifteen tugs burned in and around Albany in the 1897-1898 period (much higher than the average rate of losses). This situation indicates a downturn in business, possibly exacerbated by the arrival of Charles W. Morse's Consolidated Towing Line, or else there may have been too many tugs at Albany. It is likely (although completely undocumented) that some of these fires may have been attempts to collect insurance money.

Some time during this period it was proposed, perhaps by Captain Ulster Davis (who owned part interest in more than one of the local tugs), that the owners form a co-operative pool to eliminate some of the cut-throat competition. This was done under the guidance of Davis. Then, around 1903, the co-operative became incorporated as the Albany Towing Company, and the vessel's owners sold their assets to the newly formed corporation. Davis became its president.

In 1905, the Cornell Steamboat Company bought the Albany Towing Company, and Ulster Davis remained as president. The vessels remained under the ownership of the Albany Towing Company until 1920, but one can be sure that after 1905 the shots were called from Rondout. It is possible that S. D. Coykendall may have been the motivator for the whole co-operative—and later for the formation of the Albany Towing Company—as a way of keeping the local towing business at Albany out of the hands of his arch foe, C. W. Morse. As far as Ulster Davis is concerned, he often could be found hovering around the affairs of the Cornell Steamboat Company over the years, and this might just have been a question of hovering in the right place at the right time.

The nine small tugs owned by the Albany Towing Company at the time of the 1905 purchase by Cornell were: *Eugenia, Geo. C. Van Tuyl Jr., J. Arnold, James H. Scott, M.B. Harlow* (renamed *Geo. N. Southwick* in 1908), *Paul Le Roux, Roys J. Cram, Thomas Chubb,* and *W. B. McCulloch.* In 1912, *George D. Cooley* was purchased and placed under Albany Towing Company ownership. *Roys J. Cram*, arguably the most obscure vessel of the Cornell fleet, was destroyed by fire (not of suspicious origin) less than two months after her 1905 purchase.

Small American steam vessels like the tugs of the Albany Towing Company were issued licenses on an annual basis through 1913, or whenever a change in ownership or name occured. After a change in the documentation law in 1913, twelve annual renewals of license were permitted before a new enrollment document was issued. This documentation allows us to follow the yearly history of a vessel, and in the case of the Albany Towing Company, to peer into Ulster Davis's (or perhaps S. D. Coykendall's) mind from the perspective of towing at Albany.

Typical of the Albany vessels was *W. B. McCulloch*, built in 1899 as *A. P. McCabe, Jr.* Following is an annotated list of all documents issued to this vessel, showing how ownership changed over her lifetime.

05 Oct 1899—William P. Smith, of Rensselaer, was the original mananging owner (MO), but there is no indication of other owners. This suggests that there were other part owners, otherwise Smith would have been indicated as sole owner.

15 Dec 1900—Annual renewal. No change

21 Feb 1901—Thomas Ward (1/2) became MO. Other owners, Charles W. Lodge (1/4) and William P. Smith (1/4).

02 Apr 1901—Thomas Ward (1/20 remained as MO, with George Warner (1/4) and William P. Smith (1/4).

31 Mar 1902—George Warner (1/2) became MO, with Thomas Ward (1/2).

17 Apr 1903—Annual renewal. No change.

30 Apr 1903—Ulster Davis (1/2) became MO, Warner and Ward as copartners (1/2). There may have been a legal distinction between the designation of co-partners and showing Warner and Ward each owning 1/4, but this is unclear.

16 Jun 1903—Albany Towing Co. (ATCo) was owner with Davis as president.

25 Jun 1904—Annual renewal. No change.

17 Dec 1904—First documented as *W. B. McCulloch*. Otherwise no change.

09 Jun 1906—Annual renewal. No change.

10 Jul 1907—Davis shown as MO. This does not imply a corporate change involving ATCo, but is probably a clerical error.

14 Jul 1913—ATCo was again shown as owner with Davis as president.

20 Apr 1914—ATCo was owner with Frederick Coykendall as president.

20 Apr 1920—Cornell Steamboat Company was owner with Coykendall as president.

15 Feb 1922—No change. It was not clear why this document was issued after only two years since the last; perhaps the original had been lost, a frequent occurance.

06 Dec 1933—No change. Statutory twelve-year period expired.

The last enrollment document (1933) was surrendered on June 8, 1943 and endorsed "vessel dismantled and metal salvaged." The last renewal of this document was on Dec 6, 1934, which tells us that she was not authorized to run, and did not run, beyond a year after that date. A last renewal around 1934 is also found on the enrollments of a number of Cornell's other small steam tugs, which seems to confirm the depressed state of business during the period.

For reasons unexplained, the Albany Towing Company remained a separate corporate entitiy until 1920, when its vessels were documented under Cornell ownership.

William duBarry Thomas

Chapter Nine
Lord of Hudson River Towing

RAILROADS had overtaken the Delaware and Hudson Canal and, when it went out of business in 1898, there was virtually no coal being shipped along its 108 eight miles of dilapidated channel, locks, towpaths, and spillways. The canal had peaked in the 1870s, but in this same decade coal was being brought to tidewater far more efficiently and at competitive rates by railroad.

The canal's usefulness diminished swiftly over the next decade, yet there was still that length of waterway and rights of way, as well as considerable land along the canal that belonged to the company. At the start of the 1890s the book value of assets, investments, and improvements were estimated by the D&H Canal Company to be worth $6 million. In 1893, however, the company recorded the book value as just $100,000. Where there had been 1,400 canal boats passing through in 1870, only 250 used the canal in 1898. The coal tonnage was 500,000 in that last year, which was very little compared to the millions of tons being shipped from the Pennsylvania coal fields by rail.

In May 1899, the canal company board decided to auction the waterway, though not yet all the adjacent land. S. D. Coykendall made an offer—the only offer made at all—for $10,000 in cash and assumption of obligations that were estimated at another $90,000. Coykendall soon would purchase the extensive tracts of adjacent land owned by the canal company for another $150,000.

From the moment it began to be built in the 1820s, the Delaware and Hudson Canal had started a business boom that overnight stimulated the development of the waterfront along Rondout Creek. The canal nourished and supported all kinds of industries and businesses and gave Thomas Cornell the opportunity to apply his abilities to commerce by water and rail. Cornell had become a member of the canal company's board of directors in 1868, and his brother-in-law, Coe F. Young, served as the canal's general manager throughout its last years.

As did his late father-in-law, Coykendall recognized the intrinsic value the old canal still possessed in its rights-of-way and its considerable real estate. These could be sold, and at the same time, Coykendall's Rosendale Consolidated Cement Company would continue to use the lower section of the canal for shipments to the Hudson. With some success he worked toward merging other cement companies along the canal into his Rosendale Company. More than 1.2 million barrels of cement still came down the eastern end of the canal from Coykendall's operations.

The steamers W. N. Bavier and Norwich of the Cornell towing line arrived last night from New York with one of the largest tows of the season. When leaving New York there were ninety-one boats in the tow, and others were picked up at Newburgh and Rondout. The tow left New York Monday night and passed Hudson at 6:30 yesterday morning, arriving here at 7:30 last evening. A majority of the boats were bound for Troy where they will enter the canal. —Albany Argus, 2 May 1906

In November 1899, Coykendall was busy forming plans for yet another railroad, which would in part follow the route and rights-of-way belonging to the canal, west from Kingston. Coykendall sold some of the land beside the canal to this new company, named the Delaware Valley and Kingston Railroad, then joined the board as a director. Predictions were that Kingston would become one of the largest coal terminals in the East. Coykendall's foresight and ability to come up with cash—Thomas Cornell's own strengths—paid off in an even greater financial return, as other railroads, feeling threatened by his announced plans, bought the canal route from him piecemeal.

The canal remained in limited service until 1913, when the closing of the major cement plants eliminated all remaining business. By early in the century, Rosendale cement faced insurmountable competition from Portland cement, which dried faster and thus became the first choice for new construction.

S. D. Coykendall was one of the leading men of New York State by now, a friend of Republican governor Charles Evans Hughes, and at least twice he would be sounded out with regard to running for governor. Both times he refused.

The tug *Pocahontas* is shown as she was completed for the Ronan Towing Line by Ward, Stanton and Company at Newburgh in 1884. (She was acquired by Cornell in 1901.) Her original rig, with two boilers and two stacks side-by-side, lasted until 1911, when Pocahontas and her sister *Osceola* were rebuilt at the Cornell shops. Each was fitted with a modern Scotch boiler at this time, and the two thin stacks gave way to the assertive single one carried for the rest of the vessels' long careers. (Roger W. Mabie Collection)

The powerful *Cornell* of 1902 below the railroad bridge at Poughkeepsie with a large crowd of ladies and gentlemen aboard. The awnings sheltering them on main deck and house top, and the flags flying from the tug's mast and jackstaff and above the pilot house, tell us that this was a gala excursion to the Poughkeepsie boat races. Sold by Cornell to the Standard Oil Company of Louisiana in 1917, the vessel survived at New Orleans under the name *Istrouma* until dismantled in 1956. (Gerard Mastropaolo Collection)

Frederick Coykendall was graduating with honors from Columbia College while his father was continuing to develop Cornell and Coykendall enterprises. In 1897, Frederick received a civil engineering degree and his Master of Arts, and that same year he married Mary Beach Warrin of New York City and became secretary of the Cornell Steamboat Company. Frederick's older brother, Edward, was superintendent and a director of the U&D Railroad, and no one knew the railroad better than he did. Although all the companies were family-run, the line between Edward with the U&D and Frederick with the Cornell Steamboat Company became even more clearly delineated when Frederick was named general manager of the steamboat company in 1900.

In 1899, at Frederick's initiative, the Cornell Steamboat Company departed on another expansion, forming the Buffalo Barge Towing Company. Attempting to take advantage of increased traffic from the rebuilt Erie Canal that became part of the New York State Barge Canal System. In this enterprise, Cornell was not successful.

In 1902, S. D. Coykendall fulfilled a dream of Thomas Cornell's by consolidating the various railroads he controlled under the corporate umbrella of the Ulster and Delaware. Still, it was the towing business that was the strongest part of his family business empire. In 1903, there were sixty-three vessels and the company had a net worth of approximately $3 million. That year, Cornell bought out the Knickerbocker Steam Towage Company's Hudson River fleet, adding a number of propeller tugboats that included: *C. W. Morse, Triton, Knickerbocker,* and *Ice King.*

The most outstanding of these tugs was *C. W. Morse*, built in 1889 in Bath, Maine, as an ocean-going vessel that was designed specifically to compete with schooners in the ice trade. *C. W. Morse* was among the largest and most powerful tugs of her day, at 154 feet in length, and capable of more than 1,000

horsepower. She had towed barges packed with ice as far south as Cuba. For Cornell, she would tow coal barges from Rondout Creek to ports along the New England coastline.

During this same year, Thomas Cornell's second daughter, Cornelia Lucy Bayard, died in her forty-eighth year. She and her husband had no children.

> Robert Blaxlet, bookkeeper for the Cornell Steamboat Company of Rondout, was attacked with fever on Sabbath and died on Thursday. Fever is raging in that place.
> —*Newburgh Daily Journal*, 21 February 1885

In 1903, New York Trap Rock, the leading stone quarrying company on the river—and like Cornell tracing its roots back to the mid-1800s—made an attempt at establishing its own towing fleet. Cornell had been towing its stone barges for years, but Trap Rock wanted to improve control of the schedules of deliveries and pickups, so it began building a tug named *Wilson P. Foss*, after the company's owner. Trap Rock soon thought better of the notion, however, and sold the tugboat to Cornell. Brickmakers from time to time tried to do the same, but generally found that the towing business was not so easy, and ultimately not for them. When they wanted to sell their tugs—as was the case with the Rose Brick Company and its *Eli B. Conine* around this time—the ready buyer usually was Cornell, determined to keep other tugboats off the river.

Another upstart appeared in 1904 when John D. Arbuckle, a wealthy Brooklyn merchant, backed the new Independent Towing Company, which was operated by McAllister Brothers. This competition never amounted to much. Although the northern canal business was not panning out very well, Cornell was all-pervasive on the Hudson River, and this naturally got the attention of the Interstate Commerce Commission, which always had an eye on possible monopolies. By law, a monopoly must be broken up. For this reason, Cornell always had to be careful of not overreaching so far that the federal government would bring it into court to challenge its dominance.

The departure of old fleet members, particularly the sidewheel towboats, continued steadily, with *Austin* being retired in 1898 after forty-five years of continuous service on the river; that same year, *Syracuse* was retired after forty-one years. For decades to come, both these sidewheel towboats would endure in the memories of their former crews and their families, who for the most part lived in the Rondout Creek communities and in Kingston and Port Ewen. When, in December 1901, the sidewheel towboat *A. B. Valentine*—the former passenger steamer *Santa Claus*—was sold to the wreckers, the man after whom she was named coincidentally died that very same day. A. B. Valentine had served Cornell for fifty years, much of that time as the company superintendent at New York.

Edward Coykendall had his own mansion on West Chestnut Street, while his eldest brother, Thomas Cornell Coykendall, lived part-time at their parents' home down the street and otherwise at his suite in the Plaza Hotel in Manhattan. Although Thomas was vice president of the U&D Railroad, he was happiest while working as manager of the shops at Rondout, whether on steamboats or locomotives.

It was said that the bachelor, Thomas, had something of a drinking problem and, after working in the shop, he usually went up to the Kingston Club, where the local nabobs dined and drank together. Later that evening, Thomas would catch the trolley back to Rondout, and when his stop came, the conductor would invariably have to help him on his way, heading him up the hill toward West Chestnut Street. Thomas was highly regarded for his mechanical genius, and by the first years of the century, when the notion of burning fuel oil instead of coal was mostly talk, he would be working in the machine shop or in the bowels of tugboats, himself developing methods and equipment to convert the boats from coal to oil.

In April of 1901, the Kingston *Daily Freeman* wrote about the company's investigation into using fuel oil in the tugs' boilers:

> The owners of the Cornell Towing Line are contemplating changing the fuel of the steamers from coal to oil, but of course this innovation cannot be put into operation this season. They are anxious to get rid of the annoyance of a possible coal strike every year, and the change from coal to oil as fuel will accomplish this, and at the same time be a stroke of economy.
>
> Captain Ulster Davis, the local manager of the line, spent the past winter in the Southwest and California and Colorado, and while there investigated the efficiency of oil as fuel for river and lake steamers in that section of the country. He found that most of the steamers, both side wheel and screw boats, on the Pacific coast, use oil entirely as fuel with the best results. It is preferred not alone because of economy, but on account of cleanliness and easy handling. Captain Davis says that oil is preferable to coal, as a thousand gallons of oil produce a power equal to five tons of coal. At some points on the Pacific the crude oil, which is used on the steamers, can be secured for 45 cents a barrel, while at San Francisco it can be purchased for $1.25 per barrel.

The article said coal cost steamboat owners more than three dollars per ton, adding that Ulster Davis—who lived in Rensselaer—was investigating how to acquire oil in the East. Meanwhile, said the *Freeman*, "It is believed that the boats can be so altered that oil can be used at very little expense."

Certainly the thought of oil overtaking coal someday boded ill for the business prospects of a towing company that hauled hundreds of coal boats each year. Yet the railroads were already taking the lion's share of coal being freighted to tidewater at the terminals of Newburgh, Cornwall, and various points in New Jersey. There was no doubt that several of the staples that once had been the basis for Cornell's success were beginning to phase out or to be carried by rail instead of by water. Portland cement was a new product that set faster than Rosendale cement, and although it was not as hard in the end, it was rapidly becoming more popular. The bluestone industry was also failing these days, although the ice business was strong, with more than eighty barges towed weekly to New York. At this time, Cornell towed fifteen to twenty brick barges each week to be delivered around New York Harbor, but this industry, too, was noticeably losing its vigor as steel girders and poured concrete construction made irresistible inroads.

The tug H. T. Caswell was the first Rondout creek propeller to have an awing put on its upper deck. —*Kingston Daily Freeman*, 16 May 1888

The eighty-one man crew of the Cornell shops at Rondout poses on the tug *Cornell*, probably in the first decade of the twentieth century. (John F. Matthews Collection)

Thomas Coykendall was the man who could convert the steamers to burning fuel oil in their boilers, but the initiative to do so on a large scale was not yet there within the company. At Cornell, the switch from coal had to wait another two decades until the diesel engine.

At this time, the company had a strong construction program under way, including the steel-hulled tugs *J. G. Rose* and *G. W. Decker* in 1900, *W. N. Bavier* in 1901, *Cornell* in 1902, and *J. H. Williams* and *Wm. E. Cleary* in 1904, and also the wooden-hulled *Rob* in 1902.

In 1905, a public hearing was convened concerning the building of the Ashokan Reservoir, which for years had been in the planning in order to provide water for New York City. The reservoir's eastern end would be ten miles west of Kingston, and it would be approximately twelve miles long, virtually all of that distance including the roadbed of the Ulster and Delaware.

At the hearing, S. D. Coykendall spoke out in objection to the reservoir, which would inundate several small communities. He would not be able to stop the reservoir, which was completed late in 1913, but Coykendall made the most of the opportunity, as usual, and his cement companies sold the cement used in the project. Moreover, the U&D was well paid to give up its right of way and received $1.5 million to construct another line and new sta-

The newly-built tug *Rob* is on John J. Baisden's marine railway at Sleightsburgh, and judging from the formal poses of the yard workers and the fact that the tug's hull is newly coppered, the occasion was probably the launching of the vessel in 1902. Baisden's shipyard was located in the vicinity of the present oil storage tanks at Sleightsburgh and opposite the Cornell shops. The slip of the "Rhinebeck Ferry," located upstream of the shops, is visible just over *Rob*'s stern. (Roger W. Mabie Collection)

tions on higher ground. What was more, the U&D trains had encountered innumerable delays during the years of construction, and the railroad took the City of New York to court, suing for damages of $3 million. In the end, the settlement out of court gave the U&D $1.25 million in cash, which was established as a reserve fund for the company. The eighteen stockholders in the U&D were virtually all Cornell or Coykendall family members, but there were seldom any dividends paid out to them. The U&D had a surplus of several hundred thousand dollars in its operating account, and from this fund the Coykendall sons who were on its board received handsome salaries.

In April 1905, with the *Norwich* and the *Mary Powell* still going strong, the Cornell Steamboat Company further enlarged the fleet by purchasing nine tugboats that had been operating on the river near Albany and Troy. A rate war was anticipated between Cornell and Arbuckle and McAllister's Independent Towing Line, and it was thought that buying up the nine tugs would make it that much more difficult for the Independent to acquire or charter enough boats to handle the business they were out to take from Cornell.

Lord of Hudson River Towing

These nine tugs had been owned by the Albany Towing Company and were *Paul Le Roux, Thomas Chubb, P. McCabe Jr., Geo. C. Van Tuyl Jr., Eugenia, J. Arnold, James H. Scott, Roys J. Cram,* and *M. B. Harlow.*

The Independent Line did find tugs to buy or charter and persisted in trying to make a go of its well-publicized opposition to Cornell. To be sure, there were disgruntled clients who wanted Cornell to operate according to a schedule that favored them rather than the tugboat company. Among these clients were Trap Rock and the ice and brick companies. Cornell haughtily continued to operate as it always had, and many considered the company too inflexible.

Yet there was not much alternative to Cornell if a client wanted to move bulk freight on the Hudson River. At this time, the majority of the Cornell board of directors was constituted by S. D. Coykendall and his sons.

The propeller E. H. Mead, owned by the Cornell Steamboat Company, which was sunk near New York City in Sunday's gale, is in the Rondout Creek. Its joiner work is badly damaged.
—*Kingston Daily Freeman,* 30 November 1888

In October 1906, Cornell captain Jacob W. Dubois died at seventy-eight after a short illness. Dubois had worked for the company more than fifty years, which was not so unusual for Cornell employees because the company was reluctant to lay off men, even in difficult economic times.

Loyalty to the company was still widespread among the employees, and even though Cornell might not pay the best or give many raises, there was security as well as prestige in working for it, so like Dubois, many stayed for most of their working lives. He had been captain of the *Norwich* much of his career and had great experience with the old side-wheelers.

The Kingston *Daily Freeman* described Dubois as one who took special delight in telling stories of the *Norwich* breaking the ice at the opening and close of the sailing season. The paper said, "The death of Captain Dubois removed one of the last of the steamboat captains who plied the river 50 years ago."

A few weeks later, on December 16, his beloved *Norwich* caught fire and was almost destroyed. Being the steamboat that Mary Augusta Coykendall revered as the legacy of her father's early career, *Norwich* was rebuilt as only the Cornell shops could rebuild her—as good as new, or likely better.

Rondout lightkeeper Catherine Murdock Perkins retired in 1907 after fifty-one years of service, the longest in the United States. She was succeeded by her son, James Murdock. It was said that lighthouse inspectors considered the Rondout lighthouse the best-kept they had ever seen.

Mrs. Perkins died two years later, in 1909.

In August 1909, the pre-Civil War sidewheel towboat *Pittston* was taken out of service, having ended her fifty-seven-year career by working around Rondout Creek. One of the first boats built specifically for towing, *Pittston* had spent most of her career working in the Creek for Cornell, and before that for the Pennsylvania Coal Company, for whom she had been built.

On August 30 of this same year, *Norwich* caught fire for the second time, and it appeared she was done for. She had been at the Cornell shops in Rondout being readied for an exciting procession of hundreds of boats that would sail north from New York Harbor in the "Hudson-Fulton Celebration" that marked the centennial of Robert Fulton's first steamboat and the 300th anniversary of explorer Henry Hudson entering the river. Quick action by the Rondout firemen saved *Norwich*, but she was again severely damaged. With only twenty-five days until the parade, it appeared that the "oldest steamboat in the world," as she was called, would not be in it as so many had hoped she would.

S. D. Coykendall showed what his company could do and, in keeping with the wishes of his wife, had *Norwich* fully restored, without trace of damage. She appeared in the huge flotilla, and might have been considered the star of the show.

Coykendall was a demanding and tough chief executive, and when disobeyed after giving clear orders or warnings, he did not hesitate to dismiss men. Being involved in an accident or running a boat aground because of circumstances beyond the control of a pilot or captain was forgiven, although it was an embarrassment to the men. But if the man at the helm—or who should have been at the helm—was not doing his job, Coykendall came down hard and with finality.

In one case early in the century, the captain of *Hercules* decided to take a much-needed nap, and since the pilot was off duty, the captain allowed a deckhand to steer. It was a clear summer's day, and steering should not have been difficult, although it was illegal for a decky to do it unsupervised. This was not so unusual, though, for men other than the pilot or captain often steered for short periods, and even cooks were known to have taken charge of the pilot house from time to time. On this trip, while the captain and pilot slept, a thunderstorm came up suddenly, and the deckhand lost his way. The "Herk," as she was called, ran aground at Esopus Meadows below Rondout Creek, coincidentally close to the deckhand's home at Port Ewen.

Hercules was eventually pulled free, undamaged, and the deckhand was teased for years about trying to put the tug up in his own back yard. The captain was surely brought on the carpet, but apparently not fired, which was not the case two years later, when the *Hercules* pilot went below to work on his fishing nets, and he let a deckhand steer.

It was the middle of the night, and the boat struck a rock near Fort Montgomery, was holed, and sank in forty-five feet of water. Successfully raised and repaired, the "Herk" ran for another twelve years, but this pilot was not so fortunate. Confronted by Coykendall, the fellow admitted what he had done, and the president reportedly said, "Well, now you can go home for the rest of your life and knit nets to your heart's content." The pilot never again worked for Cornell.

There is a story told that, at the turn of the century, Captain James Monahan and his tug *John H. Cordts* took what was referred to as a "Hudson

> Only one two-pipe tug remains on the river—the Pocahontas. The Cordts and the Osceola each has but one smokestack now. —*Kingston Daily Leader*, 14 June 1901

Lord of Hudson River Towing

James H. Scott, built in 1897 and typical of the Albany Towing Company's small tugs, is depicted at her home port around 1910. The Albany tugs were painted in a different scheme from that of the Cornell fleet—a black stack, white hull and two-tone upperworks of undetermined color. (Roger W. Mabie Collection)

River sleigh ride" by riding in the wake of the Dayliner *New York*, which was heading upriver. The powerful suction of the wake pulled the "hooked up" *Cordts* along, and for miles it was as if the little tug were a match for the mighty steamboat. *New York*'s captain was proud of his vessel's reputation for speed, and the ladies aboard were always impressed by how fast she was. They were surprised when they saw the tugboat off the port-side, moving along just as fast as the steamboat.

Afterwards, disdainful ladies wrote letters of complaint to the steamboat company, declaring that if a tugboat could stay with *New York* for so long then the company had no right to claim in its advertisements that the steamboat was so fast. The line's president complained to S. D. Coykendall, who sternly warned Captain Monahan never to do it again, or he would be fired on the spot. Monahan could not resist doing it, though, and Coykendall did fire him next time.

Monahan went on to an illustrious career as master or pilot of other vessels, including the passenger steamboat *Newburgh* of the Central Hudson Line. Thanks to his abilities one snowy night in 1908, the icebound Cornell tugs *Hercules* and *Hedges* were not run down by *Newburgh*, which suddenly loomed out of the darkness, heading right at them. Then Monahan came to their aid, running his steamboat several times around the tugs, breaking up the jam-packed ice, and freeing them so they could try to get out of the way of *Ramsdell*, the next night boat, which was sure to pass by soon.

The tugs and their tow again became stuck, however, and *Ramsdell* appeared, but she had been warned by the constant sound of their whistles. The steamboat executed the same circling maneuver as *Newburgh*, and helped once more to break the tugs and their tow free. It was only temporary, however, for they soon were stopped dead again. At least there would be no more passenger steamboats coming through that night. When the tide ebbed just before dawn, the ice cleared enough for the tugs to continue their journey.

The ice business on the Hudson River was controlled by the American Ice Company, which had its own mammoth ice houses in which it stored ice cut by its own crews or bought from smaller operations. American's tugboats were operating in opposition to the Cornell Steamboat Company, which wanted all the business.

In 1910, S. D. Coykendall swung into action against American Ice by acquiring options on the production of many of the ice houses along the river. It was a dramatic struggle, made all the more interesting to the public by newspaper reports, such as the one below, entitled "Cornell Company After Ice Trust," from the pro-Cornell Kingston *Daily Freeman* in November of this year. Calling the American Ice Company a "trust" was an intentional slur, considering the fact that trusts were illegal business monopolies; making this statement showed where the *Freeman* stood on the controversy.

The subtitle of the article was "Albany Hears that the War is on, and the Steamboat People have Options on Many Ice Houses."

> The Cornell Steamboat Company is planning war on the American Ice Company and its Hudson River ice monopoly, says the Albany Argus. Captain Ulster Davis, president of the Albany Towing Company, a Cornell subsidiary which controls towing in the Albany and Troy harbors, when questioned a few days ago regarding the authenticity of the report of the plan to break into the ice business, said that he could not at the time say whether any plans had matured. Captain Davis, however, intimated that there had been displayed by the towing magnates during the summer a tendency to declare war on the American Ice Company.
>
> It is declared that the Cornell towing line has secured options on fifteen houses owned by independent dealers between Albany and Rondout. The towing business will decide within the next few weeks whether the Cornell interests will branch out so as to include ice harvesting in their business.

Cornell would do just that, and Coykendall had the financial muscle to buy the next ice crop from independent dealers, pressuring the American Ice Company to make terms favorable to Cornell—specifically to continue using Cornell to tow the ice barges to market. Cornell also wanted to be paid a rate

Pocahontas as she appeared after the installation of her new boiler in 1911, shown at the point of a tow on the river. Note that her after towing bitts are on the house top. The bitts themselves were three substantial vertical timbers (probably 16" x 16") anchored firmly into the afterbody of the tug's hull. (Roger W. Mabie Collection)

commensurate with the ice company's larger boats these days. According to the article, the original contract had been for Cornell to tow boats of 480 tons burden, while the ice barges had increased to 780 tons but demanded it pay the same rate as it had for smaller boats.

> The split between the American Ice Company and the Cornell towing line became acute last spring and resulted in the ice company bringing tugs here from Maine to tow their own boats. Before that the Cornell tugs all along the river handled the ice boats, and a special tow was sent away from Albany each night to handle the brick and ice trade. The towing of the ice boats was a big item for the Cornell company, and its loss will be felt when this year's receipts are tabulated.
>
> It is possible, however, that the American Ice Company may again contract with the Cornell people for the handling of their ice tows. River men claim that the ice company has lost money this year in engaging their own fleet of boats to do the towing. It is claimed it now takes the American boats five days to reach New York from this harbor, and that the money lost in waste will greatly outweigh the additional amount the Cornell company asked for in the new contract. Under Cornell towing the ice barge from Albany to New York was hauled in thirty-six hours. . . .
>
> The promised war to control the Hudson River ice crop will be watched with interest during the winter.

Less than three years later, in June of 1913, the *Freeman* reported that Cornell had bought all the "Ice Trust" tugs.

In 1911, the worn-out sidewheel steam towboat *Silas O. Pierce* was sold for scrap and broken up.

In May of this year, the former sidewheel passenger steamer *James W. Baldwin*, now known as *Central-Hudson*, ran aground near West Point, causing damage that was too extensive to repair in such an old wooden-hulled steamboat. *James W. Baldwin*, built in 1860 for Kingston's well-respected Captain Jacob H. Tremper, had been one of the speediest passenger boats on the river, and she had run from Rondout to New York in partnership with famous steamers such as *Thomas Cornell, Manhattan,* and *City of Kingston*.

In 1911, the former *James W. Baldwin* was bought by a wrecker, who towed her through New York Harbor to Perth Amboy, New Jersey, where this once-proud steamboat was broken up for scrap.

After the "Ice Trust" tugs were removed from competition, the Cornell Steamboat Company was the only one offering regular towing service on the Hudson River. In cases where another company might seem to be making inroads, Cornell would drop its rates so low that a competitor would be forced out of business and often would sell out—to Cornell—which was one reason the company often had more vessels than it had work for. In this time, Cornell had fifty-seven tugs in service, far more than it actually needed. One of its occasional competitors was the upcoming Moran Towing and Transportation Company, which then had only a few boats.

Cornell and the Hudson-Fulton Celebration

The Hudson-Fulton Celebration in 1909 celebrated one hundred years of steam navigation on the Hudson and the 300th anniversary of the discovery of the river by its namesake, Henry Hudson. A major event during the festivities was the Inaugural Naval Parade in New York Harbor on September 25, in which 1,595 vessels took part. Of these, 742 were in the moving parade, led by reproductions of Robert Fulton's *North River Steam Boat* and Hudson's *Half Moon* with escorting craft. The remainder were at anchor on the North River parade route, which extended from 80th Street to Fort Lee.

The moving parade was divided into four squadrons, preceded by a Scout Squadron of high-speed craft (vessels known as commuters supplied by J. P. Morgan Jr., August Belmont, W. Earl Dodge and others) and an Escort Squadron of fourteen naval vessels (predominately torpedo boat-destroyers). The First Squadron, composed of steamboats and ferries, included *Norwich* in its First Division. The Second Squadron included most of the large steam yachts in the northeastern portion of the nation, while motor yachts formed the Third Squadron.

Among the tugs and steam lighters, the Cornell Steamboat Company's fleet—twenty-three vessels strong—made up two divisions of the twenty-nine in the Fourth Squadron. Cornell's was the largest single corporate delegation in the entire parade. The Sixth Division, headed by Chief of Division Frederick Coykendall, was led by the flagship, the "Big" *Cornell*, which was followed, in order, by *R. G. Townsend, Pocahontas, Osceola, Geo. W. Washburn, John H. Cordts, J. C. Hartt, S. L. Crosby, Edwin H. Mead, Senator Rice, W. N. Bavier, John T.*

The Cornell tug *J. G. Rose* at the reception for the Hudson-Fulton Celebration Naval Parade at Newburgh on October 1, 1909. Astern of *Rose* is the steamer *Onteora* of the Catskill Evening Line. *J. G. Rose* and *Onteora* were built at the shipyard of T. S. Marvel and Company, a quarter mile to the south of this view. (William duBarry Thomas Collection)

Welch, and *Hercules*. Assisting Fred Coykendall were Fleet Captain Roland B. Bishop, Signal Officer N. J. Sinnott, and Aide Charles Lotma.

Immediately astern of the big tugs were the smaller, but no less important, members of the Seventh Division, led by *Victoria*, its flagship. Following in her wake were *Primrose*, *Knickerbocker*, *J. H. Williams*, *J. G. Rose*, *G. W. Decker*, *Edwin Terry*, *Ira M. Hedges*, *Robert A. Scott* and *Wm. E. Cleary*. The chief of division was Captain Newby S. Barritt; the fleet captain was William B. Barnett, and the signal officer and aide respectively were Timothy J. Donovan and J. J. Gilligan.

All of New York's tugboat men were represented in the Fourth Squadron, the Flag Officer of which was Fred B. Dalzell. The Morans were there as were the Tracys and McGuirls, along with Sam l'Hommedieu of White Star, Fred Russell of Newtown Creek, John M. Emery of the Lackawanna Railroad, W. B. Pollack of the New York Central, and many others.

The entire parade was organized by a thirty-man committee chaired by Captain Jacob W. Miller, a naval officer prominent in the marine world (he was one of the founders of The Society of Naval Architects and Marine Engineers and managed the construction of the Cape Cod Canal). Fred Coykendall was a member of the committee, which also included Commander R. E. Peary (who would go on to flag rank and fame as a polar explorer), Eugene F. Moran, Captain Aaron Ward, and Rear-Admiral George W. Melville. The latter two were both prominent naval officers who later had naval vessels named for them. (Eugene F. Moran scored high in this category; there were, over the years, nine tugs named for him as well as seven for his wife, Julia C. Moran.)

At the end of the day, the committee and the million or so spectators could look back at a job well done. Cornell, especially, could be proud of its impressive turnout. How the company handled the river tows during the few days of the Celebration we may never know. (One humorist has suggested that the upper river tows could only have been handled by the venerable *Oswego*, but *Ice King*, *E. L. Levy*, and *E. C. Baker*, absent from the New York scene, were undoubtedly kept busy on the upper Hudson.

Some of the participants in the parade followed *North River Steam Boat* and *Half Moon* as they made their way up the Hudson, stopping at the major riverside ports for local celebrations. Fireworks and "illuminations" were popular events at each stop. (The illuminations were searchlight displays from accompanying naval vessels. It should be remembered that electric lighting had been in existence for only about twenty-five years in most of the towns en route, and seeing the powerful beams in the spectacle was a novel experience for most observers.)

On September 25, Cornell had what must have been the last word. The man who commanded *North River Steam Boat* (erroneously named *Clermont* when the reproduction was built) was Cornell's captain Ulster Davis!

William duBarry Thomas

Chapter Ten
Loss and Transition

AFTER *C. W. MORSE*, the largest and most impressive Cornell tugboat of all was the steel-hulled *Cornell*, built in 1902, and referred to by boatmen as "The Big Cornell." She was almost 150 feet in length and had an engine of 1,400 horsepower, more than any other unit in the fleet. To turn a tugboat engine of such power required more than a ton of coal an hour fed to her two boilers, which meant unusually hard work for the men who stoked her. It was said the company had difficulty keeping firemen on the boat because the work was so demanding.

In March of 1910, *Cornell* would need every ounce of power to relieve Albany from an unprecedented flood.

An enormous ice jam had dammed up in the Hudson River below Albany that month, and suddenly the weather turned unseasonably warm, causing melting, heavy runoffs, and flooding throughout the watershed of the Hudson and Mohawk Rivers. Floodwater behind the ice dam backed into the low-lying areas of Albany and Troy, rising so high that there was danger of railroad bridges and trestles being undermined or pushed off their abutments. The federal government called on Cornell Steamboat Company to send the largest tug it had upriver to open up the ice jam. On March 3, *Cornell* was dispatched from Rondout, and the tug *Rob* went along to lend assistance.

One of the problems with sending *Cornell* was that she normally could not go so far north because the Hudson had sand bars and shoal water, and in many places was not deep enough for such a large vessel. The time of the deepening of the Hudson was still twenty years or more away, but as long as the river was in flood, there would be enough depth for *Cornell* to get back downriver again as long as she did not delay too long and allow the water level to drop. Any miscalculations by her temporary commander, Ulster Davis, the company's agent at Rensselaer, might mean *Cornell* would run aground, possibly even be capsized. *Cornell*'s captain was Tim Donovan, her pilot Irving Hayes. These two made sure the tugboat carried only a minimum load of coal and water in order to lessen her draft so she could get over those sandbars, especially the Overslaugh bar five miles south of Albany.

On *Cornell* went, battering her way through ice that in places was two feet thick, and her steel hull plating was soon scalloped and battered at the water line. It took two hard days to reach Athens, with *Rob* following close behind. They went up the western channel, for the ice there was not as thick as in the

Captain Ulster Davis of the Cornell Steamboat Company in Albany states that the tug Geo. N. Southwick is to be equipped with fire fighting facilities. The Van Tuyl now carries a hose line, but the Southwick will be the only tug in the vicinity of Albany that may be called a fire fighter. The new boat is to be so equipped especially for the Cornell line, but will be ready at any time to respond to a call along the river front.
—*Kingston Daily Freeman*, 30 December 1907

Hercules and *Rob* enjoying a well-deserved rest from their ice-fighting duties at an unknown location on January 25, 1907. Among the propeller tugs, *Hercules* was exemplary as an icebreaker, much as *Norwich* was the "Ice King" among the side-wheelers. (Roger W. Mabie Collection)

Ice was a formidable foe of Hudson River navigation. Before Coast Guard icebreakers kept the channel open to upriver points, all traffic on the river ceased at the beginning of winter and commenced once more in the spring. Cornell's tugs battled ice regularly in the company's effort to move barges and canal boats. Here *Hercules* is depicted at an unknown place early in the twentieth century. (Roger W. Mabie Collection)

eastern, and men and boys appeared all along the way to watch the *Cornell* work. Spectators came right down on the ice and walked along at a safe distance as the tugboats slowly progressed.

Cornell and *Rob* reached Rensselaer on March 6, after a three-day journey that in warm weather a passenger boat could make in a few hours. They broke through the ice jam, and it was said one could see the water dropping. The task had been accomplished, but the river was falling so fast that *Cornell* was in danger of being trapped there. There was no time for celebrating or congratulations, for she had to turn around and head home before bars and rock ledges appeared at the surface as the river level dropped.

First came the chores of hurriedly taking on coal, water, and food at Rensselaer. Then came the turning of the big tug, but the current was so pow-

This winter view looking down the Rondout Creek towards the Cornell shops shows (left to right) the chain ferry *Riverside* (known locally as the "Skillypot"), Cornell's venerable towboat Norwich and the ferryboat Transport. A number of the company's tugs are visible behind Transport. (J. Matthews Collection)

erful that *Cornell* needed help from the *Rob*, which pushed with all her power against *Cornell's* stern. It was getting dark when they were ready to go, and that posed a danger of hitting underwater obstructions in the flooded river, but they dare not wait until morning, for the water would be too low to get through by then.

The men in the pilot house had to steer *Cornell* through the dark, down the channel she had opened, and were always at risk of striking an unseen obstacle or running aground. The river was so fast that *Cornell* ran at dead slow to maintain control. If they even just scraped the bottom, they might damage the rudder or break a propeller blade, and then she would be at the mercy of the torrent driving down from astern. As *Cornell* and *Rob* approached the Overslaugh sand bar, Captain Donovan warned that it would be higher than normal because of silting from the flood. *Cornell* stopped its engine and drifted slowly. Donovan was right: she nudged onto the bar, stopped, and rolled slightly to port.

To make sure there was only sand all around and no rock ledge, the men tested the river bottom by probing with long pikes. Beneath her, fortunately, was only sand, but the water was still dropping. If she did not get through soon, *Cornell* would be grounded. Her experienced boatmen had achieved a small miracle thus far, and they had made it look relatively easy. Foresight in sending *Rob* along with *Cornell* had made it possible to turn against the current at Rensselaer, and now the *Rob* was needed again. She went ahead, being of shallower draft, and put a hawser on *Cornell's* bow. The plan was for the *Rob* to pull ahead while *Cornell* ran her engine at full speed.

Rob's hawser tightened, and the first surge heeled *Cornell* far to port. *Rob* pulled and *Cornell* inched forward, engines roaring at full steam ahead until she suddenly cleared the sandbar, leaping forward so fast that she rushed down on *Rob*, which was still on the hawser. The quick action of a *Rob* deckhand, who chopped the hawser with an axe, saved her from being rammed, and the boats narrowly steered clear of each other.

From there to Rondout and home, the tugs followed the path they had broken through the ice on their upriver journey, and the trip was happily uneventful.

Cornell and *Rob* were praised by boatmen who understood what a feat had been achieved, especially because they all knew the dangers of working in ice, whether breaking it or trying not to be trapped by it.

Early in the twentieth century, some anonymous versifier, surely an employee of the Cornell Company, wrote the following poem that is rich with inside jokes and good-natured teasing as it tells of another ice-bound Hudson River adventure:

The Breaking of the Ice Gorge
Or: Who Cleared the Narrow Channel

Listen, shipmates, and I'll tell the story
Of Davis and Scott on their quest for glory;
The ice came down with a rush and a roar,
And blocked the river from shore to shore.

Then Frank Bedell got busy, and to Cartwright he did say,
"You will have to send some tugboats to clear the ice away."
Soon the office resembled a bee hive, but in it there was not one drone.
All hands were talking together, each one had a plan of his own.
"Avast there!" then cried Cartwright, "Your jaw tackle all belay!
"We will sit down in harmony, let each man have his say."

The experts then got together; Bishop said, "We will send the Foss."
"Oh no!" said Jack Stevens, "Don't do that, it would not suit the boss."
Then Underhill said to Capt. Bearse, "It is time to show your hand.
"You've sailed the river for many years, and know the lay of the land."

Then Capt. Ed spoke up, saying, "I wish we had some boats that I've known,
"The Conqueror, Honeysuckle or Camelia, and others that we used to own."
"What good were they?" asked Billy Barnett. "They could not break much ice;
"I could beat them all with the Sammy Cornell, on that you can bet your price."

Then cried out Tommy Trollan, "I'll tell you what we will do:
"We will send the Hercules to cut the gorge in two.
"With her nickel steel armor plating and planks of oak so tough,
"She will go through all the ice there is, if they carry steam enough."

The Herkey then was ordered out, Mel Hamilton in command,
The pilot he had, John Silliman, a man both brave and grand.
Ned Bishop in the engine room, with Phinney to help him along,
They made a combination that was truly great and strong.

At break of day they left the creek, with faces grim and stern,
And, before night, passed through the gorge and started to return.
But the ice closed in around them, packed tight from shore to shore.
It was then the crew began to think they would see New York no more.

The boats of the Cornell Steamboat Company, at this point with the exception of the C. D. Mills and Norwich, have been put in winter quarters. The Mills and Norwich will be used to help the Transport in making its trips across the Hudson until the ice is of sufficient thickness to allow the running of horses and sleighs. —*Kingston Daily Freeman,* **22 December 1888**

Then word was sent to Rondout, "Send the Rob up!" was the cry,
"The Herkey is jammed fast in the ice; don't leave us here to die."
Early next morning, the Pocahontas and Rob
Were ordered to get ready and get on the job.

The Pokey was laid up, Sandy wanted to go home,
But Jack Herrick said, "No, Will can't go alone.
"Now let us get things in shape, before Ivor gets here,
"If we do what the boss wants, we have nothing to fear."

Just then Tom Hickey appeared on the scene,
And said he, "We will soon do the job up clean."
So the Pokey got ready, Irv Hayes in command,
With Rol Saulpaugh as pilot to lend him a hand.

In the engine room Sandy Hulsapple sat in state,
Will Conklin was with him, to act as his mate.
In the meantime the Rob was got ready for sea,
Gage said, "For pilot, I want Jimmie Dee.

"With Nelse Lafayette at the throttle and Willie Schultz to fire,
"We will soon pull the Hercules out of the mire."
The boat was grubbed up for two days or more,
The captain said, of potatoes, lay in a great store.

Joe Davis said Peary was no better rigged when through Arctic regions he fought,
But Chief Rafferty refused to ship on the Rob, because no chickens were bought.
The Rob got underway at noon, and reached Catskill after a hard fight.
It was there that Haysie found her, at nine o'clock that night.

When Irv came ashore and looked at his boat, he got a terrible shock,
For her copper was torn off, her planks cut through, and there was no dry dock.
But Gage had his weather eye open, and between supper time and dark,
Had met a man with a grand crop of whiskers—his name was Lewis Clark.

Then Capt. Lew said to Capt. Hayes, "Don't you lose any sleep,
"I will fix your boat in the morning, if she is not cut too deep."
The Rob left in the morning, with Gage still in command,
As guests he had Messrs. Scott, Welch and Seaman, and Smith who sells the sand.

The party arrived at Athens, after fighting more than an hour.
Before that boat touched the dock, Stewart locked up his chickens in the Tower.
Here the captain received another surprise, for the first man he met on the street,
Was Reilly Davis from Albany, who had come to take charge of the fleet.

For Denny Driscoll was very much worried, he could not sleep at night,
So he said to Reilly, "You go down, and do the job up right.
"I would take command myself, but I can't get away,
"For Haswell has so much to do, I must help him night and day."

But Denny need not have worried, for Jim Scott was on his job,
It was not the first ice gorge for him, any more than it was for the Rob.
All hands worked together and got the Herkey free;
There were more ice barons on that trip than we ever expected to see.

And when the ice was all cut out, they wore their brightest smiles,
Then the Rob went back to Catskill and picked up Mr. Giles.
She took him north, then took him south, the length of his domain;
Said he, "We have done fine business, a great crop of ice we will gain.

"Now, Captain, take your boat home, for we have reached our goal."
"All right," said Gage, "we will go and hang up Branigan for some coal."
Then here is success to Davis and Scott. May their shadows never grow less,
For they are jolly fellows, to that we will all confess.

Six hundred loaves of bread are consumed weekly by the crews of the towboats of the Cornell Steamboat Company. —*Kingston Daily Freeman*, 10 June 1889

The reputation of *Hercules* as an icebreaker was made in 1912, when she and *S. L. Crosby* were working in tandem to break unusually heavy ice that was preventing the movement of barges of crushed stone from the quarries at Rockland Lake, south of Haverstraw. The barges were frozen in the ice, and to release them, the tugboats took turns slamming into a track they were trying to shiver open with perfectly placed blows.

First one tug drove at full throttle into the ice, which was more than seven inches thick. After it had gone as far as it could, it backed off, and the other came charging forward to slam against the same spot. They were slowly working their way toward the dock where the scows were, when *Crosby* made a decisive crack in the ice before she ran out of forward momentum. *Crosby* had done the job, but when *Hercules* followed up and opened the crack wide, it appeared to onlookers that *Hercules* had just performed an amazing feat of icebreaking.

Crosby had made the crack, but Frederick Coykendall, general manager of Cornell at the time, had been watching on the dock, and from his perspective *Hercules* had won the day. He had not seen the first crack made by *Crosby*. Enthusiastic about what *Hercules* appeared to have done, Coykendall ordered the company shops to fit her bow with extra stout oak planking and steel straps to make her even better as an icebreaker.

It was reputed from then on that *Hercules* was the best icebreaker in the Cornell fleet, but *Crosby*'s captain, Aaron Relyea of Bloomington, flatly disagreed, saying his boat was the better of the two. Years later, *Hercules* captain, Mel Hamilton of Port Ewen, conceded to William O. Benson, an up-and-coming captain himself, that *Crosby* was indeed the better icebreaker.

As Benson related it, Hamilton added with a wink, "Never argue with the boss."

River towing had its many hazards, but one of the worst Cornell accidents happened at sea, off New Jersey's Sandy Hook, when the steam-propeller tug *Ice King* was wrecked, fortunately without loss of life.

On the night of December 26, 1913, while towing two garbage scows to an offshore dumping site, the ocean-going *Ice King*—formerly the *Greyhound*, built in 1877—reportedly had her towing hawser entangled by a drifting log, resulting in her propeller becoming fouled and badly damaged. The housing around the propeller began to take on water so fast that the captain, Charles Thobea, had to run her ashore at Sandy Hook. The crew was safely taken off the grounded tug. The barges had to be cast adrift, their sea anchors dropped to prevent them being blown ashore. Then a heavy northwest gale blew up and for hours pounded the *Ice King* to pieces, and she was a total loss.

On January 14, 1913, S. D. Coykendall died unexpectedly at his home in Kingston at the age of seventy-six.

A simple service was held at the residence, with pallbearers chosen from employees of long standing in the Cornell companies: George Gage of the tugboat *Rob;* John Herrick of the Cornell machine shops; Thomas Hickey, superintendent of the Cornell boiler shop; John B. Cook, superintendent of the Consolidated Rosendale Cement Company; William D. Cashin, superintendent of the Hudson River Bluestone Company; Conductor Patrick Phillips and Engineer John Rothery, two of the oldest employees of the U&D railroad; and Chief Engineer Douglas Fowler of the ferryboat *Transport.*

The Rev. A. R. Fuller, former pastor of the Wurts Street Baptist Church that once had Thomas Cornell as a deacon and benefactor, gave the eulogy, saying, "Whether trustee of a little church or a large college, director of a bank or great corporation, he was the faithful and efficient executive. He was much more than a successful businessman who had accumulated property. He was a clean, true man of high ideals and moral integrity. . . ."

Even Coykendall's enemies in business had to agree that he was of transcendent personal character and stature, for all that he was a hard and relentless competitor. As was Thomas Cornell before him, S. D. Coykendall had been a leading light and a dynamo for Kingston and Rondout and Ulster County. No one came close to matching Coykendall's accomplishments or improving on them, not even the six Coykendall sons, who had been brought up to leadership and inherited a great business empire. That empire had a strong foundation, but it faced a new age of electricity and oil and swift change, and with that change came great adversity for the Cornell Steamboat Company, although in 1913 it was as yet unforeseen.

The tug boats Columbia and C. D. Mills have a large white C placed upon their smokestacks. These were placed there by the crew, but the company intends putting them on all their boats.
—*Kingston Daily Freeman*, 1 September 1892

With the death of S. D. Coykendall, his sons moved into new responsibilities. The directors of the Ulster and Delaware Railroad elected Edward president, and certainly he had the most experience of all, having served as its superintendent since 1895. This meant bypassing fifty-three-year-old Thomas, who had been vice president of the U&D under his father. Thomas remained a director and was well paid by the U&D, as were other brothers, but he was no longer very active in the company. He continued in the capacity of director in several Cornell companies.

Frederick succeeded his father as president of the Cornell Steamboat Company and soon moved its headquarters from Rondout to New York, where he lived. Frederick, who was forty years of age when his father died, had been secretary of the company since 1897, becoming manager in 1900. With his home in New York's famous "Dakota" apartment building, he seldom spent time in Kingston, where Edward and Frank lived. Thomas came

The Metamorphosis of a Tugboat

Named for a prominent Rondout business man, the tug *John D. Schoonmaker* is depicted at various stages of her long career in the company fleet (1888-1951) showing how the vessel's personality changed as she was rebuilt. (Top) We first see her as she was built. We do not know what the occasion was, but she is shown in holiday regalia—colors flying at jackstaff and mainmast and an awning rigged on her foredeck. (Center) Another view from her early days as she is headed down the Rondout Creek towards the Cornell shops with two coal barges alongside. The side-wheel steamboat *Mary Powell* may be seen at the left. (Bottom) As the *Schoonmaker* looked when she was running on the Barge Canal around 1930, with a low and extended pilot house and a very low stack.

(Top) Here she is shown in her canal rig with a stack extension added. The temporary coal bunkers used in the canal—her "saddle bags"—can be seen alongside the deckhouse. Note that her freeboard approached zero with the added coal. (Center) Next, the vessel back on the river about 1940, with her low pilot house and a new, moderately high stack. (Bottom) Our last image shows the *Schoonmaker* in 1951 in her last rig—high pilot house, the same moderately high stack and her deckhouse panels replaced with plywood.

(Photographs from Roger W. Mabie and William duBarry Thomas Collections)

Loss and Transition

The case of the Cornell Steamboat Company against Patrick Hanley of Ellenville for $41, which the plantiffs claim is due them for towing, was settled before Justice Clare, before whom the case came for trial Wednesday. He paid the full claim with $1.50 court costs. —Kingston Daily Freeman, 8 March 1894

and went between New York and Kingston, but Harry and Robert had been more New Yorkers than Kingstonians, and the New York's social register early in the century includes these Coykendalls and their wives.

Shortly after the loss of her husband, Mary Augusta Cornell Coykendall would have more than her share of personal sadness, for in September of this year her youngest son, Robert, died at thirty-six. A year later, in October 1914, Harry, too, passed away; he was forty-six.

Of all the Coykendall sons, only Frederick would have a child, daughter Ursula, born at the turn of the century. The Coykendall daughter, Catherine, went on to marry E. Hunt Herzog, and have children, but she was not active in the Cornell companies, although she received a regular stipend from the Thomas Cornell estate. The Herzogs lived in New Orleans.

Three of the Coykendall sons had propeller tugboats named after them: *Harry* (1892), *Frank* (1893), and *Rob* (1902). These were similar in design and were of the smaller type that worked in Rondout Creek and as helpers.

There was strong sibling rivalry among the Coykendall brothers, especially between Edward and Frederick, who were not close. S. D. Coykendall had shown a certain favoritism in his will, by naming Edward, who was forty-one, executor of his estate. That meant Edward controlled the voting rights of those shares that remained in the estate, and this gave him power over the various enterprises, including the Cornell Steamboat Company. Although Frederick was president of Cornell and nominally in charge of operations, brother Edward could step in and, with his control of the majority of shares, could overrule Frederick at any time.

For the moment, Edward had his hands full running the U&D and managing his father's estate, but there was no guarantee for Frederick that things would stay that way. Yet, he had plenty to occupy him, too, with the steamboat company thriving and his other various directorships demanding attention, such as the Kingston-Rhinecliff ferry and the banks. Of all the family enterprises, the Cornell Steamboat Company was the most famous, having one of the most stellar reputations of any business in the Hudson River Valley or in the state.

In 1913, Cornell made another acquisition from Knickerbocker Steam Towage Company's Hudson River fleet, buying *Delta, Perry, Britannia, Imperial, Princess, Bismarck, Charlie Lawrence, Wm. H. Baldwin, Ralph Ross, E. D. Haley,* and *Woodbridge*. Several of these, such as *Britannia, Imperial, Princess,* and *Bismarck,* which were eventually sold to the Cahill Towing Company and others, did not stay long in the Cornell fleet.

Although the Cornell Steamboat Company had only been incorporated since 1878, its history on the river went back to 1837, when Thomas Cornell bought his first sloop and entered the river freight business at Rondout. More than a hundred vessels had come and gone in the Cornell fleet by the first years of the twentieth century, and their accomplishments and their colorful boatmen had become an enduring part of the Hudson's maritime lore and heritage.

In 1914, as Europe was swept into World War I, Isaac M. North died in his seventy-fifth year. North had been a Cornell superintendent of operations since 1878, until retiring a few years before his death.

About this time, the mighty line steamer *Cornell* was sold to Standard Oil Company of Louisiana, which converted her to an oil burner and renamed her the *Istrouma*. She was put into service on the Mississippi, out of Baton Rouge.

In the years around World War I, the movement of barges of oil on the Hudson River began to become more important. Cornell occasionally towed some oil barges for Texaco, but Frederick Coykendall was worried about being sued as a monopoly because of his company's control of most other Hudson River towing. For that reason, Coykendall was not aggressive in going after oil barge business, which was not especially large as yet. Furthermore, the oil companies demanded that Cornell deliver their barges—which were very costly to build—more promptly than was possible with the existing system of large tows moving slowly down the river while helper tugs fetched waiting boats along the shoreline. And the oil companies wanted their empty barges returned quickly from Albany to be reloaded, but once again Cornell declared that it would determine when and how tows were made up and scheduled.

The result was that the oil companies found other towing contractors to do their work, including the ambitious and willing Moran Towing and Transportation Company. Michael Moran, the founder, had started out as a laborer with the D&H Coal Company at Rondout. His determination to succeed with his towing company was beginning to pay off.

One reason for the increase in the oil business was the advent of the automobile. As roads were improved and paved, trucks carried more and more freight, thus becoming another competitor to Cornell. Thomas Coykendall continued experimenting with dieselizing steam tugs. He could have lived the easy life, enjoying his inheritance and serving on the boards of directors of the various companies and gallivanting with New York and Kingston society, as brother Frank did. Instead, he was in the shops with the mechanics much of the time, putting his Columbia engineering degree to practical and brilliant use.

In July 1916, *C. W. Morse* was lost at sea with all hands. In 1912, she had been sold to McAllister Brothers towing company, which in turn had sold her again. On the very day of the resale, July 17, *C. W. Morse* had departed from New York, heading for Puerto Rico and then on to Africa. After leaving New York, however, she was never heard from again.

A more common end to a vessel's career—although with its own poignancy—came in 1917 for *Mary Powell* and in 1919 for *Norwich*. The fifty-seven-year-old *Mary Powell* had been running for the Day Line on special trips from Rondout to New York or Albany. Her last captain, the youthful Arthur Warrington, had started with her fifteen years earlier as a bootblack. In this

> The tugs Schoonmaker and Hartt got up steam this morning, and the Schoonmaker has been amusing herself running about the creek this afternoon. —*Kingston Daily Freeman*, 10 March 1894

*John H. Cordt*s as she appeared after the fire on November 3, 1907 which badly damaged the tug and destroyed Cornell's coal pockets, located downstream of the Rondout shops. Two weeks after the fire, the engine and boiler of the *Cordts* were removed and the hull taken to Conrad Hiltebrant's shipyard in South Rondout for repairs. By late June 1908 she was back in service. The coal pockets were hastily replaced with a similar structure located at Whiteport, which was torn down and re-erected at Rondout. (Roger W. Mabie Collection)

The little *Geo. C. Van Tuyl, Jr.* at work with a tow near Lock 40 on the Barge Canal at Little Falls, New York, in 1911. This image offers proof that the tugs of Albany Towing Company, a Cornell subsidiary, could be found on the canal well before Cornell's venture there two decades later. What constituted the deck load on the head barge is a mystery, as is the identity of the man standing atop its lading—and why he was there at all. (T. I. Brooks Collection, courtesy of William duBarry Thomas)

last season, it was extremely difficult to find men willing and able to work on her, because so many were joining the military as the United States entered the war. This meant that what men could be found were able to demand much higher wages than usual, and that put financial pressure on her owners.

The scrapping of *Mary Powell* in full view of the Rondout community might have caused a public furor and trouble that the Day Line did not want, so after she was sold, the steamboat was towed by *Rob* far up Rondout Creek for gradual dismantling over several years. It was said the owners had refused an offer of $100,000 from a film company that wanted to set *Mary Powell* on fire as part of a movie production. The actual sale was likely for only a few thousand dollars, but for years to come, much of *Mary Powell* was sold off, bit by bit, to collectors.

In her last years, *Norwich* had worked as a helper tug in the upper part of the Hudson River, sometimes in charge of tows, but more often cooperating with the stronger *Oswego* or *Pocahontas*. Even her reputation as an icebreaker had been eclipsed by the more powerful propeller tugs, most of which were better at it than she.

On March 19, 1917, while at the Lindsley dock, her winter berth near the Cornell shops in the Ponckhockie section of Rondout, *Norwich* sprang a leak and sank. She rested on the bottom of the shallow slip, and it was fully expected that it would not be difficult to raise her when the tide went out, then tow her to dry dock and make repairs. It was not so easy. Several efforts to raise her failed, and a diver had to be brought up from New York to go down and patch her up.

The Kingston *Daily Freeman* reported daily on the week-long efforts to raise the "Old Ice King." On the 27th, the newspaper wrote: "Efforts to raise the sunken *Norwich* have so far proved unsuccessful, but another pump will be installed and an effort made to free the hull of the Ice King to float her."

Loss and Transition

The twilight of a towboat's career. The side-wheeler *Oswego* is depicted in lay-up in the slip at the lower end of the Island Dock, probably sometime around 1918 or 1919. Moored along *Oswego*'s starboard side are three unidentified Cornell tugboats and a canal boat. The railroad tracks in the foreground are sidings of the Ulster and Delaware Railroad. (Roger W. Mabie Collection)

It was not until April 4, that *Norwich* was finally raised and towed to Hiltebrant's dry dock across the Creek at South Rondout, where her hull was to be repaired. A couple of days later, she was towed by the tug *Rob* to the Cornell shops for an overhauling. She would go back in service, but her days were numbered.

Perhaps *Norwich* endured so long—into her eighty-third year—only because she was the sentimental favorite of the Coykendalls. True or not, her career on the river ended shortly after Mrs. Coykendall died on June 7, 1919. Then *Norwich* was taken to Port Ewen, the graveyard of so many boats like her. A few years later, in 1923, she was sold to Port Ewen salvager Michael Tucker, who dismantled her.

Laid Down But Never Completed

In the summer of 1907, the Cornell Steamboat Company placed an order with T. S. Marvel Shipbuilding Company for a steel-hulled tug measuring about 105 feet in length overall (or 95 feet between perpendiculars) and having a beam of 23 feet and a depth of 11 feet 6 inches. The shipyard was to build only the hull of the vessel, and Cornell was to install her engine and boiler, construct the deckhouse and pilot house, and otherwise complete the tug, much in the same manner as that employed for *J. H. Williams* and *Wm. E. Cleary* (Hull Numbers 154 and 155) three years before. The contract price for the hull was $35,800.

It was intended that the hull of the new tug should be fitted with the engine of *W. E. Street*, built for Cornell in 1881 in Philadelphia. Her boiler was either to come from the older vessel or to be a newly-constructed one, probably from the Cornell shops. *W. E. Street* was the first of a quartet of new-generation wooden-hulled tugs built in Philadelphia for Cornell between 1881 and 1883, the others being *R. G. Townsend*, *S. L. Crosby*, and *J. C. Hartt*. These four vessels were the first in the fleet to be fitted with compound engines and condensers, and therefore can be considered to be Cornell's first modern tugs. *Coe F. Young* and *Thomas Dickson*, the previous screw-propeller tugs built for the Rondout company (by Morgan Everson in Sleightsburgh in 1872), were fitted with condensing single-cylinder engines in accordance with the practice of the 1870s.

In October 1907, work commenced in the drafting room and mold loft on Hull 192, and her keel was laid shortly afterwards. Work progressed through the erection of a number of midship frames and at least one transverse bulkhead during the month of December, and then ceased when the contract was canceled. Nearly all the materials on hand were set aside for use on later contracts.

The abandonment of construction of Hull 192 marked the first time in the twenty-nine years of the Marvel yard's existence that a vessel was canceled and not built. The financial condition of the country that led to the Panic of 1907—and the downturn in business that followed—had affected Cornell's towing business along the Hudson. Traffic in the principal commodities carried in Cornell tows—coal, brick and stone—inevitably followed the fortunes of business, and the company found that, in the conditions of the times, it could simply not afford the new vessel.

Although the Marvel yard survived the panic of 1907, some well-known shipbuilders were forced out of business. Neafie and Levy and the Delaware River Iron Ship Building and Engine Works are perhaps the best known. Others, such as John H. Dialogue at Camden, were able, like T. S. Marvel, to hang on for a few years more, but for various reasons were not able to keep their businesses viable until the boom time of World War I.

William duBarry Thomas

Frederick Coykendall, the third and longest-serving president of the Cornell Steamboat Company, was a graduate of Columbia University and served as chairman of the university's trustees. (Courtesy of Columbia University)

Chapter Eleven
Dissension in Cornell

THE SIDEWHEEL TOWBOAT *OSWEGO*, built in 1848, also ended her career in 1919. Frederick Coykendall was trying to have her rehabilitated over that winter by rebuilding the paddle wheels, making them smaller so the boat would theoretically be easier to manage. At $20,000, the cost was high. The story goes that Frederick was standing on the dock one day, watching work being done on *Oswego*, when Ben Hoff, one of his oldest captains, objected.

"Freddie, it's no good to spend all that money," Hoff asserted. "She will turn up too fast and fill the wheel houses with water and not do anything at all, not even as good as she used to. It's just money thrown away."

Captain Hoff had known "Freddie" since the Coykendall sons were children and had no qualms about addressing him that way. Frederick did not mind, but disagreed, saying, "Well, Captain Ben, it's our money we're spending. Let's see who's right."

Captain Hoff was right. *Oswego*, with her smaller paddle wheels could not handle a heavy tow, making her useless to the company. So the towboat Thomas Cornell once had accepted as part of a trade for *Mary Powell* was sold for scrap and broken up. This period of disappearing sidewheelers was indeed the end of their era.

On September 30, 1918, at the end of World War I, a new era seemed to be beginning in Rondout Creek, as the wooden-hulled freighter *Esopus* was launched at the shipyard of the Island Dock for the U.S. Shipping Board. The largest vessel ever built in the Creek, she was constructed of wood because the Shipping Board held the belief that wooden ships could be built faster and in greater quantities than steel ships.

More than 15,000 persons gathered to watch, crowding hillsides and wharves, standing in boats, and looking out from windows. Everyone anticipated that the four additional freighters that had been contracted by the government meant a new shipbuilding industry would develop in Rondout Creek. As *Esopus* slid down the ways and splashed into the water, the Creek erupted with cheers and the ringing and clanging of bells, from light trolley car bells to the distant Rondout lighthouse bell and deep church bells, all mingling with boat and factory whistles. The passenger steamboat *Benjamin B.*

The large towing steamer C. W. Morse of the Cornell line left today for Galveston, Texas, having been chartered by a Texas oil company to tow oil tank vessels to New Orleans and other southern ports. —*Kingston Daily Freeman*, 24 May 1906

Odell (1911) was docked at the Central Hudson Company's wharf, and her pilot cheerfully sounded her whistle in salute to *Esopus*. Almost seventy years of Hudson River steamboat history was in Rondout Creek that day, including *Oswego* (1848), *M. Martin* (1863), and *Mary Powell* (1863). In a few weeks the Cornell tug *Pocahontas* would take *Esopus* down to the East River, where a coastwise tug would assume charge for the rest of the trip to Providence, Rhode Island. There, the boilers and engine would be installed.

Prospects looked bright for Island Dock, but with the armistice to end the war having taken place that November, two of the contracts were canceled, one was completed as a schooner, and the other remained an unfinished hull. There was no further call for wooden-hulled ships. The shipyard at Island Dock had proven more than worthy of the task, but not until World War II would shipbuilding on such a scale resume in earnest in Rondout Creek.

> **The steamers Mead and Washburn left Rondout last night for New York where they will be inspected today by officials of the United States Navy with a view to ascertaining if they will be of value to the government in case of war with Spain.**
> —*Kingston Daily Freeman*, 6 April 1898

In May of 1922, Edward Coykendall's wife, Isabel Hutton Coykendall, died.

Just a few days later, Edward suffered another blow as the U&D Railroad had its worst accident ever, with six men killed. The railroad and its owners always had taken special pride in its almost accident-free record.

A year later, the last and largest dividend was paid by the U&D to the eighteen stockholders, an astounding $1.25 million, which was the entire reserve fund that had been received as the settlement with New York City after the litigation related to the building of the Ashokan Reservoir. Railroad bondholders whose bonds were due in 1928 were angry at the U&D dispersing the reserve instead of keeping it ready to pay off their bonds. The U&D still had $800,000 in surplus, but operating costs had been consistently in the red for the past several years, and that surplus was evaporating rapidly.

Not only had Edward Coykendall lost his wife, but his cherished U&D was about to fail.

After a long winter, boating on a coal-fired Cornell tug at the springtime start of a new season meant following a ritual of preparations that brought Rondout Creek and company wharves and shops to life. As eloquently described by longtime Cornell captain William O. Benson's series of historical articles edited by Roger W. Mabie and published in the *Freeman*, the first day back was always exhilarating:

> On a tugboat, the crew would report aboard in the early morning. All the new lines, supplies for the galley, mattresses, blankets and sheets and other supplies were brought aboard. The cook would be rushing around getting the galley ready and cooking the first meal, which usually had to be prepared quickly. Generally, he would go over to Planthaber's on the Strand in Rondout and order his supplies for the first few days. When these came down to the dock, they always looked as if they would last a month.
>
> Then the tug would go down to the coal pocket and coal up. The smell of dried new paint in the fireroom and on top of the boilers, the soft hiss of the steam, and the pleasant aroma of the soft coal smoke made one so hungry, he could eat almost anything that was put before him.

Outside, the freshly painted cabins and coamings, the big shiny black smokestack with its yellow base, the glistening nameboards, and the new pennant on the jackstaff gently waving in the clean spring air suddenly made everything right with the world.

When the tug started away from the dock for the first time, to feel and hear her softly throbbing engine, and the gentle wake of the water around her bow and stern were all sounds a boatman never forgets.

Down off Port Ewen, the tug would generally blow a series of salutes on the whistle. It seemed there was always someone in the crew from Port Ewen. Often you could see someone on shore, or from the upper window of a house, waving back with a towel or maybe even a bed sheet. How clear and pleasant the whistle would sound in the early spring evening. It was great to be back in commission.

Benson tells how it was the same with all the Cornell tugs, savoring that first meal on board, renewing old friendships, and sleeping on fresh sheets in a newly painted cabin. For that one first day in commission, at least, even lowly deckhands on the great passenger steamboats enjoyed "the freshness of it all";

you would completely forget all the white paint you would have to scrub, all the brass you would have to polish, all the decks you would have to wash down, all the lines at all the landings you would have to handle, and the thousands of deck chairs you would have to fold up and stow before the new season would come to its end in the fall.

By 1924, with Thomas Cornell Coykendall as the leading light, the steamboat company was a pioneer in efforts to dieselize tugs, just as it had been forward-thinking in using steel hulls. Most tugboat companies in the East were reluctant to convert their boats to diesel or to build new ones powered by it.

The Cornell Company had fifty-six boats on its fleet roster at this time, too many for the amount of work available. Some tugs had been sold off, such as *Levy, Baker, Imperial,* and *Princess.* Some old tugs might be laid up for years, then put back in service when they were needed *J. C. Hartt* had been hauled out at Baisden's boatyard in the Creek before being extensively rebuilt and launched in the spring of 1917 to accommodate the boom in business during and after World War I. Likewise with the elderly tug *Eugenia,* formerly *Saratoga,* built in 1865. Put back in commission at the same time as *Hartt, Eugenia* had Alfred Davis of Milton for her captain, which was fitting because Davis was the most senior captain in terms of service in the company.

Cornell bought two big diesel tugs, *Jumbo* and *Lion.* Their hulls had been built at the end of the war, but they were completed in 1924 and 1925, respectively, for New London Ship and Engine Company (Nelseco), the engine builder. The steam tug *Charlie Lawrence* was converted to diesel in 1924 and renamed *Cornell.* Company policy was to give all converted diesel tugs the name "Cornell" and a number—the number being its numerical designation in the fleet. In 1926, *Eli B. Conine,* built in 1900, was also converted and renamed *Cornell No. 41.* So, too, was *Frank,* which became *Cornell No. 20.* In

1929, *Cornell No. 21* followed, with the dieselization of *J. H. Williams*. All four conversions had Nelseco engines.

Not every conversion was fully successful. For example, when *Cornell* was transformed into a diesel she was also lengthened at the same time. John Baisden, operator of the shipyard at Sleightsburgh, objected to the tugboat's new design, saying she should also have had her hull deepened to make her more seaworthy. Baisden's warnings were not heeded, and *Cornell* always sat precariously low in the water, sometimes in danger of being swamped when the river was rough. So much water flowed over her deck at times that her crew nicknamed her "The Submarine."

Most of the dieselization was extremely successful, and at one point Thomas Coykendall was working with a progressive diesel manufacturing company to put a new, state-of-the-art diesel hydraulic propulsion plant into one of the boats. This work was never completed, however. Perhaps family rivalries interceded, or Thomas's drinking habits got in the way of his mechanical genius.

There was considerable adversity for Cornell and the Coykendalls at this time, with the bulk shipment of building materials by water in a sharp decline as the economic depression that would strike hard in the early thirties developed momentum. Progress, too, stymied the towing company, as Portland cement almost completely replaced Rosendale cement by now, and there was little call for Rosendale to be shipped. Portland was being manufactured locally, but even Cornell's work towing boatloads of this cement would diminish because the railroads developed technology to carry it more efficiently in covered hopper cars. Anthracite coal being moved downriver by towboat was a thing of the past, as railroads also took over there. Further, electric refrigeration abruptly shut down the once-lucrative ice industry, which had been another major client for Cornell. Hay was still being shipped from Canada to New York City, which might seem surprising, since horses, too, were disappearing. Perhaps in these years hay remained a regular commodity because illegal Canadian whiskey was often smuggled under the bales as a way of eluding 1920s' Prohibition laws that forbade the sale of alcohol.

Ominous plans were underway for the "Deeper Hudson" program, by which the federal government would dredge a deeper channel all the way upriver to Albany, thus opening the way for sea-going vessels to pass through. This would further reduce the need for tugboats, whether steamers or diesel, to tow the barges and lighters that previously had taken commodities between New York Harbor and the New York Barge Canal System—the name for the former Erie and Champlain canals.

Around this time, the company attempted to get a foothold in the canals, collaborating with shipping agents in Buffalo to generate business. This required a number of Cornell tugboats to be modified for operations in the canals, which had low bridges that would not permit Hudson River steam tugs with their high stacks and pilot houses to pass through. Pilot houses of several tugs were replaced with shorter ones, and stacks were cut down as well before the vessels were sent north to the canals. The pilot houses were

Many ice men have been made fighting mad by the old Ice King, the Norwich, going up and down the river during the past week. The ice men claim that her trips were uncalled for and were made for the purpose of breaking up their fields of ice. —*Kingston Daily Leader*, 14 March 1900

kept at Sleightsburgh, in case they might be of use on the tugs again. In several cases, they would be.

With the coming of the Great Depression, and in the face of stiff competition with towing companies that owned tugs built specifically for canal work, Cornell never did develop enough business to continue operating in the northern canals. The boats that had been cut down to work there were, for the most part, brought back to Rondout Creek, some to be refitted with their original tall smoke stacks and pilot houses.

For all the strength of railroads in general, the Ulster and Delaware was swiftly losing ground as the tourists stopped going to the Catskill resorts, causing the hotels to close up one after the other, and some burned down. The Coykendalls' Grand Hotel was through by the 1930s. Private automobiles and "auto trucks" were also coming into their own, taking business from both railroads and towing lines.

The U&D surplus fund was virtually gone for paying operating costs by 1928, the year the bonds came due, and in 1931 the railroad went into receivership. It ultimately would be sold to the New York Central, repaying the bondholders in part, but leaving Coykendall and Cornell family stockholders with shares that were worthless. Not only that, litigation began against those U&D stockholders in an attempt to force them to repay to the bondholders the entire $1.25 million that had been taken as a dividend. That litigation eventually would be settled in favor of the stockholders, but it would grind its way through the courts until 1937.

Edward Coykendall had suffered severe blows, losing his wife and his beloved railroad. Then, in August 1934, at the age of sixty-seven, Thomas Cornell Coykendall died in New York City after a short illness.

In 1932, the Cornell Steamboat Company's balance sheet showed a net worth of $2.48 million, with much of that value in its tugboats, many of which had grown old. The 1933 fleet of forty-five tugboats had at least twenty-four that were pre-1900, with three of them (*Earl, Eugenia,* and *Pratt*) from the 1860s or earlier. Ten or so were between 1900 and 1910, with the remaining nine having been built after 1910 or converted to diesel after that date. The boats in service were scrupulously maintained by the Cornell shops, which employed approximately 200 men in this time and could carry out any task required for the fleet. They kept engines humming, boilers in first-class shape, hulls, deckhouses, and pilot houses painted for each new season, and even fabricated hempen bow bumpers.

Yet, the coal-burning steamers had serious shortcomings compared to diesels, which were becoming steadily more powerful, while the coal burners seldom topped 1,000 horsepower. When they did generate that sort of horsepower, as with the "Big Cornell," it was difficult to find firemen willing to work on them, because the toil was so grueling. On the other hand, a working diesel tug refueled only once every ten days or so. In addition, too much turnaround time was involved in coaling up and watering steam tugs. A diesel could make a trip down and back between Rondout and New York without needing to take on fuel, but a steamer had to take on coal for the fires and water for the boiler after each leg of the trip.

In New York Harbor, for example, the last stage of the tow usually went like this: the big tug—also called a towing steamer or a line tug—and a helper brought the loaded scows to "The Market," the name for docks near West 38th Street. The tow was met by several smaller harbor tugs, which took off boats that had been consigned to customers in places around the harbor, such as Bayonne, Brooklyn, around to the East River, Staten Island, and Long Island. The Cornell towing steamer and the helper then landed the rest of the tow at The Market, and the cook of the line tug got onto the helper to be shuttled to the Cornell Steamboat Company offices at West 53rd, where he would go ashore and order groceries for the crew's return trip.

Meantime, the big tug and the helper went over to the coal pocket at Hoboken, New Jersey, and refueled. When that was done, they went to take on boiler water near The Market. This process consumed several hours. Tugs sometimes would be ordered to take on short-term towing work in the harbor that the company dispatcher had lined up for them.

At the same time, the main uptow was being made up and waiting at one of three company stakeboats, those floating docks anchored out in the middle of the harbor. The big tug and helper would arrive and hook up with the tow, usually "light"—empty—scows and barges to be brought back to their owners. In the old days, the uptow would have had a good proportion of loaded boats with pulp wood, molasses, scrap metal, and even boatloads of horse manure for the thriving mushroom business in the Hudson Valley—these last were called "fruit boats" by the boatmen. With the river being deepened, larger vessels were carrying most of these commodities all the way up to the Barge Canal and out to the Great Lakes and beyond, so there was not much need for tugboats to tow anything upriver any more.

That Cornell's fleet consisted of mainly steamers was a marked disadvantage in the face of dwindling business and increased competition from the likes of Moran Towing and Transportation Company. Moran had built its own solid reputation by now, especially in New York Harbor.

In the mid thirties, the major commodity by far was "trap rock," crushed stone of various dimensions and types that was used for large-scale construction, such as for foundations, roads, and airports. Colonial Sand and Stone was among the largest buyers of this material and it had one of the best docks in the Port of New York, where Cornell delivered scows regularly. These scows belonged to New York Trap Rock Corporation headquartered in Nyack, in Rockland County. Trap Rock by now was Cornell's most important customer. Like the oil companies, Trap Rock wanted faster service delivering stone and turning around their empty scows. If Cornell did not efficiently deliver empty scows to the Trap Rock stone-crushing operations—there were several along the mid-Hudson shoreline—then the company sometimes had to shut down its works while waiting for scows to get there. The delays

Three stalwart and powerful tugs—*E. L. Levy*, *E. C. Baker* and *J. C. Hartt*—are shown at the Rondout shops early in the twentieth century. *Hartt* was built for Cornell in 1883 and remained in the fleet until 1949, although she was inactive for many of her final years. *Levy* and *Baker* were purchased from C. W. Morse's Consolidated Towing Line in 1901 and sold in 1917. (Hudson River Maritime Museum Collection)

Edward Bishop, of Port Ewen, spent nearly his entire working life aboard the tug *Hercules*. He was a crew member of that vessel for fifty-three years—from 1878 to 1931—and chief engineer for forty-two! It is said that when *Hercules* entered the creek one day in 1931, Bishop went ashore in retirement and his tugboat never ran again. (Roger W. Mabie Collection)

caused by coaling and watering were annoying to Trap Rock and other Cornell customers, who complained about the drawbacks of steamers.

Further, with Edward Coykendall assuming more and more control of day-to-day operations, the innovative ideas of Frederick, the president, were not being adopted. Time and again Edward vetoed his brother's plans to dieselize boats or buy new ones or change the towing schedules or methods to accommodate customers such as Trap Rock or to win oil company business. As long as Cornell continued its policy of one big tow starting out at Rensselaer (across the river from Albany) in the evening and working its way leisurely downriver, getting larger and slower as it went, waiting for every customer to have his scow picked up, then those clients who needed more speed and frequency of tows would become all the more frustrated.

Yet Cornell was still the boss tower on the river, having the best boatmen and still able to win rate wars against upstart competitors. In cases where competition from another place came into the Hudson River, Cornell would send tugs to work in that company's home waters, such as it once did along the New Jersey coast, and charge extremely low rates until the competition agreed to withdraw from the Hudson.

Rivalry could appear in unexpected ways, as it did one foggy day around this time when the steamer *J. C. Hartt* was in charge of a big tow heading upriver from New York. *Hartt*'s tow was overtaken near Tarrytown by a New York City-based tugboat hauling an oil barge destined for the Barge Canal. The captain of this tug took advantage of the dense fog and hooked up to the last barge in *Hartt*'s tow—something small canal tugs were known to do from time to time.

The oil tug held on until Bear Mountain, when the fog cleared, and then the captain let go and headed on upriver past *Hartt*. He thought he had pulled a fast one on Cornell, but when he got back to his home office in New York he was called in and asked whether he had been holding on to a Cornell tow. Startled, the captain sputtered a vague answer, but when shown a $65 bill for towing, which Cornell had sent his company, he admitted everything, with this excuse: "I was caught in a fog . . . and you know those Cornell men know the river in a fog better than anybody. I knew I'd be safe hanging on and sailing along with them."

The steamer Norwich and the tug C. D. Mills have returned. During the past six weeks they have been up the river endeavoring to break up the ice gorge. —*Kingston Daily Leader*, **26 March 1900**

Relations were mostly good between Cornell employees and administration, for the company was reluctant to lay off men, even though there was no union representing the workers. Cornell was known for keeping wages low, however, with few raises. Early in the century deckhands and firemen earned only a bunk, food, and a dollar a day for a twelve-hour day, working seven days in a row. The boatmen in that time used to say, "Thirty days and thirty dollars."

At least the men usually could count on steady work, especially in the Rondout shops, where the company made a point of making work if there was not enough coming through by normal channels. Edward Coykendall bought a tug called the *Watchman* and had her laid up at dry dock across in Sleightsburgh. This boat was said to have been a rum runner during the Prohibition era, avoiding the maritime authorities while bringing in illegal alcohol from Canada. For years, the company shops spent time on this vessel, but for one reason or another she was never finished and did not go into service.

Of course, all was not perfect between employees and Cornell, and the boat crews were most liable to layoffs when there was no work to be had in winter. In years past, they had found ready work at the ice houses during the winter, but those days were long gone by the 1930s. The need for winter employment convinced the crew of *S. L. Crosby* to agree to work on Christmas Day, 1930, and for one of its deckhands, a young fellow named William O. Benson, it was his first time away from home during the holidays.

Benson was blue about it, as were the rest of the "down-in-the-face" crew. They had been told that if they took a tow of five brick scows, five cement boats, and two scrap iron scows to New York, they would be assured of being employed all winter. It was nostalgic for the men as they started out at 5:00 A.M. Christmas morning, which was bitterly cold, with the river iced up. By the time *Crosby* was rounding the lighthouse, they could hear church bells ringing and chimes sounding out Christmas carols. Benson was homesick as could be.

The journey south was bucking ice all the way to Storm King Mountain, and then there was heavy fog and rain the rest of the way. That night they arrived at New York Harbor, "put the tow away" at Hoboken, New Jersey, and went over to the company office on Pier 93, North River, at the foot of

West 53rd Street. There they were dismayed to learn they had been laid off after all—probably because of the heavy ice that was gripping the river.

During this time, there were no fringe benefits of any kind for the men, no unemployment insurance, not even overtime pay or extra pay for working holidays. This unexpected layoff was a sorely felt blow by *Crosby*'s crew and was one of the last straws that led to the move in 1935 to unionize.

Through the 1930s Edward Coykendall was increasingly asserting his authority as executor of S. D. Coykendall's estate, which gave him control of the voting stock in the company—meaning he had virtual control of the steamboat company if he wanted to take it.

He soon did.

While brother Frederick urged dieselizing steamers or replacing them with diesels, Edward flatly opposed it. Some thought he simply was a sentimentalist who favored steamers. Others thought that after his own failure with the U&D, he was not genuinely concerned with promoting the interests of the steamboat company, and that jealousy was behind his reining in Frederick. By the mid-thirties, Frederick was head of the Cornell Steamboat Company in name only, and, disgusted by interference from his brother, he spent less time at the office and more time with his first love: Columbia University.

In 1916, Columbia had appointed Frederick an alumni trustee, and in 1922 a life trustee. He had been active in alumni affairs ever since graduation in 1895, earning his Master's degree two years later, and he became invaluable as a member of the trustees' finance and education committees. Frederick's most enduring personal ambition lay with the Columbia University Press, which he helped found. He served on its board, and was a well-known bibliophile, a scholar and collector, with more than 6,000 volumes of poetry, early periodicals, and seventeenth and eighteenth century romance writers. Frederick's particular interest was in the English illustrator Arthur Rackham, about whom he compiled and published a bibliography.

In 1933, while Edward's once-promising U&D Railroad was languishing in receivership, Frederick had the glory of being named chairman of the board of the Columbia University trustees.

Because of Edward interfering, Frederick's administrative ability was not given free rein with the Cornell Steamboat Company after 1930, and for the rest of their lives the brothers shared a bitter mutual antipathy. The company suffered from it. For years, Clarence W. "Bill" Spangenberger, one of its rising new executives, found himself in the middle between the Coykendall brothers, and sometimes he felt he was directly in the line of fire.

Spangenberger joined the Cornell Steamboat Company in February of 1933 as a collector of past-due accounts. Not only was business suffering in the Great Depression—the Cornell fleet had abruptly gone from sixty tugs in service to twenty—but outstanding bills were seriously mounting. It was

> John Lynn, mate of the tug C. D. Mills, fell in the creek Sunday night while attempting to step from the dock on the boat. Fortunately he grabbed the stringpiece of the dock and was able to draw himself up. —*Kingston Daily Leader*, 21 August 1900

Spangenberger's task to approach clients delicately and induce them to pay while at the same time retaining them as Cornell customers.

A native of Rondout, Spangenberger had worked for the Ulster and Delaware Railroad during high school in the early twenties, serving as a ticket agent and car cleaner. In 1924, he was the summertime station agent at the U&D's station at the Laurel House Hotel in the Catskills, selling tickets and checking baggage. Later, he was ticket agent at the Kingston Point landing for the Hudson River Day Line, where the Kingston trolley line ended. Young Spangenberger also handled paperwork for the railroad, including bills of lading, and he had the job of checking the number of coal cars that were dumping their loads into the barges.

Twice a day, once for the down boat to New York at 1:00 P.M. and again at 2:25 P.M. for the up boat to Albany, he sold tickets at the dock. Then he had to balance the ledger and receipts and by 4:00 P.M. was walking with a black bag full of cash toward the Cornell offices at 22 Ferry Street. There were times when Spangenberger carried as much as $3,000 in that bag, and he was uneasy about it because he was sure everyone knew what he had. It was harrowing, although he was never accosted. Later, the company sent a small motorboat to pick him up at the end of the day and take him safely to the Ferry Street wharf.

Spangenberger's father, Lawrence, was on the company payroll as the barber who regularly shaved Edward Coykendall. Lawrence got his school-age son his first job with the Cornell Company, which was to work in the gardens at the Coykendall's Greenkill Park, a cottage and clubhouse resort west of Kingston. In 1927, Spangenberger earned a degree in business management at New York University, afterwards taking a sales job with the Standard Oil Company. The Great Depression caused him to lose his position there, but Edward Coykendall offered him the collector's job, and he took it, knowing it would be difficult.

From the start, Spangenberger was considered by the office staff at Cornell headquarters in New York as a spy for Edward in Kingston. Whenever he came to the office, employees hid their work from him so he could not see what they were doing. Frederick, too, was not forthcoming at first. As Spangenberger proved successful in collecting bills due, and it was apparent that he was no spy for Edward, his relationship with Frederick became a good one. He began to be the trusted go-between for the brothers, and every Saturday morning went up to Kingston from New York and conveyed messages from Frederick. Invariably, whatever Spangenberger said caused Edward to become angry, and the messenger was the one who bore the verbal brunt of the wrath. When Spangenberger had taken enough, he confronted Edward, asserting that all he was doing was relaying a message, and he would accept no more abuse for it. From that moment on, although he continued as the go-between, Spangenberger was never personally stung by the hostility between the brothers.

As collector, Spangenberger experienced first hand the complaints of clients who wanted better service and special express tows when needed, and he heard their disgruntlement with tugs being late because they were wasting

Edward Coykendall, the third eldest of S. D.'s sons, was head of the family's railroad interests and executor of the Cornell estate. (J. Matthews Collection)

time coaling and watering. Customers wanted more flexibility from Cornell, and they were particularly frustrated by the company's hide-bound daily schedule of one big tow down and one up. Spangenberger even noticed how the Hutton Brick Company near Kingston was favored over other clients because Edward's late wife had been a Hutton. It often happened that Hutton Brick scows were not ready when the Cornell tow came by, but the tow would wait, sometimes losing part of the ebb tide, and therefore being delayed getting downriver. This was not done for other customers.

After a couple of years as collector, Spangenberger's duties were essentially completed, and he was given responsibility over the company's engineers, acting as liaison between them and the president and seeing to it that their jobs were done right and that they were given support to carry them out. This troubleshooting was Spangenberger's first management position, and he soon was confronted with a successful move by the employees to unionize. In 1935, the employees joined Local 333 of the International Longshoremen's Union, and Spangenberger became the company's liaison with the union agents. Now there would be an eight-hour day instead of twelve, with three crews assigned to a tug instead of two, as it had been previously. Each crew would work two weeks on duty and have one week off.

The company also named Spangenberger assistant to the president during this year, giving him much responsibility for being the eyes and ears of Frederick, but with no authority other than what accrued to his continuing supervision of the engineers.

In the doldrums of the ongoing Great Depression, Cornell's fortunes took another downturn as the Hudson River channel was dredged to allow deeper-draft ocean-going ships to sail all the way to Albany and unload their Cuban sugar, Florida phosphate rock, sulfur from Texas, wood pulp and pulp wood from Scandinavia—all commodities that once had to be transferred to barges and lighters that were towed by Cornell.

Further, those ships could load grain at Albany and sail back downriver, again taking over shipments that once had given Cornell a steady stream of work. The Port of Albany thrived as a result, but Rondout Creek was suffering.

S. D. Coykendall's Bête Noir

No history of maritime activities on the northeastern coast of the United States during the first decade of the twentieth century can avoid mentioning Charles Wyman Morse. This native of Bath, Maine, has been variously described as a cunning and egocentric scoundrel, a megalomaniac, and—to the many victims of his methods—the ultimate in snake-oil salesmen.

In his obituary in the *New York Times* in 1933, Morse was described as having "appeared in the financial sky like a meteor, often leaving a searing path, and dropped into apparent oblivion behind the walls of the Federal Penitentiary at Atlanta in 1908." The "searing path" that led to Atlanta touched banking, Hudson River steamboat lines, the ice industry, coastwise passenger and freight steamships, shipbuilding, and towing.

Born in 1856, Morse entered his family's ice and towing business after graduating from Bowdoin College in 1877. In his undergraduate days, it was rumored that he had amassed a fortune of a half-million dollars dealing in ice. By the 1890s, he had targeted banking and in a short time gained control of thirteen of these institutions. From there, it was an easy task to engineer the takeover of Maine Coast steamboat lines to form the Eastern Steamship Company. Later, his attention turned to the coastwise steamship lines and, by 1906, he had added the Clyde, Mallory, Ward Line, and New York and Porto Rico house flags to those of Eastern and his newly incorporated Metropolitan Steamship Company under the title, Consolidated Steamship Lines.

Meanwhile, he had returned to his roots in the ice business by turning his attention to the Hudson River after having gained control of a number of New York ice companies. These—including the American Ice, Knickerbocker Ice, and other smaller companies—were amalgamated to form Morse's Consolidated Ice Company.

Moving the ice to market from upriver ice houses was a critical part of the business, and when C. W. Morse first began his affair with Hudson River ice in the 1890s, he chose not to use Cornell's services. Instead, he bought a competitor of Cornell, the Ronan Towing Line, and entered into an operating agreement with another competitor, Lake Champlain Towing Company.

Ronan and Lake Champlain had built up successful businesses, concentrating on the traffic from the Erie and Champlain Canals. Ronan's founder, Patrick Ronan, had died suddenly in 1886, after having built a substantial fleet of tugs, the crown jewels of which were two large and powerful tugs—*Osceola* and *Pocahontas*—built in 1884 by Ward, Stanton and Company of Newburgh. The fleet also included *Ellen M. Ronan*, *G. C. Adams*, *Saranac*, *Victoria*, and *Mabel*. Ronan's estate continued the business until Morse appeared and made his offer in 1897. The offer was quickly accepted and the Consolidated Towing Line made its appearance on the river.

The "Consolidated" aspect of the business stemmed from the inclusion of the Lake Champlain Towing Company's two modern iron-hulled tugs, *E. C. Baker* and *E. L. Levy*, which had been built by the noted Philadelphia firm of Neafie and Levy in 1888 and 1889 respectively. Unlike the Ronan tugs, *Levy* and *Baker* were not purchased by Morse.

Consolidated competed with Cornell for about four seasons until its tugboats—and Lake Champlain's two vessels—were purchased by the Rondout company in 1901. S. D. Coykendall was determined to rid the river of Morse and Consolidated, and his attractive buy-out offer was exactly what Morse wanted. The Kingston *Daily Leader* for May 9, 1901 reported, "The largest tow of the season to pass this city went up the river Monday morning. It consisted of 69 canal boats and barges, and was in tow of the steamers Pocahontas, Adams, Ronan and Levy."

It was certainly an impressive tow—and it was a Consolidated one. A short time later, all four of those tugs would sport Cornell's colors.

After 1901, Morse still remained in the ice business, but was left without tugboats. He then began to bring his Knickerbocker Steam Towage Company tugs to the river from Bangor and Bath. It was then that four large, powerful tugs—*Ice King, Knickerbocker, C. W. Morse,* and *Triton*—appeared on the river. Two years later, in 1903, the wily Morse and the equally wily Coykendall were at it again, and the latter acquired these four boats from his arch-nemesis. All were "outside tugs," but *C. W. Morse* proved to be much too large and unhandy for river towing. Cornell disposed of her to McAllister Brothers in 1912.

The handsome tug *Ice King*, built in 1877 at Philadelphia, was purchased by Cornell from Charles W. Morse's Knickerbocker Steam Towage Company in 1903. Her career in the Cornell fleet lasted only ten years, for on December 26, 1913, she stranded on the New Jersey shore a mile and a half below Sandy Hook while on an offshore towing assignment. (William duBarry Thomas Collection)

The melancholy finale of this tug's career began on July 17, 1916, when she was sold by McAllister to Sugar Products Shipping Co., Inc., of New York. On that same day, *C. W. Morse* cleared New York for an African port via San Juan and was never heard from again. She was twenty-seven years old, had a wooden hull, and was presumed to have foundered.

After the 1903 sale, Morse continued his headlong monopolistic quest, gradually rebuilding the tugboat fleet on the Hudson River. Eventually, this new tug fleet, all from Knickerbocker's Down East fleet, consisted of *Delta, Perry, Bismarck, Britannia, Charlie Lawrence, E. D. Haley, Imperial, Princess, Ralph Ross, Wm. H. Baldwin*, and *Woodbridge*. These vessels were brought to the river between 1903 and 1910. It is of interest that *Charlie Lawrence*, nearly forty years old when she came to the Hudson, would outlast them all. This vessel ran until 1955, when, as the dieselized eighty-one year old *Cornell*, she sank in the Tappan Zee off Tarrytown.

S. D. Coykendall went on Morse's trail again, the "Ice King's" fleet having by this time become once again a thorn in his side. Unfortunately, Coykendall did not win this last battle, for he passed away in January 1913. Later that year, his son and successor, Frederick, was able to extinguish the Morse flame once again, purchasing the above nine vessels and marking the end of the Morse-Cornell towing wars. By this time, Morse was rebuilding his life after having been released from a federal penitentiary. He had served two years of his original fifteen-year sentence before being pardoned by President Taft in 1910.

Some of the boats acquired in 1913 were useful to Cornell's business. Others were not, and a few were sold when market conditions were right. If anything, Cornell may not have needed those nine additional vessels in its fleet. Peter Cahill bought *Imperial* and *Princess* in 1916, after having taken *Bismarck* from the 1903 group two years earlier. When S. D. Coykendall sold tugs, he was careful to dispose of them in such a way that future competition would not be an issue.

Morse's business philosophy was reflected in his corporate titles—Consolidated Steamship Lines, Consolidated Ice Company, Consolidated Towing Line. In 1897, *The Nautical Gazette* had stated that the Consolidated Ice Company "absorbed all the big ice companies of New York City, including the old Knickerbocker Ice Company." And so it went throughout Morse's career—buy and merge, buy and consolidate.

In retrospect, it might be said that the methods of Morse and Coykendall were quite similar. Neither man suffered competition to persist, but their views of the world were entirely different. Samuel D. Coykendall wished to dominate Hudson River towing, and in this he was successful. Charles W. Morse, his bête noire for nearly two decades, had a decidedly different—and much larger—vision of what he considered his domain. Despite his voracious appetite for companies and his impressive consolidation in water transportation, in the end Morse found that the world was indeed bigger than he had bargained for.

William duBarry Thomas

Chapter Twelve
From Coal to Diesel

DURING the heady, thriving days after World War I, the Cornell Company acquired the hull of what would become its fleet's most powerful tugboat. Ordered by the wartime federal government, *Perseverance* had been under construction at Somerset, Massachusetts, near Fall River, but since there was no more need for her, the hull was sold to Cornell.

Towed to the Creek in September 1920, the "Percy," as she later would be nicknamed, had her joiner work completed and was outfitted with a coal-burning propulsion plant that would generate as much as a thousand horsepower. *Perseverance* would be renowned for her towing ability, and soon after going into service would tow, on her own, an astonishing 110 loaded grain barges from Albany to New York City.

Another large steamer built at the very end of World War I was *Stirling Tomkins*. First known as *Artisan,* she was acquired by Cornell early in 1930 and given her new name, which honored one of the leading figures in the family that originally founded New York Trap Rock Company. Year after year, New York Trap Rock's business with Cornell increased steadily, as the quarrying company grew and the other commodities available for shipment by water diminished. Along with *Geo. W. Washburn, Stirling Tomkins*, and *Perseverance* were the stalwarts of the Cornell Line by the 1930s. Named after a leading Glasco brickyard owner, *Washburn* was the fastest of the company's tugs, and her sleek hull lines made her look every bit as speedy as she was. Some said she was maintained by Cornell like a yacht.

According to river lore, *Washburn* was steaming upstream without a tow one day in 1926, and just ahead was the steamer *Homer Ramsdell* of the Central Hudson Line. *Washburn*'s captain, James Dee, and chief engineer, John Osterhoudt, began to give chase to *Ramsdell*, whose own captain and chief engineer, well known to the Cornell men, saw her coming. *Ramsdell* was a fast boat, and she poured on the steam, as did the pursuing *Washburn*. One of the most memorable, and last, steam-powered races of the twentieth century on the Hudson River was underway.

It was a glorious sight to Hudson River steamboat men to see two old-timers like *Washburn* and *Ramsdell* racing at full throttle. *Washburn*, which had been completely rebuilt in 1921, stayed at *Ramsdell*'s stern for ten miles, past Stony Point, Iona Island, and Anthony's Nose in the Hudson Highlands. In years gone by it was a common sight to see passenger steamboats racing to be

The tug *Lion* and her helper, *Cornell No. 41*, lying alongside a New York pier in the 1940s. They had recently arrived with a southbound tow and were enjoying a well-earned rest before preparing to assemble a northbound tow at the stakeboat. The diesel-propelled *Lion* and her sister *Jumbo* were used as line-haul tugs almost continuously from around 1925 to the mid-1950s. They were powered by 600-horsepower Nelseco diesel engines. (Gerard Mastropaolo Collection, Courtesy of Hudson River Maritime Museum)

G. C. Adams and *Osceola* are passing the mouth of Esopus Creek at Saugerties with a northbound tow in this classic scene captured in 1930 or shortly before. The active lives of these two venerable tugs would soon be over. *Osceola*, the younger, dating from 1884, was around forty-five years old; she was scuttled at Port Ewen late in 1930. *Adams*, built in 1878, was dismantled in 1937 and her hull joined that of *Osceola*—and others—in the Port Ewen graveyard. (Photograph by R. Loren Graham. Roger W. Mabie and William duBarry Thomas Collections)

the first to get to a landing to pick up the people and collect their fares, or just to win bragging rights about being the fastest on the river. Such races were the cause of too many accidents and were illegal by now. But a race between a tugboat and a steamboat was more or less a friendly rivalry, and there would be no side-swiping or risk of over-heating boilers. This race ended when *Ramsdell* had to slow and turn off for her landing at Highland Falls. *Washburn* raced past, steam still up, both her crew and *Ramsdell*'s well aware of her remarkable performance.

Cornell's coal-fired steamers were state-of-the-art, but they were still not as efficient as diesel tugs, two of which—*Jumbo* and *Lion*—were acquired by Cornell after World War I in the company's initial pioneering forays into oil-engined vessels.

Despite the early promise of the post-war years, Cornell financial reports from 1923-32 tell a cold, hard story of steady and inexorable business decline. The Great Depression was a major factor in the decline over the latter portion of this period, but the loss of so much towing work on the river was taking place no matter what the business climate.

In 1923, Cornell's gross earnings were approximately $2.13 million, with an operating expense of $1.8 million, and net income after miscellaneous additions and deductions was almost $181,000. That ratio remained fairly constant for the next three years, with gross earnings varying as much as $200,000 more or less than the 1923 figure. Then in 1927, with gross earnings at $1.9 million, the net income plummeted to approximately $64,500, which was about two-fifths of the 1926 net income. In 1929, the company operated in the red, with a shortfall of more than $92,000. For at least the next three years (figures for the following fifteen years are not available), Cornell still operated in the red, with the net income for 1932 being approximately a negative $196,000, against gross earnings of approximately $818,000.

In these years, the Coykendall family members were receiving regular stipends from their grandfather's trust, at times with quarterly payments in the neighborhood of $4,000 for each of the surviving Coykendall sons and sister Catherine. In addition to this, in 1933 the Cornell Steamboat Company was paying a monthly salary of $1,750 to Frederick, the president, and $1,250 each to vice president Thomas, director Edward, and treasurer Frank. Except for the salary to Thomas, who passed away in 1934, these salary payments remained the same into the 1940s even though the company's revenues were falling.

Frank Coykendall was minimally active in the day-to-day affairs of the steamboat company. He had been president of the failed Hudson River Blue Stone Company, treasurer of both the Ulster and Delaware Railroad and the Kingston Ferry Company. Like the rest of his siblings, Frank was a trustee of his father's estate, for which Edward was executor. Frank was active in the Kingston community, serving as president of the Kingston City Library and being involved in the local Red Cross chapter. He was a golf enthusiast,

This striking portrait of the diesel tug *Cornell*, built in 1874 as *Charlie Lawrence*, offers proof positive of her negligible freeboard, an attribute which caused the sobriquet "The Submarine" to be bestowed upon her. *Cornell* had just been launched from the marine railway at the Island Dock and was being moved to the Cornell shops under tow when this photograph was taken on September 21, 1954. (Photograph by William duBarry Thomas)

which absorbed much of his time, and was also president of the Twaalfskill Country Club.

In 1938, Edward Coykendall became a trustee at the State University Teacher's College at New Paltz, just south of Kingston, a position he held for the rest of his days. Like his father at Vassar and to a much lesser degree Frederick at Columbia, he was active and valuable as a college trustee. In time, a science building would be named in his honor. Even after the death of his wife, Edward maintained the handsome mansion with its beautiful gardens on West Chestnut Street. He was active in community affairs, including being a charter member of the Ulster County Historical Society, serving as president of the Board of Managers of the Kingston Hospital and as a trustee at the Kingston museum, the Senate House. An art collector whose home has been likened to a fine gallery, Edward brought a number of important works to the Senate House, including several by local painter John Vanderlyn, one of the best-known American artists during the early and middle nineteenth century.

Edward Coykendall was the most prominent socialite in Kingston and had much influence regarding who was accepted at the Twaalfskill Country Club. Well regarded in the community, kind-hearted to children, some of whom would remember his small acts of generosity all their lives, Edward carried on the Cornell and Coykendall tradition of being a pillar in the Kingston-Rondout and Ulster County communities. There were those who believed he really had the best interests of the Cornell Steamboat Company at heart in the decisions he made, misguided though they came to appear.

Whatever Edward had in mind as he superseded Frederick in the company's hierarchy, the result was the same: because Cornell did not switch fast enough to diesel, the company lost its place as the dominant tower on the river as oil barges increased in number and most of the traditional bulk commodities virtually vanished from the Hudson by 1940.

Of course, all was not worry, conflict, and travail between brothers Frederick and Edward Coykendall. Their shared college loyalty brought out high spirits whenever the Columbia rowing crew was matched against other colleges on the river at Poughkeepsie.

For these annual intercollegiate regattas, the Coykendalls arranged to have one of the company tugs get the Columbia shells at the university boathouse on the Harlem River and transport them upriver to a boathouse north of Highland, just below Krum Elbow. Cornell tugs also were available to pick up Coykendall friends and take them to see the races, and the company maintained an old D&H Canal boat, which was painted each season, then towed by the well-known Rondout Creek tug *Rob* out to the finish line and anchored to serve as the "finish boat." On this barge was a signboard, and when a race was over, the results were posted on it for all to see.

The river would usually be crammed with boats of all sizes to watch the colorful regattas, especially before the Great Depression, when Day Line and Central Hudson Line steamboats were on hand along with yachts and small motor boats, and even navy destroyers with midshipmen aboard came up from the Naval Academy. Regattas attracted large crowds along both shores of the Hudson, and many other spectators watched from a special passenger train that ran slowly along the West Shore tracks, staying with the shells as they raced.

Among the most privileged spectators, however, and perhaps the ones who had the best view, were not the guests of the Coykendalls, but the friends and family of officers and crew on *Rob*. Captain John Lynn was from Port Ewen, and a number of his guests came from that town, including Roger Mabie, grandson of retired steamboat pilot and Cornell captain, William Mabie. Then a young boy, Roger was allowed to stand high up on the pilot house of *Rob* beside the gilded eagle most Cornell boats carried, and from there could watch the races. The boy was inspired enough to go on to become a member of the Syracuse University crew.

At the end of the races, while virtually all the sightseeing boats went downriver in a mob toward New York, *Rob* made its way back to Rondout Creek towing the finish boat, which was put away for another season.

One of the chores that faced steamer crews at this time was coaling up. Cornell's boats went to Rondout's East Strand coal pocket, a large waterfront building with hundreds of tons of coal stored in bins. Railroad cars came by

The freshly painted *Perseverance* at the Cornell shops shortly after she was completed in 1921. The steamboats *Homer Ramsdell* and *Newburgh* may be seen at the extreme left, and the tug *John H. Cordts* lies immediately upstream of *Perseverance*. (Collection of The Mariner's Museum, courtesy of Roger W. Mabie)

and dumped coal into the pockets, and in turn the coal was chuted down into the tugboats. Watching tugs being coaled was a favorite pastime for children who lived along Rondout Creek, but in 1935 they got more excitement than they had bargained for.

The tugboat *Empire* was following the usual routine of taking on coal at her starboard side and was gradually heeling over as the crew carefully watched to see when she was full on that side. It actually looked as if *Empire* might turn right over and sink, and that was part of the thrill for kids, but the experienced crew and pocket workers knew how much a tugboat could take—under normal circumstances. Then the tug was to leave the dock and turn around, still heeling precariously over, to fill with coal at her port side. This soon would balance the weight and right her again. This day, however, circumstances were not normal: no one realized *Empire* was being held up by unseen underwater pylons, so she was loading far more coal than she should have on that side.

When the crew began to turn her, she lay further over, suddenly taking on water that poured through her deck scuttles, and she sank. *Empire* was soon raised and put back in service, but this type of freak accident was another example of the hazards of boating and of the drawbacks of steamers.

Another hazard was fire, and many a tugboat was damaged or destroyed this way. So, too, were coal pockets, with their tons of fuel that created fiercely hot blazes difficult to fight. Sometimes, pocket and tugboat burned together, as was the case with *John H. Cordts* in 1907, when the coal pocket it was moored beside caught fire. The pocket was a total loss, but quick action by

J. C. Hartt and her helper tug, *Cornell No. 41*, bound upriver in the lower Hudson in the late 1930s. Cornell's helper tugs routinely worked alongside the line-haul tug when not dropping off or picking up barges during their trips up and down the river. (Photograph by Roger W. Mabie)

the Kingston firemen saved the *Cordts*, which was badly damaged but could be repaired and was restored to service for another twenty years. The same happened to the *Geo. W. Washburn* in the 1920s, and this time the firemen saved both boat and pocket. Again, in 1936, a coal-pocket fire called out firemen from two districts, but the pocket was destroyed.

After this fire, with Cornell turning more and more toward diesel tugs, there would be no more company coal pockets built on Rondout Creek.

In 1936, another major freshet struck the Creek, causing even more damage than the memorable flood of spring, 1893. At 7:30 A.M. on March 12, the ice dam below Eddyville surged downstream, dragging away a small passenger steamboat, a derrick boat, and several barges and lighters from Hiltebrant's shipyard at Connelly. Next, the flood and grinding ice swept off two scows tied up at Island Dock, driving this unmanned fleet before it and through an eerie fog that rang out with the snap of lines and the cracking of ship timbers and docks.

A drifting barge struck the tug *Rob*, tied up near the Rhinecliff ferry slip on Ferry Street, and heeled her over until she capsized and sank. Eleven Cornell tugboats tied up across the Creek at Sleightsburgh broke free and were set adrift. Eleven more moored at the Cornell shops were forced downstream, one other somehow remaining secured. At least thirty tugs and barges were moving downstream, vanishing into the murky fog. Farther down the Creek, nine more Cornell tugs and a steam derrick by the Sunflower Dock at Sleightsburgh were buffeted as the swirling ice rushed past. The outermost tug, *Coe F. Young*, was holed and sank, serving as a barrier for the other tugs, which stayed put. Two days later, one of these, *Wm. E. Cleary*, unexpectedly rolled over and sank.

Once again, as in 1893, *J. C. Hartt* was there to rescue the fleet. She, herself, had been saved by the alert captain of a brick scow that she had bumped, for he had leaped aboard her and tossed a line to men on shore to make her

The tug *G. C. Adams*, forlornly high and dry after running aground on Red Hook Island in October 1930. In predicaments such as this, the preferred solution was to let nature assist. *Adams* floated off on a later high tide. (Roger W. Mabie Collection)

fast. Then a crew came aboard, got up steam, and went after the rest of the boats one by one. All the drifting vessels were rescued, and *Rob* and *Cleary* were raised before too long, but the old *Coe F. Young* was done for. She was left on the bottom of the Creek, just off the Sunflower Dock, which used to be the winter home of *Mary Powell*.

As late as 1958, coal barges were still being built in Rondout Creek to supply coal-burning electric-generating plants.

Much of the coal that was being carried by boat and tug these days was for contractors who were supplying major power plants with their main fuel. For a time in the mid-1950s Island Dock was kept busy building coal boats for such clients as Jersey Central Power and Light, which was purchasing and transporting its own coal to its power plants.

In 1939, World War II began in Europe, and the United States benefited from the military buildup of the Allies. With the Cornell fleet having dropped to only twenty in operation during the Great Depression, many tugs had been laid up or scrapped. *Rob* now was laid up at Sleightsburgh. There was an anticipated need for tug boats in the near future, however, and *Rob* was sold. Another Cornell tug, the *W. N. Bavier*, had a hull so rusted that she sank at her dock in 1942.

By the time the United States entered the war at the end of 1941, the towing business had picked up, and Cornell saw an increased volume of trap rock, in particular, for there was a leap in construction of airfields and navy yards in the New York City region. That business soon dried up, however, as the American war effort turned to guns, oil, and steel, and some domestic industries such as construction slowed almost to a halt. The oil shortage and gasoline rationing of the war years combined with the effects of the Mid-Hudson Bridge that had opened at Poughkeepsie in 1930, to cause the closing down of the Kingston-Rhinecliff ferry after its last trip on December 15, 1942.

That year, the ferryboat *Kingston* carried almost 29,000 private automobiles, while just the year before it had carried more than 59,000.

Interviewed at that time by a Poughkeepsie newspaper, Edward Coykendall reportedly said of the ferry, "I don't see any future," and slowly shook his head as he added, "The ferry hasn't paid for eight or nine years. . . No, I don't see a future."

Transport, one of the long-running ferryboats, was already out of service, having been laid up from late 1938 until mid-1941, when she was dismantled at the Cornell shops and towed to New York Harbor to serve as a stake boat. She remained there until late in the 1950s. *Kingston* was sold to the government late in 1943 and was sailed down the Atlantic Coast to the Gulf of Mexico and Texas. The following year, the Coykendalls dissolved the Rhinebeck and Kingston Ferry Company, Inc., and the responsibility of running the ferry service devolved upon New York State. Service was restored in 1946, with the state paying Cornell $40,000 for the deeds to the ferry landings. The service closed in January 1957, when the river froze over. This was a month before the Kingston-Rhinecliff Bridge opened.

When the time came early in the war that the federal government was looking to buy tugboats of any kind, C. W. Spangenberger brought the news to Frederick that several of the big coal-burning steamers could be sold for a good price. Frederick, in New York, agreed wholeheartedly, but when Spangenberger laid the proposal before Edward in Kingston, the latter vetoed any sale.

It was never made clear precisely why Edward refused—perhaps he had hopes of an economic resurgence that would employ his boats—but the Cornell tugs would not be sold. Since there was no work for them, most were laid up, including the three magnificent old steamers *Perseverance*, *Stirling Tomkins*, and *Geo. W. Washburn*

Rarely has the elegance and grace of a handsome tug been captured as in this classic view of *Geo. W. Washburn* by an unknown photographer, probably in the 1920s. *Washburn*, built by T. S. Marvel at Newburgh in 1890, was the first modern, iron-hulled tug in the Cornell fleet. Powerful, commanding and fleet, she could evoke only admiration from those who knew her. (T. I. Brooks Collection, courtesy of William duBarry Thomas)

At the end of 1943, Cornell had twenty-six boats, but twelve were inactive and laid up. The active boats included the six diesels: *Cornell, Cornell No. 20, Cornell No. 21, Cornell No. 41, Jumbo,* and *Lion*. Among the inactive boats were such former stalwarts as *J. C. Hartt*, built in 1883, but which had not run since 1937, and *S. L. Crosby*, built the same year, but which had not run since 1935. Their splendid careers were now over.

Although no longer working on the Hudson, one of the best-known company tugs was still in service during the war. Roger Mabie of Port Ewen, now a naval sub-chaser commander, was visiting a shipyard in New Orleans when he was surprised to see the "Big" Cornell in an adjacent dry dock. Now she was Standard Oil's
, long ago converted to oil as fuel, but still familiar to Mabie, whose childhood had been spent watching tugboats come and go in the Creek. On her forward plating she had scallops—known as the "hungry horse effect" because one can "see the ribs"—from that battle with the Hudson River ice in 1910, when she had opened the channel to free the floodwaters at Albany and Troy.

Mabie went aboard and saw her brass capstan caps still inscribed with *Cornell*, and in the engine room her vacuum gauge faces were etched with "Cornell Steamboat Company, Rondout, N.Y."

In 1945, C. W. Spangenberger was named general manager of the company, working under both Edward and Frederick, although Frederick was even less in the New York office and ever more busy with Columbia University. He was not only chairman of the Columbia University Trustees, but in another year would be named president of Columbia University Press. Back in 1941, Frederick had been the guest of honor of the trustees and the university press at a banquet commemorating his twenty-five years of service. Previously, he had received other awards of achievement, and Hamilton College in upstate New York had given him an honorary doctorate. In 1946, Frederick took a cut in pay, from $1,750 a month to $1,250 to help the company's balance sheet a bit.

The new position C. W. Spangenberger assumed in 1945 finally gave him authority within the hierarchy of the company, and he took more and more of the day-to-day responsibilities for running Cornell. It was a struggle, for financial shortfalls occurred almost every year, and business did not pick up again until 1947. At this time, government-built diesel tugs were available at a very low price, and Spangenberger went to the Coykendalls to urge them to replace their outmoded steamers with these diesels. Other operators, such as Moran Towing Company, were acquiring numbers of these government tugs and becoming extremely successful with them. Cornell had to do the same if it wanted to be competitive. Fred agreed. Edward did not. Spangenberger was overruled. The company would not acquire more diesel tugs. Steamers were good enough, as far as Edward was concerned.

Spangenberger continued to try to persuade Edward that diesels meant not only quicker turnaround time and more efficient towing, but fewer men in the rotating crews—two captains, two engineers, one oiler, two deckhands, and a cook, along with the four other men who rotated in for their own shifts. In time, with business steadily sinking and the steamers losing their worth as collateral for the operating loans always needed at the start of each towing season, it appeared Edward was beginning reluctantly to agree.

Yet, in those first years after World War II, no decisive action was taken to modernize the fleet.

In January 1948, C. W. Spangenberger wrote a report outlining his concept of Cornell's operating needs for the following year. It was a plan to increase the number and frequency of the company's tows and to add tugs to the three main service areas—the Hudson's "upper end," between Clinton Point and Troy, the "lower end," which was down to New York Harbor, and the harbor itself.

As a key step, Spangenberger recommended acquiring a large diesel tug, increasing the number of tows to meet the needs of the rejuvenated brickyards, and going after more business in the "shifting" of boats from place to place in busy New York harbor. He was particularly concerned about the persistent question he was hearing repeated by customers: What is Cornell doing about acquiring new or improved equipment? He wrote in the report, "There is a feeling of doubt among our customers as to whether we plan to continue in the towboat business. This feeling I speak of is not imagination on my part,

Cornell tugs frequently served during the Intercollegiate Rowing Association's races at Poughkeepsie, an event widely known as the Poughkeepsie regatta. Here the Columbia University shell is being loaded aboard diesel tug *Cornell*. The time: The late 1940s. The place: The Columbia University boathouse on the Harlem River. (Roger W. Mabie Collection)

as it has been expressed to me personally several times by many of our customers."

New York Trap Rock, now Cornell's single most important customer, was especially up in arms over the delays in getting empty scows back to their quarries in time to reload them. Too often, Trap Rock was forced to stop operations at a plant and send men home because their boats were all loaded, but there was no Cornell tug there to pick them up. Sometimes a tug arrived four or five hours late, or a passing Cornell tow was going too slowly for the needs of Trap Rock, and then Spangenberger was the one who caught the brunt of the complaints.

The 1948 report showed the potential savings from the reduced number of personnel required on diesel tugs, and also from the diesels being more flexible in operation and having quicker turnaround. Furthermore, it was difficult to find quality crewmen for steam tugs, he wrote: "This is especially true of any type of labor you get for firemen. They will walk off the job any time, which means the boat would be out of service, as the attitude of crews today is not what it used to be."

Spangenberger personally knew the difficulties of finding firemen for the steam tugs, because he was often telephoned in the middle of the night at his home in New York City and told there was a lack of men, and a boat could not go out. Then he would have to make his way through local waterfront bars, asking for tugboat firemen who wanted to come to work. For the most part, the firemen he found were Spaniards or Portuguese, who were eager to work, while Americans were unwilling to do such difficult labor.

After reading the report, Frederick Coykendall enthusiastically agreed with Spangenberger about the company's needs, while Edward praised the quality and foresight of the plan and said, "But we're not going to do it."

That seemed to be the end of yet another enterprising effort at saving the company, but later in 1948, Edward one day called in Spangenberger and unexpectedly asked where they could get a big diesel tug. He had changed his attitude at last. Inspired with hope for the company's turnaround, Spangenberger chartered *Harry Card*, a 1,250-horsepower diesel built in New York in 1944. *Harry Card* belonged to McAllister Brothers Towing and would be the largest tugboat operating on the river, able to do the work of several big steamers.

That November, Edward suffered a stroke and went into a coma and did not come out of it. In contrast, a month previous his brother Frederick had joyfully officiated at the installation of the new Columbia University president, war hero General Dwight D. Eisenhower. Before 20,000 applauding spectators, Frederick handed the university's historic charters and keys as symbols of authority to General Eisenhower, who in a few years would become the thirty-fourth president of the United States.

Edward Coykendall died on February 7, 1949, at the age of seventy-eight—just weeks before the diesel, *Harry Card*, officially came into the Cornell fleet.

Storming the Barge Canal

In the late 1920s and early 1930s, the Cornell Steamboat Company wished to extend its domain beyond the waters of the Hudson River and New York Harbor. Such opportunities were limited, but the traffic through the New York State Barge Canal system from Waterford west beckoned. Although the beginning of a drop in the company's river-generated business was to be seen with the onset of the Great Depression, there was still sufficient traffic through the state's waterway to and from the West. It made an attractive prospect. The black and yellow stacks of Cornell tugs might just become a common sight as far west as Buffalo, and the traffic they brought through the guard lock at Waterford would ensure that the southbound tows from Albany always contained canal boats loaded with grain for New York's hungry elevators.

The Barge Canal required small tugs. At that time, the Cornell fleet included enough small tugs to equip a fleet sufficient to move a tow eastward through the canal every second or third day. That they were steam tugs did not really seem to matter. They would be able to draw boiler feed water from the canal itself, and coal was readily available almost anywhere throughout the length of the route to Buffalo.

Cornell therefore determined that, with appropriate modifications, they might be able to place eight or more vessels in the proposed canal service. The minimum clearance under bridges along the canal route was fifteen feet, but the tugs proposed for the service—vessels like *G. W. Decker, J. G. Rose, Wilson P. Foss, R. J. Foster, Primrose, Saranac, John D. Schoonmaker,* and *Geo. N. Southwick*—were all much too high to be suitable. Not only were their masts and stacks well over the fifteen-foot mark, but, more important, their pilot houses were all located on the upper deck.

Masts and stacks could be, and were, cut down to the appropriate height, which was established with prudent conservatism as fourteen feet six inches. In the case of the pilot houses, the ingenuity of the artisans at the Rondout shops was tested to the limit. On at least three of the tugs—*Saranac, Hance,* and *Wm. H. Baldwin*—the original handsome rounded pilot houses were installed on the main deck, well below the maximum height. This stayed with the vessel until the end of her career. On most of the remaining tugs, square "chicken coop" pilot houses were fashioned for their upper decks or were installed on the main deck ahead of the existing deckhouse. There was barely enough headroom within these singularly ugly, cramped structures to permit the pilot to sit comfortably at the wheel, and in some of the upper-deck alterations it was necessary to drop the deck level several inches below the upper deck. This encroached severely upon the headroom in the galley below, but it was possible to create a tug on which all of the fixed parts were below the clearance line.

Serious thought was also given in Rondout to augmenting this fleet. In the spring of 1931, Tom Coykendall's men proposed that the venerable *Coe F. Young* be cut down in a manner similar to that considered for the eight small vessels. Even with a pilot house having a dropped deck (to produce six feet of headroom), the height of the vessel above the water line (called "air draft") was well over the safe maximum of fourteen feet six inches. The solution was to ballast the *"Youngs"* forward to a working draft of nine feet seven inches, which resulted in the fore deck being perilously close to the water surface. As long as she remained in the canal, she might be safe.

Next, the question of coal consumption had to be considered. The small vessels had limited bunker capacity, and as long as they were working around Rondout Creek or Albany Harbor, they were always within range of coal pockets, and these vessels probably "coaled up" every day or two. Running the length of the canal brought with it a serious problem in logistics.

To satisfy themselves that the use of these tugs was feasible, the men at the shops calculated the coal consumption of each tug and, from that, the range based on a speed of 2.1 miles per hour and the consumption of ninety percent of the vessel's bunker capacity. The results were not encouraging, ranging from 43 miles for *Geo. N. Southwick* up to 82 miles for *Primrose*. It was then suggested that additional coal could be piled on deck, extending each boat's range, so that the worst case, *Wilson P. Foss*, might make 90 miles and *Primrose* all of 134.

It was a gamble, but the decision was made to place at least some of these vessels on the canal. The venture was short-lived. By 1934, the experiment had been given up, and those vessels with their low stacks and chicken-coop pilot houses all returned to the shops. Some of them—for example *John D. Schoonmaker, J. G. Rose,* and *G. W. Decker*—had their previous pilot houses reinstalled to make them handsome tugboats once more. Others, such as *Coe F. Young, Primrose,* and *Saranac*, kept their canal appendages. These three vessels, along with *Empire,* ended their lives tied up alongside the Sunflower Dock, where they apparently had been placed upon returning to the Creek.

Aside from the problem of keeping fuel supplied to the boats, there was the question of competition. Moran was well established in the canal by that time, and John E. Matton and Son of Waterford, had run in the canal for years with a well-proven system in place. Matton was also converting his fleet to diesel propulsion, which was, in the end, the solution to successful canal operation. Other operators, such as the Canal-Lakes Towing Corporation (Calatco), with its fleet of small diesel tugs designed from the keel up for operation between Albany and Buffalo, had a measure of success on the canal from the 1920s through the end of World War II.

Even for Moran, Matton, and Calatco, the early 1930s must have been lean days, and for Cornell to attempt to storm the canal as the Great Depression was slowing the nation to a crawl—and with a fleet of what can only be termed ill-suited vessels—was a venture which, in retrospect, was ill-fated from the start.

William duBarry Thomas

Chapter Thirteen
Last Act for the Coykendalls

ONCE AGAIN, the death of a leading Cornell-Coykendall family member was a sad blow to the Kingston and Rondout Creek communities. Like his grandfather and father before him, Edward Coykendall had been warmly regarded by many, most of whom had known him all their lives.

The majority of his estate went to brother Frank, with Judge Harry H. Flemming of Kingston, longtime Cornell director and Ulster and Delaware legal counsel, named executor. Flemming was also to be the beneficiary of the remainder of Edward's trust fund upon Frank's death. It was said that Flemming had been financially assisting Edward in the last few years.

Edward left much of his prized art collection to the State of New York, part for the Senate House Museum in Kingston and part for the New Paltz campus of the state university. He also left the sum of $2,500 for the care and upkeep of the Cornell-Coykendall family plot at the Montrepose Cemetery, which stands on a hill high above Rondout Creek.

With the death of Edward, Frederick Coykendall returned to involvement with the company, of which he was chairman and nominally president; Frank remained on the board. Chase National Bank, the main lender to Cornell, had its own ideas for the future, and could not be ignored. For Chase to continue financing the company, which was essential, there would have to be changes on the board and in the company's executive leadership. Three board members who had been close to Edward resigned: William C. Hussey, Cornell assistant treasurer; Harry Flemming, who had been board secretary; and his brother, T. W. Flemming, who had been vice president of the board and Cornell's superintendent of operations at Kingston.

Frederick arranged to have two friends join the board: stock broker Albert G. Redpath of Auchincloss, Parker and Redpath, and attorney Henry W. Proffitt of Barry, Wainwright, Thacher and Symmers. Proffitt's firm proceeded to handle Cornell's legal work, eventually bringing in expert admiralty lawyer Edward Kalaidjian to lead in the considerable amount of litigation that was part of a tugboat company's daily operations. This litigation ranged from large and small accidents and damage claims to Interstate Commerce Commission cases and would involve a United States Supreme Court decision.

The machinery will be taken from the tug Lavergne, which was damaged by fire, and the hull will be broken up. —*Kingston Daily Leader*, 17 September 1900

Proffitt became secretary of the board, turning his high-powered talents to the development of Cornell, and accepting remuneration that was far less than his usual fees as an attorney. There was something about Cornell—and about Frederick's capacity for attracting loyal friends—that urged men like Proffitt and Redpath to do all they could to assure that it survived against all the odds. There was also the appeal of benefiting from Frederick's considerable influence and connections as chairman of Columbia University's trustees.

For many years prior to Edward's death, highly regarded Kingston attorney, Harry H. Flemming, had served as Cornell's legal arm, with an office at the company's Ferry Street headquarters. Flemming was a close friend and advisor to Edward Coykendall, and as executor of the estate, was now authorized to dispose of or sell, at his own discretion, all Edward's real estate. Flemming also was given authority to exercise the voting rights of Edward's stock in Cornell. The voting rights to the S. D. Coykendall estate's stock in Cornell—two thirds of the total shares—went to Frederick and Frank as surviving sons. This gave them total control, although the stock was worth nothing in 1949.

At the same time, C. W. Spangenberger, who had been named to the Cornell board just before Edward died, was appointed executive vice president, with administrative authority. The bank had at first suggested he assume the title of president, replacing Frederick, but Spangenberger felt that would be disrespectful. Whatever his title, Spangenberger had operational oversight of Cornell and the support of the board and Chase National Bank.

The new members of the board brought a fresh dynamic energy to the company on behalf of their friend, Frederick Coykendall, who was able to enlist the support of other influential Columbia University alumni, including executives at Chase—after 1955 called Chase Manhattan. Chase had a shaky customer in Cornell Steamboat Company, but one which carried considerable prestige, not only because of Frederick Coykendall, but because there was sentimental attachment to Cornell after all these years it had been in business.

Chase lending-officer trainee Charles Fiero broke in around this time with Cornell as a client, and he recognized this attachment, well aware that purely financial reasons for backing Cornell were not especially strong. Fiero, who would rise to become a Chase Manhattan assistant treasurer and vice president, was keenly aware of this attitude on the part of Chase superiors as he watched men such as Earl Allen—loan officer and head of the district office—work to find ways to keep Cornell afloat long enough for the new board to turn it around. Allen was one of the few remaining old-style bankers who would personally meet with clients rather than just look at their financial statement.

Certainly, Chase had the option of foreclosing on its loans to Cornell and liquidating the assets, but in reality, that would have been a poor return for the bank. The decision was made to attempt to rescue the company insofar as the trustees and administration were willing and able to try to do so.

Fiero and Harry Proffitt worked closely with Spangenberger to prepare documentation for secure existing loans and for opening new ones. In 1950,

All the tugs and towing steamers in this vicinity are using soft coal [instead of hard coal], and when the air is heavy the smoke is dense over the river and creek. A tug makes a stream of smoke a mile or two in length. Sometimes this smoke goes straight up in the air, and it is certainly very picturesque. Last evening a body of smoke hung over Rondout and pilots said it was a sure sign there would be heavy fog this morning. —*Kingston Daily Leader*, 27 September 1900

The Cornell repair shops along Rondout Creek in a photo take from Sleightburgh about 1910. The building at the left was the boiler shop, the large building in the center the machine shop, and the large structure at the center right the coal pocket. In the photo—probably taken in early March—26 tugboats are visible. (Roger W. Mabie Collection)

Cornell's net worth was $806,000, with New York Trap Rock providing about eighty percent of the annual gross revenues, and brick-towing constituting another ten to fifteen percent. There was a foundation there, and the long-range financial plan for Cornell was eventually to underwrite and issue stock, but first the company had to right itself and expand operations beyond the Hudson River as per Spangenberger's 1948 plan. The first essential step was to modernize the aged fleet, which also meant selling or scrapping the remaining coal-fired steamers. At the same time, the bank needed collateral to back the operating loans it gave Cornell, and those steam tugs had constituted most of that collateral.

To improve its balance sheet, it was necessary for Cornell not only to get rid of old steamboats, but to close up work shops, sell real estate, and begin the process of laying off many of its long-term employees.

That last, most difficult task fell to Spangenberger.

Spangenberger told every single one in person. Some had known him since he was a boy collecting tickets at Kingston Point. Cornell had seldom laid off employees, keeping them on at wages that even more seldom ever were raised, but keeping them on just the same, like a family. In one case for Spangenberger, the firing was of very close family: No termination was more poignant than that of Spangenberger's own father, Lawrence, who had been salaried as Edward's personal barber.

Over the next year, there was a steady attrition at Cornell shops, offices, and on the tugboats. A call to come into Spangenberger's office often meant the worst, but there was no other choice.

The diesel *Harry Card* was purchased outright in 1950, after two seasons under charter, and she was renamed *Thomas Cornell*. By then, the company was in the midst of the wholesale selling or scrapping of the coal-burning steamers. The mighty *Perseverance* and *Stirling Tomkins* were the two last big towing steamers to go, both sold for scrap early in 1950. Although four small helper steam tugs remained in the fleet—*Edwin Terry, R. G. Townsend, John D. Schoonmaker,* and *J. G. Rose*—this virtually was the end of the steam era.

The question was whether it had come too late for the long-term survival of the Cornell Steamboat Company, which soon would own no more steamboats.

During this time, the shipyard on Island Dock in Rondout Creek was prospering as the federal government ordered seventeen landing craft and twenty-one steel-deck barges to be built. These were completed at a rate of one every three weeks, and then they were delivered to Brooklyn Navy Yard. Roger Mabie was the Island Dock general manager, and William duBarry Thomas and Robert M. Wilkinson were the firm's naval architects.

Mabie, Thomas, or Wilkinson would travel downriver to deliver the new vessel, and for their pilot they hired one of Cornell's top captains, William O. Benson. On their trips, longtime Rondout Creek men Mabie and Benson often got to talking about a favorite subject: ships and boats. They especially enjoyed trading stories from Cornell's long history, but the younger men did not have the fund of anecdote and legend of Captain Benson, whose entire life since the early thirties had been spent on a tugboat. When friends urged Benson to write down his stories as he recalled them during trips back and forth on the river, he got himself a large log book and began to write. Benson eventually filled three of those books and, working with Mabie, who edited the stories, eventually published them regularly in the Kingston *Daily Freeman*.

After 1949, at the insistence of Chase National Bank, Frederick Coykendall was to be inactive in the day-to-day management of the Cornell Company. Frederick remained chairman of the board of trustees and president, but without real power, which was now in the hands of Profitt, the board's secretary, and Executive Vice President Spangenberger, who was fully in charge of operations. Frank Coykendall remained on the board as vice president but likewise had nothing to do with management.

Chase worked closely with the board members during this time to reorganize and refinance Cornell. To protect its loans and hold out some hope of further financing, Chase took a chattel mortgage—meaning it had a lien on everything the company owned.

Cutbacks were the order of the day at Cornell, along with finding a way to acquire diesel tugs to replace the steamers. Property was put up for sale, including the offices at 22 Ferry Street, the shops and warehouses along Rondout Creek, shipyards at Sleightsburgh, and facilities at Watervliet, above Albany. The steady sale of property over the next five or six years would help provide cash with which to periodically repay Chase Bank's loans, totaling more than $100,000 at their peak. Cash that came in from sales of property or tugs was not available to Cornell for down payments on new tugs, but with Chase's backing, new purchases were made, and at the same time old tugs were scrapped if they could not be sold off.

In 1949 alone, five old steam tugs were scuttled in the boat graveyard off Port Ewen, among them *Watchman* and Edward Coykendall's personal favorite, *Wm. S. Earl*, which had been kept going for decades beyond its time, and at ninety years of age probably had been the oldest tug still operating in the country. *G. W. Decker, Bear,* and *J. C. Hartt* also were scuttled off Port Ewen in 1949, an underwater graveyard that held nineteen Cornell tugs by then, including *Pocahontas, Osceola, Hercules,* and *S. L. Crosby*. Other boats scrapped at this time included *Wilson P. Foss* and *Wm. E. Cleary*.

Getting rid of old tugs meant there was less need for maintenance, thus less need for the shops and their employees. It was thought that, in time, maintenance and repair could be contracted out to other shipyards. With the reorganization of 1949-50, terminating employees was expected to save at least $23,000 in salaries annually. This was in addition to further Coykendall brother salary cuts, which amounted to a savings of $7,000 annually. Drastic layoffs at the offices and shops would, by 1956, leave only eight from the original forty who had been there in 1949. Reducing the number of employees and selling off property and boats would also reduce taxes and insurance payments, and the cumulative effect of making Cornell more lean might persuade

Stirling Tomkins and *Perseverance* laid up at the Rondout shops on April 3, 1948. By this time, the era of the large steam tug on the Hudson had ended; these vessels would be sold and dismantled in a few years. (Photograph by Donald C. Ringwald, Roger W. Mabie Collection)

Perseverance at a New York coal pocket, probably in the late 1930s. The hull of *Perseverance*, built by Crowninshield Shipbuilding Company at Fall River, Massachusetts, was acquired from the United States Shipping Board in 1921 and the vessel was completed at the Rondout shops. She had a standard Shipping Board 1000-horsepower triple-expansion engine and two Scotch boilers. (Photograph by Robert G. Fuhr. William duBarry Thomas Collection)

C. William Spangenberger, the fourth and last president of the Cornell Steamboat Company. (C. W. Spangenberger Collection)

Chase to open up new lines of credit or take second mortgages on the best tugs in the fleet in order to provide funds to purchase new equipment.

And so it went. Cornell estimated it needed approximately $30,000 in cash over and above income from operations to see it through the slow time of winter. The company was also wrangling with the longshoremen's union over wages, but it was inevitable that Cornell's annual salary expense would rise approximately $7,900 as a result. Further, until Cornell proved itself solidly on its feet in every way, there was little chance that it could require customers to pay higher rates to cover rising expenses. Still, Cornell pushed ahead, and when in March 1950 it acquired *Harry Card* outright from McAllister Brothers for $85,000 and the steam tug *J. G. Rose*, Chase provided the financing.

Meanwhile stiff competition had developed in the brick-barge towing business from one-time customer Callanan Road Improvement Company, which started a towing operation. Cornell sued to compel Callanan to stop towing, asserting Interstate Commerce Commission regulations that Cornell believed forbade Callanan from freighting on the Hudson. Callanan had quickly taken four of Cornell's major brick-barge clients, and the brickyards that went with them asserted that the reason for doing so was Cornell's inefficient and old equipment. The litigation with Callanan would go on for years, ultimately to the Supreme Court, and in 1953 would be decided in Cornell's favor, but not before much towing business was lost.

Cost-cutting included reducing the monthly salaries of the Coykendall brothers to approximately $540, and Spangenberger's new responsibilities and authority earned him for the first time a salary equivalent to the two Coykendalls.

In 1950, former trustee T. W. Flemming and a partner purchased the Ferry Street office building for $25,000. Cornell's legacy at Rondout would be further diminished by the sale of its boiler shop, too, but at least the company kept going.

There was a severe blow to operations in June 1953 when the Trap Rock employees went out on a seven-week strike, and towing for that company stopped cold. It was as if Cornell were working for Trap Rock these days, because everything that affected the quarrying company rebounded on Cornell. By the same token, Trap Rock was constantly demanding better service, express tows, quicker turnaround, but all the while fought hard to keep Cornell from raising its rates. Those seven-weeks were tough on Cornell and then, as soon as the quarry strike ended, truck drivers went on strike, further preventing the delivery of stone to the waterfront.

For all the daily troubles it faced, Cornell reported a net profit of approximately $18,000 in August of 1951 and $11,000 in September. There was hope. Month after month showed a net profit, small but consistent, and the main Chase loan was steadily paid down by the sale of property or tugs, while new loans to purchase equipment were provided by Chase. At the same time, Cornell opened negotiations for a three-year contract with Trap Rock, which was not eager to come quickly to terms that would be favorable to Cornell. In one report of a 1952 meeting of Cornell's trustees, Spangenberger told about union negotiations and added that negotiations with Trap Rock were not going well, for "it appeared that it is going to be extremely difficult to negotiate any increase in rate for 1952, notwithstanding that our labor cost for this year will probably increase by at least $24,000."

In future board meeting minutes, it would be recorded that the Cornell trustees encouraged Spangenberger to "make reasonable efforts to procure some increase in rates from the New York Trap Rock Corporation in a tactful way, having due regard for the fact that Cornell Steamboat Company would be obliged to accept such terms as the New York Trap Rock Company Corporation might specify."

Trap Rock was difficult to deal with, but on the other side of the coin Henry Proffitt's law firm put little pressure on Cornell for payment of its own account, and when the legal bills did come in, they were far below the normal rate. Proffitt wanted to see Cornell survive. Meanwhile, his close relationship with Frederick Coykendall certainly was in his favor when Columbia

Thomas Cornell at the Rondout shops in the mid-1950s. She and her nearly identical sister, *Mary A. Cornell* (named for Thomas Cornell's daughter, who was the wife of S. D. Coykendall), handled most of Cornell's line-haul towing assignments during the 1950s. These two diesel-propelled, wooden-hulled vessels started life as United States Army "LTs" (the Army's designation for "large tugs"). (Photograph by William duBarry Thomas)

From Coal to Diesel

University named him an alumni trustee in 1955, and in 1959 he would become the university's head counsel.

At the end of 1953, Cornell showed a net profit of approximately $30,000, which included purchasing *Jack* for $122,500—$7,500 down payment—a diesel tug that was renamed *Mary A. Cornell*, after S. D. Coykendall's wife. *Mary A. Cornell* was almost identical to *Thomas Cornell*, being sister ships with similar engines.

In the fall of 1954, the Association of the Alumni of Columbia College notified Frederick Coykendall that he would be the recipient of the association's annual Alexander Hamilton Award for 1955, which honored distinguished service and accomplishment.

On Tuesday, November 16, he was unusually absent from the regular Cornell board meeting. Two days later, on November 18, and just four days from his 82nd birthday, Frederick Coykendall died at his home in the Dakota.

As the nineteenth chairman of Columbia, Frederick would be sorely missed by the university. So, too, did the Cornell Steamboat Company miss him, for he had presided over virtually every board meeting since the company had been reorganized in 1949, and his personal prestige had gone far to win support from the likes of Henry Proffitt and the Chase Bank.

Now Proffitt was elected chairman of the board, and Spangenberger president. Frank Coykendall would remain vice president, though his future participation in board matters and his attendance would be almost nil. Edward Kalaidjian became secretary of the company.

In December 1954, the Cornell Steamboat Company had eight tugs, all diesel, seven of which were engaged in regular operations, while an eighth was in reserve. More would be needed, because Trap Rock predicted a heavier volume of scow loadings during the coming year. Brick and scrap-iron customers also predicted more volume for Cornell. During the 1954 season, the company had towed approximately 4.4 million yards of stone, as compared to 3 million in 1953 and 3.2 million in 1952.

Trap Rock was regularly asking whether Cornell intended to raise its rates in the coming year, and at the same time Spangenberger calculated that wages would again rise because of the 1954 union contract. Read into the minutes for the December board meeting was part of a complimentary letter from Wilson P. Foss III, president of Trap Rock: "I am quite frank to say that the services which your company has provided Trap Rock have, year by year, grown to be more satisfactory, and from my personal point of view have gotten to that happy stage where I can think of other matters. Needless, of course, to say—I hope it will continue just that way."

Foss had good reason to hope, for his company's four-year projections indicated an increase of more than forty percent in business because of recently approved state and federal road-building legislation. With Cornell's steady

The iron-hulled tug *Duke* lying at the Cornell shops in September 1951. *Duke* was never owned by the Cornell Steamboat Company but was operated on charter from Robert B. Wathen, of Baltimore, Maryland. Built as *A. C. Rose* for the Baltimore and Ohio Railroad in 1888, she was re-engined with a 600-horsepower Atlas Imperial diesel engine in 1943. (Photograph by William duBarry Thomas)

recovery, its trustees and employees had every right to expect that its service would get even better.

In August 1955, Frank F. Walker was elected the new trustee to replace Frederick. Walker was the husband of Ursula Coykendall Walker, daughter of Frederick and Mary Warrin Coykendall (Mary was still alive). Ursula was the only S. D. Coykendall grandchild; she had one child, son Frank. Her husband, Cornell trustee Frank Walker, would seldom attend board meetings, for he was far across the country, an executive with the brokerage house Dean Witter in San Francisco.

Spangenberger now was anxious to acquire or charter three newer tugs and to get rid of five uneconomical, old-line vessels: *Lion, Jumbo, Cornell No. 41, Edwin Terry,* and *Cornell*. *Edwin Terry* was sold in October of that year, the last steam tug to run for Cornell Steamboat Company. *Edwin Terry* and *Ira M. Hedges* had been built in 1883 and were among the first iron-hull tugboats in the Cornell fleet, which had acquired them both a year later. The *Edwin Terry* lasted for seventy-two years in Rondout Creek. When she sailed away, the Cornell Steamboat Company no longer had any steamboats.

Of those other old tugs whose days were numbered, the converted diesel *Cornell*, sometimes nicknamed "The Submarine" because she was so low in the water, went out her own way. On November 4, 1955, while in the Tappan Zee near Tarrytown, she foundered in extremely heavy weather and sank. The crew members scampered onto a scow that was alongside and were rescued, but *Cornell* went down in forty feet of water. She, too, could have been considered a pioneer in the Cornell operation, for in 1924, when she was still the 1874 *Charlie Lawrence*, her conversion to diesel by Thomas Coykendall had made her not only the first such tug for the company, but one of the first diesel tugs on the East Coast.

Lion and *Jumbo* had been two of the first diesel-built tugs purchased by the company. At the end of 1955, *Lion* was scrapped, its spare parts used to refurbish *Jumbo*, which was similar in design. *Jumbo* continued in service on the Hudson until 1957.

A three-year contract for towing Trap Rock's boats was finally agreed upon, but Trap Rock soon would be making new demands to try out different towing schedules. At the same time, Spangenberger wanted to investigate the new push-type tugs that were said to have so much more power and currently were widely used on the Mississippi, although not in the East.

Early in 1956, Cornell bought the tug *Magnetic* for $100,000 and did Trap Rock the honor of allowing the company to rename her. A Trap Rock employee won the naming contest, and with the crash of a champagne bottle at that company's dock in Tomkins Cove, she became *Rocktow*.

The next year, 1957, was Cornell's 120th anniversary as a towing company, one of the very oldest firms in the United States.

A view of the shops on 17 August 1950. As was frequently the case in the company's latter days, and in contrast to the heady days earlier in the century, only one tug—*Cornell No. 20*—was in the creek. The shop complex consisted (left to right) of the boiler shop, the carpenter shop, the machine shop and the storeroom, the latter adjacent to the dockside crane. The coal pockets, which burned on several occasions—the first time in 1907 and the last in 1936—were located downstream (to the right) of the shop buildings and crane. (Photograph by Donald C. Ringwald. William duBarry Thomas Collection)

City of Kingston's Second Accident

City of Kingston's second accident during her five years on the Hudson happened just short of two years after the first. On the afternoon of June 5, 1888, the steamer left her North River pier at Harrison Street bound for Rondout. Opposite Fourteenth Street, Captain Van Keuren and the pilot noticed the steam yacht *Meteor* in the middle of the river ahead of them. *Meteor*, a 95-gross ton vessel built in 1881, was according to *The New York Times*, "wedge-shaped and turtle-backed" and "the model of a steamer designed to cross the Atlantic in five days." According to Van Keuen, who stated that the yacht was lying still when first sighted (a fact later confirmed by *Meteor's* owner), he blew a two-blast whistle signal, indicating that he was altering his vessel's course to port to pass to the west of the yacht. No reply was heard from *Meteor*. Again, a two-blast signal was sounded with a single blast, which meant that she was sounded by *City of Kingston*. This time *Meteor*, apparently now under way, responded with a single blast, which meant that she was intending to cross the bow of the steamboat, but a moment later, as if her helmsman had finally seen what was coming, the yacht blew two blasts.

Under these circumstances, the danger signal was called for, but by this time it was too late. With a collision now certain, both vessels rang "full astern" to their engine rooms, but they came in contact less than a minute later, fortunately without injuries, and suffered from little more than badly bruised joiner work around the point of contact. Her damage was repaired the following day by the carpenters at the Cornell shops at a cost of less than a hundred dollars.

During the investigation which followed, there were the usual disparate accounts of the collision from the men aboard *Meteor* and *City of Kingston*. The maritime rules of the road, finely tuned as they are after years of use and countless tests in the world's courts, are the best we have. Sometimes, however, they fail even the most prudent mariner. The wonder of it all is that in those days before radar and instant bridge-to-bridge communication, the rules worked as well as they did.

In reporting the accident on the 7th, *The New York Times* pontificated, "There will be a rigid investigation made, for it is held that if there is an utter disregard in answering signals a serious smash-up may occur any day, particularly as the excursion season is just opening." Fortunately, the "serious smash-up" prophesied by the *Times* never occurred.

William duBarry Thomas

What Became of *Hance* and *Baldwin*?

The tugs *George B. Hance* and *Wm. H. Baldwin* were among those which received low pilot houses at the time of the ill-starred venture of the Cornell Steamboat Company to work in the New York State Barge Canal in the early 1930s. They returned from upstate joining many fleet mates in layup along the Rondout Creek.

Unlike many of the canal tugs, *Hance* and *Baldwin*—as well as *Saranac*—were fitted with handsome rounded pilot houses. These were either the boats' original structures relocated from atop the deckhouse, or, less likely, they might have been pilot houses taken from other members of the Cornell fleet. (*Saranac*'s lowered pilot house looks much too wide to have been on her originally.)

As it was with many of the smaller Cornell tugs, the annual renewals of license of *Hance* and *Baldwin* stopped in 1934, implying that neither vessel operated after that year. From the official record, it would seem that both languished in the Rondout Creek until early 1942. The last enrollment documents of both, showing Cornell as the owner, were surrendered at Albany on February 26, 1942, with endorsements stating that they had been "abandoned." Unlike nearly all of the Cornell tugs disposed of during the 1930s and 1940s, there is no clear record of what became of this pair. A photograph shows *Hance, Baldwin,* and *Saranac* lying in the Creek on December 9, 1938, but they were not cast aside in the Rondout area, and they were never documented under the ownership of others.

There was a persistent rumor in Rondout many years ago that *Hance* and *Baldwin* were taken to New York to be sold to Newtown Creek Towing Company. That company owned a small fleet of "low air draft" tugs similar to the two Cornell vessels and operated on the upper reaches of Newtown Creek, separating Long Island City from Brooklyn. The many low bridges over the creek made low pilot houses and stacks necessary.

Perhaps *Hance* and *Baldwin* were sold to Newtown Creek sometime in 1939 or later and were never used. It is possible that they were towed to New York and the Newtown Creek Company then decided that they did not need the vessels after all and sold them for scrap during the winter of 1941-1942 without redocumenting them. Less likely, they might have been disposed of by Cornell for scrap in New York or elsewhere, without the intercession of Newtown Creek, and the documents were retained at Rondout until it was convenient to transmit them to Albany.

We can only speculate on the fate of *George B. Hance* and *Wm. H. Baldwin,* but *Saranac,* the third member of the handsome triumvirate, was left to rot away and eventually sink at the Sunflower Dock on the south side of Rondout Creek. In the 1950s, she and the other boats at the Sunflower Dock became the targets of maritime predators—scrap merchants. The vessels' engines, boilers and other metal parts were removed and sold for junk. The remains of the thusly eviscerated hulls were removed later during a clean up of the Creek.

William duBarry Thomas

Chapter Fourteen
Recovery and Close

CHARLES HENDERSON—the new Cornell vice president in charge of sales, who had been hired at Chase Manhattan's suggestion as a second to Spangenberger—celebrated the company's 120th anniversary by distributing some commemorative items, including calendars that indicated the ebb and flow of tides.

Henderson also suggested a promotional campaign, including advertising, to announce Cornell's move into harbor and general towing in addition to flotilla towing on the Hudson River. General towing was an important new direction for the company to take, and for the first time in recent history, a Cornell tug towed a Hess Oil Company barge to New London, Connecticut. Another Henderson idea was to publish, starting in 1956, a regular newsletter keyed to praising the performance of employees—especially on the tugs, and especially with regard to good safety records. This last idea caught the interest of Cornell captains and crews, who were regularly honored with a bonus and a banquet in their honor if they excelled in safety.

Accident liability costs were historically a major drain for Cornell, which was largely self-insured and had to pay claims out of pocket, often after costly litigation. The Cornell newsletter and its praise for good accident records resulted in a dramatic drop in accident claims from then on. Compared to damage claims of more than $61,000 in 1954 and $52,000 in 1955, the claims in 1956 amounted to only $25,664. Spangenberger believed the captains and pilots were not so much interested in the bonuses or banquets as they were proud to show their families that they were on that month's list as being accident-free.

In the first six months of 1956, the company's gross income was approximately $502,000, a little ahead of the previous year despite the fact that Trap Rock revenue ran slightly lower in this period. This income was achieved thanks to the increase in general towing, including towage of oil barges and hauling steel to the Kingston-Rhinecliff bridge construction site. Net monthly operating income continued to hold steady through 1956, and in August was more than $31,000, the highest for that month in recent years.

That same month, as if it were a symbol of newfound inspiration, the company inaugurated a design for a new Cornell insignia "to clearly distinguish

The coal pockets which stood near Whiteport have been torn down and are being rebuilt where the coal pockets of the Cornell Steamboat Company were burned on November 3.
—*Kingston Daily Freeman*, 12 November 1907

Cornell boats from all others," said the newsletter. It was a a white "C" around a red bullseye, and would be attached to the stacks of its tugboats.

In 1956, there were 104 employees in Cornell boats, shops, and offices. As a way of communicating with them, the Cornell newsletter offered a short feature about one of the employees, giving a brief but vivid picture of the people who worked for the company. During this time, most of the women employed by Cornell worked as secretaries, clerks, or telephone receptionists, and they were duly noted with expressions of appreciation for their cheerfulness and announcements of their marriages. It was the boatmen and shopmen who were featured in the newsletter, among them William B. Hornbeck, port engineer for Cornell.

Hornbeck had joined the company in 1902 as a deckhand on the tug *Edwin H. Mead*, and later switched to fireman on *Hercules*. His career flourished after he became a master engineer, intimately knowledgeable regarding every tug and every engine put in or taken out, rebuilt or scrapped. It was said that Hornbeck could remember which engine had been in which tug fifteen or twenty years back. He was an expert with both coal burners and oil burners, a troubleshooter who had to be ready at any moment to respond to the latest crisis.

Also featured in a newsletter was seventy-year-old Lawrence Gibbons, who had been an infant on his father's canal boat on the D&H Canal in 1887. Gibbons had started out driving the towpath mules that pulled the family boat; he went on to rise up through the Cornell ranks, becoming captain of *Cornell No. 21*. The newsletter made a statement about Gibbons that was true for virtually all the Cornell boatmen, especially the captains: "His feeling for his boat is only surpassed by his love for the River."

Another child of the canal was Frank Kennelly, who started his career "decking" for Gibbons on *James H. Flannery*, and in 1917 became a pilot under this captain's guidance. Also featured was Andrew Tubby, sixteen-year engineer of *Cornell No. 41*, and from a long line of Cornell men. Tubby said, "As long as the Cornell Company has been around, there's always been a Tubby working for it." Typical of many of these boatmen, he started out as a decky— he was on *Mary Powell*—and learned engine-room skills on the ferryboat *Kingston* before becoming a full engineer on *Cornell No. 20* in 1938, then three years later moving over to *Cornell No. 41*.

The tugboat cook with the longest term of service was John Golgoski, who spent thirty-five years on famous tugs such as *Washburn*, where he started as a deckhand, and also on *Osceola* and *Pocahontas*. From a family of Kingston boatbuilders, Golgoski was highly praised as a cook, and the newsletter said, "Chefs at the Waldorf could take lessons from John, and if proof is needed, ask any man who has ever been on a boat where John was in the galley."

Seventy-six-year-old office worker Thomas Duffy was another employee of amazingly long standing. Duffy began his boating career in 1889 as the captain of a brick scow, then became the union delegate for the brick scow captains. In 1920, he went to work for Cornell in its New York office at Pier

The push towboat *Rockland County*, en route to New York with a flotilla of twenty-one barges loaded with crushed stone from the quarries of the New York Trap Rock Company, was the first of her kind on the Hudson. *Rockland County* was powered by a pair of diesel engines which delivered 1,800 horsepower to her twin propellers–technology light-years distant from that of Cornell's early side-wheelers. (C. W. Spangenberger Collection)

93. Duffy was ever proud to say he had voted for Grover Cleveland as president in 1892.

The newsletter also contained frequent quips to stimulate a spirit of caution and thus reduce accidents and damage claims: "A careless moment can be a costly one." And: "Constant repetition breeds carelessness until an accident happens, and then it's too late!" It also explained that "One broken end plank in a deck scow costs from $300 to $500 to replace."

In 1956, the newsletter reported on the July *Sunday News* feature about family life aboard the Cornell stake boat anchored in the Hudson River off 69th Street. Donald and Shirley Culjak, who lived on the boat, were said to be "viewed by thousands every day going to and from work, as well as by thousands of sightseers each day. . . ." The story caught on, and in May of 1957 the Culjaks and their two boys were interviewed aboard the stake boat by NBC Television's *Tonight Show*.

> In answer to the rumors about the Ulster & Delaware Railroad and the Cornell Steamboat Company, Mr. Coykendall said that these properties were not for sale, neither have negotiations been pending for their sale. There have been many rumors that the business of the Cornell Steamboat Company would remove to either Newburgh or Albany.
> —*Kingston Daily Leader*, 17 January 1901

In 1957, New York Trap Rock anticipated an increase of another thirty percent in volume for the next three years, meaning an increase from approximately 4.4 million yards to more than 6 million yards. In an anxious position as it faced this promising but challenging prospect, Trap Rock created a committee that included representatives from its several towing providers, a transportation expert, and a member of its own staff. This committee was to evaluate what had to be done to meet the anticipated demand, which included hurriedly finding additions for its fleet of more than 200 boats.

Cornell would have to find a way to keep up with Trap Rock, and to add more power to its towing fleet or lose the business to other towing companies. At the same time, Trap Rock's president, Wilson P. Foss III, was inquiring insistently about the availability of push-boats instead of towboats. What was Cornell doing about looking into it? Studying and testing a push-type towboat was another problem altogether. And in this booming period it would be difficult enough to even charter another tug for the Cornell fleet, let alone buy or build one with company resources that were already stretched too thin.

Proffitt and Spangenberger turned to Frank and Ursula Walker, trying to convince them to agree to loan Cornell $30,000 from the S. D. Coykendall Trust to help with the purchase of a new tugboat. Letters to the Walkers told of the company's turnaround: how in 1949 Cornell's indebtedness of $247,000 had been secured by assets worth only $183,000, while in 1956 indebtedness of $274,000 was secured by assets worth $645,000, a net improvement of $461,000.

One letter said that "Over the same period there was paid by way of salaries and bonuses to the family [Edward, Frederick, Frank, and Frederick's widow, Mary Coykendall], who contributed very little in the way of service, a total of $133,000, and we paid out in damage and insurance premiums $476,000."

Company financial tables indicated that in 1949 Cornell owned twenty-six tugs, with an average age of fifty-one years and valued at approximately $102,000, while in 1956, there were seven tugs, with an average age of twenty-two years and valued at $605,000. Proffitt added that this "pretty remarkable performance" also made "a striking addition to the value of the Company's stock." Impressive as his argument might be, the Walkers refused to agree to the loan.

Enough Coykendall estate money had been poured into the Cornell Steamboat Company over the years, they said. Furthermore, the company still owed the estate and Coykendall family members more than $107,000, and this debt that had been subordinated to the Chase Bank loans. They conceded that everything had changed for the better since 1950, but said it was high time there was some financial return from the Cornell Steamboat Company rather than the family having to come up with more money to keep things going. They flatly objected to Cornell taking on more short-term, high-interest debt in the form of a loan to buy a new tug.

Frank Walker wrote: "What was once a very large estate has been almost drained dry, in large part by the Steamboat Company, and I feel strongly that the small amount of cash remaining should be retained for the time being as an emergency fund."

In April 1957, there was a general tugboat strike in the East, and Cornell had no choice but to lay their boats up at Rondout Creek, cover their stacks against the weather, and hope it would soon be settled by the union and the leading shipping companies and passenger lines in New York Harbor. Cornell had little influence on the strike's outcome, since it had only seven tugs. On the other hand, Moran Towing, the company's longtime Hudson River competitor, now had fifty-two.

The tugboat strike lasted only a few weeks, with the major shipping companies caving in to union demands, and Cornell found its labor costs rising once again.

Cornell's gross income in 1957 showed a ten percent increase over 1956, with the May gross of $149,000 being the highest in any recent period. The company was stable, but it hung on every whim of Trap Rock, which virtually dictated rates and the methods of towing and schedules of tows. Matters were so touchy that Trap Rock asserted that if Cornell could not perform according to the quarrying company's future requirements, then Trap Rock demanded the right to cancel the forthcoming contract.

Collaborative studies by both companies were made of push-type towboats, and in the late spring of 1957 Cornell chartered the pushboat *Papa Guy* of the Steuart Transportation Company, based in Washington, D.C. Cornell had to evaluate her merits on the Hudson River, with its tides, channels, and sudden changes, not to mention its ice. Most pushboats were to be found on the Mississippi, which had a placid current that was far different than the Hudson's changing waters.

In June, Spangenberger went to Paducah, Kentucky, and then to Chicago to observe push-type tugs in operation. He went all the way to Wisconsin to

The flag on the Cornell Steamboat Company's office is at half mast in honor of the late John J. Groves, who was the company's representative at Newburgh. The boats of the company also display their flags at half mast.
—*Kingston Daily Leader*, 9 May 1901

discuss the cost of building such a tug, and Cornell began to take bids from various sources. The cost would likely be around $350,000 for the boat. Chase Bank, with lending officer Charles Fiero as Cornell's best advocate, was favorably inclined to finance the new boat, perhaps even three, if Cornell could bring in more equity in the form of cash investment. The Walkers again were sounded, but refused, though they agreed that push-boats were the future for the company.

That year, Cornell could point to $250,000 in loans repaid and $460,000 in new equipment bought and paid for. The company was getting back on its feet. So no wonder it was a shock to Spangenberger when, in the fall of 1957, he was called to a meeting with Trap Rock and told in no uncertain terms that the quarrying company wanted "to make a marriage" with Cornell.

Trap Rock aimed to acquire the Cornell Steamboat Company outright and in this way control its own towing, thus meeting its growing needs without having to depend on an independent company. Spangenberger and the principals at Cornell, including Frank Coykendall and the Walkers, knew full well they had no other choice but to sell out to Trap Rock, for if they lost that business, everything would collapse.

The Cornell Steamboat Company employs 88 at boat repairs, etc. —*Kingston Daily Leader*, 7 January 1901

In March 1958, New York Trap Rock Corporation acquired all the stock, part of the assets, and the towing franchises of the Cornell Steamboat Company, which would become a wholly owned subsidiary. Cornell would keep its name and remain a corporation.

Other board members and executives were finished with Cornell, but Spangenberger stayed on as president of the company. He also served as president of a new, temporary, company, called Lenroc Towing Corporation. Lenroc was Cornell backwards, without one "l." Proffitt, Redpath, Frank Coykendall, and Walker were all with Spangenberger on the board of Lenroc, formed solely to liquidate all the company's remaining assets, which monies would be paid to Cornell's former stockholders. Approximately seventy percent of the income from this sale would go to the Walkers as the largest stockholders. Trap Rock retained only the *Rocktow* and one of the stake boats in New York Harbor, and everything else, including the other six tugs, was to be sold by Lenroc.

Now Trap Rock wanted to charter larger tugs or build new ones. At the same time, the company ordered fifty new steel crushed-stone barges to add to their fleet in order to meet expected future operations and to replace old boats. The flotilla-type of towing with eighteen or twenty barges would be ended, and a system of twice-a-day towing of no more than eight or ten barges would be initiated, with the purpose being to speed up Trap Rock's deliveries.

By the fall 1959, Spangenberger was in charge of the entire Trap Rock fleet of 239 boats, the largest of its kind in the country, and he served as the company's director of transportation.

The sale of Cornell stirred up shipping-trade publication journals to speculate that Trap Rock might soon become a major player in the New York area's stone industry, and that the Cornell Company would be wholly reconstituted and rebuilt, with the introduction of push-type towboats as its first innovation. In this last speculation, the journalists were exactly right.

Trap Rock's president, Wilson P. Foss III, and Cornell's Spangenberger combined their expertise to work with naval architects to design and build the right push-type tug for the Hudson River. The new boat was ordered in May 1959, and the builder was the Dravo Corporation of Pittsburgh. This boat, which cost $750,000, would be the first tug ever built entirely from scratch by the Cornell Steamboat Company.

In the spring of 1960, *Rockland County* was named in a celebration at the Trap Rock Haverstraw dock, with more than 200 guests on hand. *Rockland County* then entered the Hudson River as the first push-type tugboat ever based there. She would also be the first Cornell Steamboat Company tug not to bear the hailing port of "Rondout, N.Y." on her stern. Instead, it was just "New York."

The Cornell Steamboat Company continued for another four years as a valuable subsidiary of New York Trap Rock Company, but much like the Cornell of old, even such an established giant as Trap Rock faced severe competition that it could not overcome. Its main client, Colonial Sand and Gravel of New York City, opened its own quarries and began to ship most of its own stone. Trap Rock was faltering.

In December 1963, Spangenberger met with Foss and was told the gloomy news that Trap Rock intended to sell out next year to Lone Star Cement Corporation. That meant the Cornell Steamboat Company would be closed down after 127 years on the Hudson River. Spangenberger's own position was no more, and he was not to stay with Trap Rock when it was sold. He was asked to tie up loose ends at Cornell in the next few weeks and sell off the one remaining boat, *Rockland County*.

Spangenberger soon sold *Rockland County*, the Cornell Steamboat Company's last boat, to Red Star Towing of New York City.

**The largest tow of the season to pass this city went up the river Monday morning. It consisted of 69 canal boats and barges, and was in tow of the steamers Pocahontas, Adams, Ronan, and Levy.
—*Kingston Daily Leader*, 9 May 1901**

Chapter Notes

Chapter One: Cornell's Last Boat

Rockland County's performance trials were conducted under supervision of Sparkman and Stephens, Inc., New York City naval architects who worked with Cornell to design her.

She was 105 feet long, with a thirty-two-foot beam and depth amidships of eleven feet nine inches; she had two Fairbanks-Morse engines with a combined 1,800 shaft horsepower. Her twin seven-foot stainless steel propellers were mounted in welded steel Dravo Kort nozzles, which in effect were hydrofoil sections surrounding the propellers, increasing the boat's push-power by approximately twenty-five percent. *Rockland County* had two hydraulic-operated steering systems, one for the flanking rudders and one for the steering rudders. The hull differed from that of a typical harbor tug of the day in that the bow was somewhat spoon-shaped instead of being pointed.

Chapter Two: Canals, Coal, and Steam

Artist, engineer, and inventor Robert Fulton designed *North River Steam Boat,* launched in 1807 and the world's first commercially successful steamboat, and also the first to ply between New York and Albany. In 1817, a biography of Fulton, who had died two years earlier, erroneously called the sidewheeler *Clermont.* In most history books, the new name stuck.

The Cornell boys who died in infancy were Peter Gedney Cornell, July 31—September 16, 1846, and Hiram Schoonmaker Cornell, April 29—May 2, 1849.

After Rondout Creek, David Mapes went to the Midwest, where he recovered financially, becoming a founder of Ripon, Wisconsin, and writing a memoir of his days on the Hudson River.

M.V. Schuyler was said to have been the first propeller tug to come to Rondout; she was very small, and it was said that although she could tow anything in the Creek, using her sometimes required much patience.

Chapter Three: Thomas Cornell's Rise to Power

Rhinecliff was originally called Shatzell's Dock, and the Hudson River Railroad station built there around 1850 was named Rhinebeck Station, after the village of Rhinebeck, two miles away. The railroad company renamed the station Rhinecliff in 1861, but for years afterward locals often referred to it as Rhinebeck.

The term "Pass" in the poem about Rondout harks back to the long-lasting Dutch influence in the Hudson Valley, for it refers to *Paasen*, the Dutch word for Easter.

George Washington Murdock was born in 1853 in Sing Sing, N.Y., now Ossining, which at the time was an important port for steamboats. Murdock's life and career spanned the era of the great passenger boats, and he knew most of them, working on several, including *Mary Powell*, where he was a fireman. He survived the 1875 wreck of *Sunnyside,* and he also worked in the salvage business, dismantling such passenger boats as *Thomas Cornell, Rip Van Winkle,* and *New Champion.* His personal interest in the lore of boats, boatmen, and the Hudson River inspired him to collect photographs and illustrations of steamboats and tugs, and until his death in November 1940, he kept extensive notes on the biographies of virtually all the steamboats that plied the Hudson.

Chapter Four: War, The Mary Powell, and S. D. Coykendall

Because of its place of honor as one of the first regiments to volunteer for federal service, the 20th New York State Militia lobbied successfully to retain its original militia designation throughout its service, and thus came to be recognized as both the 20th NYSM and the 80th NY Volunteer Regiment.

Manhattan served the government on the run between Cape May, New Jersey, and Philadelphia until July 1864, when she was briefly sent south with a load of troops, returning to the same run. During fall and winter of 1864-65, she carried government and soldier mail between Washington, D.C., and City Point, Virginia. After May 1865, *Manhattan* was in the Gulf of Mexico, running between Mobile, Alabama, and New Orleans for several years until she sank in Mobile Bay. She was raised and brought to Wilmington, Delaware, to be broken up for scrap.

In 1864, Thomas Cornell bought the eighty-eight-foot towboat *Walter B. Crane* from veteran captain Peter Dubois of Rondout. Dubois had just built a propeller tugboat, *John Dillon,* to tow coal boats for the D&H Canal Company. The days of sidewheel towboats were numbered, as propeller tugboats proved more maneuverable and even more powerful, while their design steadily improved and boatmen learned how to handle them.

Although *Mary Powell* did not carry freight, most steamboats depended on cargo for making a profit: On one trip in 1858, Cornell's *Manhattan* shipped more than twelve hundred firkins of butter, worth $27,000; on one trip the next year, she carried 36,000 baskets of raspberries, and on another 1,000 domestic animals. The swift *James W. Baldwin* once carried 90,000 baskets of raspberries from Marlborough to New York.

Chapter Five: Railroads and Tugboats

The Kingston-Rhinecliff ferry also benefited from its association with the steamboat company, such as when ice choked the river and tugboats had to break open a crossing; *Rob,* in particular, was known to carry passengers across when the ferry could not run in foggy or rough weather.

Chapter Six: The Last Passenger Boats

Among the many large and small boatbuilders and dry docks in the Creek were the Island Dock Shipbuilding Company, Conrad Hiltebrant, Dwyer Brothers, John D. Schoonmaker, Jacob Rice, Feeney Company, Baisden, Donovan, D&H Canal Company, and Cornell. At their peak of activity, more than a thousand men were employed in the boatyards.

Chapter Seven: Tugboats

The incident with the deckhand tossing the hawsers off occurred on the line steamer *Perseverance* in 1937.

A piece of the cabin paneling from *City of Kingston* was sent back to Kingston by one of the crewmen who had gone out west with her. Cornell shops put the piece in an oak frame, and eventually it went to Port Ewen's Captain William Mabie and then to his grandson, Roger W. Mabie.

City of Kingston's trip was an epic journey through the Straits of Magellan. A duplicate of her was built in the Northwest and called *City of Seattle.*

There are few extant photos of *Thomas Cornell* on the water, but several from the 1882 crackup. Two paintings of *Thomas Cornell* were done by James and John Bard; one, an oil, is privately owned, and the other, a watercolor, is at the Senate House Museum in Kingston.

The Beverwyck and Ronan lines were both based in Albany.

City of Kingston was rammed midships by the British-flag freighter *Glenogle.*

Chapter Eight: Coykendall's Reign Begins

The ferryboat *Riverside* was also nicknamed "Skillypot," a corruption of the Dutch *schildpad,* meaning turtle.

Transport originally had been built for the Camden and Amboy Railroad in New Jersey.

State Senator Jacob Rice, a local boatyard owner after whom a Cornell tug was named, bought the Cornell mansion on the southeast corner of Wurts and Spring Streets. Around 1942, after Rice's two maiden daughters left the mansion, it was torn down. Part of the former mansion grounds was donated by the Cornell family to the city and named Cornell Park where, in 1943, an eagle from a Cornell pilot house was set on a pedestal as a war memorial. The Rice family donated the park's decorative urns, which once had been on grounds near the original Cornell home.

Iron- and steel-hulled tugs which came into the fleet in these years consisted of *Edwin Terry* and *Ira M. Hedges* (1884), Geo. W. Washburn (1890), *Edwin H. Mead* (1892), *Thomas P. Fowler* (1893), *G. W. Decker* and *J. G. Rose* (1900), *W. N. Bavier* (1901), *Cornell* (1902), and *Wm. E. Cleary* and *J. H. Williams* (1904). *Terry* and *Hedges* were built in Camden, New Jersey; *Bavier* in Port Richmond, New York; and Cornell in Shooters Island, New York. Others were from Newburgh's T. S. Marvel and Co.

In 1904, Cornell bought two steel-hulled tugs that had been under construction from New York Trap Rock; both tugs were subsequently sold before they ever ran for Cornell.

In 1905, each week Cornell towed an average of fifty to seventy barges of coal, seventy to eighty of ice, twenty-four of cement, six to eight brick scows, and five bluestone barges.

Chapter 10: Loss and Transition

In one of his Kingston *Daily Freeman* articles, published on March 25, 1973, William O. Benson said he was told that the company decided "it was not feasible to convert *Cornell* to an oil burner, since it wouldn't be possible to install sufficient oil storage capacity aboard her." Benson wrote that the Standard Oil Company of Louisiana allegedly sent men to masquerade as firemen aboard her so they could investigate whether she could be converted to oil; apparently the answer was in the affirmative, and Standard Oil made the purchase, keeping her, as *Istrouma*, in service for another thirty years.

The origin of the poem, "Breaking the Ice Jam," is unknown; these verses were found in the collection of steamboat historian Roger W. Mabie of Port Ewen and used with permission.

Chapter 11: Dissension in Cornell

Nelseco engines were known for sending up smoke rings whenever they were started or stopped, according to William duBarry Thomas.

At Kingston Point, Cornell had a dynamometer anchored to the end of the landing; it was regularly used to test the towing power of the tugs.

Chapter 12: From Coal to Diesel

Roger Mabie remembered working as a teenager selling household items for the Fuller Brush Company, and among his customers was Edward Coykendall's secretary at Cornell's Ferry Street office; one day, Edward arranged to bring his houseman down from the mansion to see the young salesman's wares. That turned out to be Mabie's best sale of all.

Some who knew Edward went so far as to say that his refusal to get rid of the steam tugs in favor of diesels was really because he was a sentimentalist at heart, a man who loved steamboats, and that it was not so much pure vindictiveness against Frederick.

Even once-delightful Kingston Point Park had steadily declined, closing in 1948, when the Hudson River Dayline ended its upriver operations.

In the early 1950s, when Frederick Coykendall was no longer able to continue borrowing operations funds simply on the strength of his signature, Chase gave a chattel mortgage that covered everything Cornell owned as security. Every boat carried a framed notice announcing that it had been mortgaged.

Rob was still running in New Jersey as late as 1960.

When the building at 22 Ferry Street was sold in January 1950, the company moved its accounting operations to the repair shops at 120 East Strand, Kingston. The Ferry Street building was purchased by Edward T. Shultis and Thomas W. Flemming. At one time, more than a hundred employees had worked at Ferry Street, including clerical workers for the Cornell Steamboat Company, the U&D, the ferry, and other operations, including the office of Coykendall general counsel Harry Flemming. The building was later bought by Ulster County and then sold to the Kingston Urban Renewal Agency. In the fall of 1966, it was demolished along with about three hundred other structures to make way for urban renewal.

The shops on East Strand were bought, for the most part, by Miron Building Products Company in January 1958.

Catherine Coykendall Herzog died on January 30, 1948.

Chapter 13: Last Act for the Cornells

The company chartered the diesel tug *Duke* and others as needed.

Charles Fiero of Chase had a personal interest in this long-lived Hudson River towing company because his family was originally from the Catskill area.

In 1949, company shares were held as follows: Estate of S. D. Coykendall, by Frederick Coykendall and Frank Coykendall, trustees: 10,039. Estate of Edward Coykendall, by Harry H. Flemming, executor and trustee: 2,599. Frederick Coykendall: 1,526-1/2. Frank

Coykendall: 2,758-1/2. Total: 16,923 shares.
In later years, C. W. Spangenberger bought a total of 525 shares of Cornell stock from Frederick Coykendall.

Frederick's widow, Mary Warrin Coykendall, died on September 3, 1958.

Frank Coykendall died on June 29, 1964 at the age of 87; he lived in semi-retirement at the Union League Club on Park Avenue until some time before his death, when he moved to Sky View Haven, Croton-on-Hudson.

Cornell's main competition for towing Trap Rock stone were: Turecamo Coastal and Harbor Corporation; Red Star Towing and Transportation Company; Gowanus Towing Company; Jamaica Bay Towing Line Company, and the Bronx Towing Line Company.

Edwin Terry left Rondout Creek on October 8, 1955.

Chapter 14: Recovery and Close

The law firm that in the last years handled Cornell's legal matters and the sale to Trap Rock was Thacher, Proffitt, Prizer, Crawley and Wood of New York City.
The February 28, 1958 sale price of the Cornell Steamboat Company shares, a stake boat, and miscellaneous furniture and supplies was $68,200, paid to the shareholders. The tug *Rocktow* was purchased by Trap Rock from Lenroc Towing Corporation for approximately $84,000, and Lenroc assumed Cornell's damage claim liabilities of approximately $35,000 as well as another $107,000 indebtedness to the Coykendall family and trust. Terms were arranged whereby Lenroc gradually compensated the family from the subsequent sale of Cornell assets. In time, Ursula Walker became Lenroc's president, and her husband, Frank, treasurer.

Spangenberger continued as president of Cornell, which became a wholly owned subsidiary of Trap Rock; he also served as director of transportation of the parent corporation and as vice president and general manager of another of Trap Rock's wholly owned subsidiaries—Rock-Air, Inc., a helicopter company that provided the company with transportation and made aerial surveys of the Hudson River. Spangenberger also became director of real estate for the Trap Rock Corporation.

Appendix A
Technology Along the Rondout Creek
An Appreciation of Thomas Cornell Coykendall

From the early days of the industrial revolution, the world's engineers have created an endless procession of technical marvels which have both dazzled us and made possible life as we know it today. The steamboat was the archetype of those seminal developments in technology, and the history of the Cornell Steamboat Company is marked with milestones in the application of steam—and, later, diesel—power to tugboat propulsion.

Today it is difficult to imagine that the Cornell Steamboat Company was a leader in the application of technology throughout much of its corporate existence. This aspect of the company's activity was centered at the machine shop, foundry, and boiler shop buildings on Rondout Creek. "The Shops," as these imposing structures were universally and collectively known, were erected in the late days of the nineteenth century to house the mechanical heart of the organization. Within their red brick walls, teams of men—machinists, boilermakers, foundrymen, ship carpenters, patternmakers, storekeepers, painters, and other artisans of the times—were assigned the all-important tasks of maintenance of the fleet of Cornell tugs and steamboats and the development of new methods, new materials, new ideas.

For us to appreciate how important these men were to the Cornell fleet, we must examine the state of the art in tugs and towing throughout the nearly 130 years that Thomas Cornell and his tugs and towboats—and later the corporation which was his legacy—were active on the river. From its earliest days, the Hudson River towing industry was focused primarily upon two types of traffic. One was the line-haul towing of canal boats, mainly carrying grain bound from the eastern terminus of the Erie Canal to New York. The other was the movement of a constant procession of ice, brick, and stone barges from way landings on the Hudson as well as sailing vessels carrying coal from the Delaware and Hudson Canal terminus on the Island Dock at Rondout, all bound to the metropolis or beyond.

Other local freight from riverside towns—such as the produce which fed New York—was generally handled by the steamboats hailing from those places. From south to north: Haverstraw, Ossining, Peekskill, Newburgh, Poughkeepsie, Rondout, Catskill, Hudson, Albany, and Troy, as well as many of the smaller communities, all had their steamboats to serve New York, and a further network of lesser steamers, sometimes called "yachts," connected many points along the route.

We may have lost sight of a number of facts which determined the size and shape of river traffic in those days. Ice amounting to hundreds of thousands of tons a year was needed in New York City alone, and this perishable commodity was in what is now termed a "just-in-time" basis. Brick served as the building material of choice, if not necessity, in New York's pre-skyscraper days, and nearly every brick laid in the city during the late nineteenth and early twentieth centuries came from the brickyards which dotted the river banks from Haverstraw to Albany. Finally, coal was the predominant fuel for the manufacture of gas, for commercial and domestic heating, and for industry. Although much of the area's coal was brought by the railroads serving New York from eastern Pennsylvania, the Hudson River formed a part of a "coal pipeline" through its transfer points at Rondout, Newburgh, and Cornwall. In short, as the premier towing company on the river, the Cornell Steamboat Company was an important element of New York's lifeline.

The earliest towing steamers were side-wheelers which had been converted (or "cut down," as the boatmen would say) from obsolescent passenger boats. Thomas Cornell's first towboats were such craft. They were typically propelled by walking-beam engines, variously also called vertical-beam engines or simply beam engines. A few of his earliest steamboats (including *Norwich*, which survived in Cornell's fleet until 1923) were equipped with crosshead engines.

In the walking-beam engine, a diamond-shaped iron assembly (the "beam") pivoted atop a wooden gallows frame. (The name is derived from the oscillating, or "walking" motion of the beam.) The piston rod of the engine's single, large, vertically-mounted cylinder was connected to one end of the beam by a connecting rod, while the other end of the beam transmitted power to a crank on the paddle wheel shaft by means of another connecting rod. Thus, the reciprocating motion of the engine's piston was converted to rotary motion at the crank. In a crosshead (or "square" engine), the two connecting rods were joined at the top at a crosshead which moved vertically in guides as the piston rod moved. Both the beam engine and the crosshead engine were outstanding examples of early steam engineering, the former having been used in the early shoreside engines of James Watt and Thomas Newcomen.

The propeller tug came on the scene at Rondout about 1850 with the steamer *M. V. Schuyler,* and by the start of the Civil War such vessels were used by Thomas Cornell to shift canal boats in the Rondout Creek, where they worked alongside the small sidewheelers such as *Maurice Wurts, John F. Rodman, Pittston,* and *P. C. Schultz.* The earliest propeller tugs were inefficient affairs, using a technology—the screw-propeller—which remained one of those inaccessible corners of "black magic" until after the turn of the last century. Later vessels of the type, whose propellers were much improved, found employment first as helper tugs on the Hudson's line-haul express tows and later still as the line-haul tugs themselves.

About 1880, Cornell's towing fleet consisted of a mix of side-wheelers and small propeller tugs having single-cylinder engines. *Coe F. Young* and *Thomas Dickson,* built in 1872 at Morgan Everson's yard in Sleightsburgh, across the Creek from the Rondout shops, could be classed as the most modern of the propellers when they were built. Their engines were equipped with condensers. The smaller boats were of the "high-pressure" type in which exhaust steam went from the cylinder to the atmosphere with a characteristic sound—"chuff-chuff-chuff"—and a white plume of water vapor. The *Young* (boatmen always referred to her as "the Youngs") and *Dickson* condensed the exhaust steam, reusing the water in the boiler. The high-pressure boats operated without difficulty in the upper Hudson, where boiler feed water could be drawn from the river; below Poughkeepsie, the brackish-to-salt water made it necessary for the engineer to replenish his water tanks from ashore on a regular and frequent basis.

The compound engine, in which steam is expanded successively in a high-and-low-pressure cylinder, made its initial appearance in the United States in the early 1870s. The double expansion increased the fuel efficiency of the engine to a marked degree. Later developments in marine engineering brought the triple-expansion and quadruple-expansion engines. The use of the "triple" was limited to larger tugs, while the "quad," where the increase in efficiency was nearly matched by increases in maintenance cost because of the multitude of moving parts, was never used in a Cornell tug. There were but three "triples" in the Cornell fleet in the latter days: *Perseverance, Stirling Tomkins,* and *Triton.*

During the early 1880s, Cornell went to the Delaware River shipbuilders for a fleet of four tugs propelled by compound engines, and the first, *W. E. Street,* was delivered from the Neafie and Levy yard in Philadelphia in 1881. She was followed by *S. L. Crosby, R. G. Townsend,* and the stately and powerful *J. C. Hartt* in 1883. These four tugs represented a giant step in building a modern fleet, and there is little doubt as to what motivated The Cornell Steamboat Company in choosing this new type of power.

The Neafie and Levy quartet had wooden hulls, the nation's material of choice in shipbuilding prior to this period. Our iron industry was not as advanced as that of Great Britain, but since the Civil War the Delaware River shipyards were rapidly being converted to build from this superior material. The Washburn Steamboat Company of Saugerties contracted with John H. Dialogue and Son, of Camden, New Jersey, to build two iron-hulled tugs to be used in competition with Cornell. The Washburn firm was owned by the Washburn brothers (George W., J. Tyler, and Richard C.), prominent Saugerties brick manufacturers who wished to participate in the river towing bonanza, as well as to haul their own product to market.

The two iron tugs, named *Edwin Terry* and *Ira M. Hedges,* were delivered to Washburn in 1883 at about the same time as the last of the Neafie and Levy quartet arrived in Rondout. The following year, Cornell absorbed the Washburn fleet, and it cannot be denied that the performance of the two iron hulls must have influenced Cornell's future plans.

We can only speculate as to when Thomas Cornell ("Tom") Coykendall, a son of S. D. Coykendall and a grandson of Thomas Cornell, became involved in the molding of the future fleet. When the Washburn tugs were acquired, he was eighteen years old and headed for an engineering education at Columbia University. With his inquisitive nature and mechanical skills, he must have commented to his father about the positive attributes of *Terry* and *Hedges.* Although his chosen discipline—civil engineering—was more concerned with land-based issues such as bricks and mortar and surveying, an engineer is an engineer. Coykendall adapted quickly to the world of water and steel and steam.

When the side-wheeler *George A. Hoyt* was hauled on the marine railway at Newburgh in 1889 and her wooden hull, only seventeen years old, found to be so deteriorated as to make repair economically unfeasible, it is quite possible that Tom Coykendall, then finishing his studies at Columbia, urged a switch-over to iron hulls. Cornell would support the local wooden shipbuilders for a few years with orders for smaller vessels, but the die had been cast—and it came up iron and steel. The company was ready to build powerful iron-hulled propeller tugs to replace the aging side-wheelers, and it turned to the eminent firm of T. S. Marvel and Company of Newburgh for the first of the truly modern vessels in the fleet.

Three tugs were built at Newburg, starting with *Geo. W. Washburn*, launched into the frigid Hudson on March 8, 1890. She was fitted with a massive compound engine of about 800 horsepower having cylinders 24 and 48 inches in diameter with a piston stroke of 36 inches, and with this remarkable power, the vessel would prove herself over and over throughout a long career. She was to be in Cornell's service for more than half a century. Next came *Edwin H. Mead* in 1892—a little smaller, but built, as old-time shipbuilders would say) "to the same mold." The trio was completed in 1893 with the delivery of *Thomas P. Fowler*, smaller yet, but still an outstanding vessel.

Cornell would return to the Marvel yard in 1900 for helper tugs *J. G. Rose* and *G. W. Decker*, and again in 1904 for *J. H. Williams* and *Wm. E. Cleary*. A last vessel, designed to utilize the engine from *W. E. Street*, was laid down in 1907, but canceled, probably because of a severe downturn in business caused by that year's financial panic. Ironically, the panic was due in part to the machinations and manipulations of Charles W. Morse, who was Cornell's *bête noire* during the 1890s and 1900s. Otherwise, the company sought the expertise of Burlee Dry Dock Company and Townsend and Downey, both based on Staten Island, for the only other steel tugs they ever ordered. The former built *W. N. Bavier* in 1901, and the latter, the enormous *Cornell* the following year. *Cornell*, more than 150 feet in length, was propelled by a gargantuan compound engine. She was a powerful puller but may have been too much tugboat for the river. *Cornell* was sold to Standard Oil Company of Louisiana in 1917 and ran as *Istrouma* until after World War II. (Roger Mabie recalls seeing her in New Orleans in the early 1940s.)

Most of these vessels had been completed at the respective builders' yards. Starting with *Cornell*, the hulls were built outside the Creek and towed to Rondout for installation of engines, boilers, and upperworks. The engines were built in the shops, and the detailed design and installation of the machinery plants were under the watchful eye of Tom Coykendall and his staff.

The newbuilding program may have been truncated at this time because of the number of eminently serviceable tugboats, large and small, that entered the fleet through acquisition of other companies. Nine small "high-pressure" boats came with the Albany Towing Company in 1905 and the various purchases related to Morse ice interests—in 1901, 1903, and 1913—brought such useful craft as *Imperial, Princess, Osceola, Pocahontas*, and many more. In all, forty-six tugboats were incorporated into the Cornell fleet by purchase between 1900 and 1913.

From 1904 through the Great War of 1914-18, the shops concentrated on keeping the fleet running—routine repairs of hull and machinery, occasionally an extensive rebuild of an engine, and the continuing task of keeping the steamboat inspectors satisfied. Tom Coykendall's men must have done their work with skill. Machinery will inevitably wear out, but other than the boiler explosion aboard *H. P. Farrington* in 1882, there were few, if any, serious accidents attributable to mechanical failure.

One of the most critical—and bothersome—tasks faced by the shops was in keeping the boilers of the great fleet in good repair and capable of satisfying the standards of the Steamboat Inspection Service and its legendary Albany inspection team, Robert Keller and Andrew Gaul. Mr. Gaul, the boiler inspector, would make many trips to Rondout each year to ensure that a replay of the *H. P. Farrington* explosion would not be seen. (It wasn't.) The inspection would includ the testing of safety valves, sighting of such important elements as staybolts and stay tubes, and the all-important hydrostatic test in which the boiler was filled with water, sealed tight, and pressurized to a specified amount above the working pressure. As boilers aged and became increasingly weaker, a lower working pressure might be mandated at each inspection, the end coming when Mr. Gaul condemned the boiler. At this point, the shops might be called upon to build a new boiler, a major task which they did from time to time prior to the 1914-18 world war.

During the period immediately following the war, Tom Coykendall and the Cornell Steamboat Company took advantage of the bargain-basement prices asked for by the United States Shipping Board for both surplus vessels and uncompleted hulls. At this time, Cornell purchased *Bear* and *Burro*, sisters built at Leathem & Smith Towing and Wrecking Company's yard in Sturgeon Bay, Wisconsin. These vessels, to the Board's Design 1086, were 100-foot harbor tugs each equipped with a 450-horsepower compound engine and a Scotch boiler. Despite the impending arrival on the scene of the diesel tugboat, they were state of the art. So successful was this design that a majority of the sixty-plus vessels completed (out of the 104 originally ordered) survived in commercial service at New York and elsewhere until the mid-1950s.

Also acquired from the Shipping Board at this time was the unfinished hull and engine of a 150-foot wooden-hulled seagoing tug of Design 1055. This vessel, named *Perseverance* by the Board, was one of fourteen ordered from Crowninshield Shipbuilding Company of Somerset, Massachusetts, of which only five were completed. The remaining nine, including *Perseverance*, were canceled. The vessel was brought to the Rondout shops and finished as the magnificent, two-stacked, 1,000-horsepower tug which enjoyed a successful quarter-century career on the Hudson, far from the coastwise coal-towing business for which she had been designed.

As a running-mate for *Perseverance*, Tom Coykendall engineered the reconstruction of *Geo. W. Washburn*, a thoroughbred among tugs, which was, as stated above, Cornell's introduction to modern towboats when she was built at the Marvel yard in 1890. About 1921, she was equipped with a pair of modern water-tube boilers purchased from the Shipping Board's surplus stock. The new boilers had a working pressure of perhaps 150 pounds per square inch. By that time, the steamboat inspectors had probably reduced the allowed pressure of Washburn's original boilers below 100 pounds per square inch and a change was needed. It was a rejuvenating experience for this thirty-year-old workhorse.

Washburn, with her new two-stack profile, resulted in a handsome and capable consort for the larger—and slightly more powerful—*Perseverance*. At that time, the installation of water-tube boilers in coal-burning tugboats was unusual, but the *Washburn's* machinery was to perform admirably for another twenty-five years in the face of increasing competition from diesel-powered towboats.

It was the diesel engine, however, that caught the attention of Tom Coykendall in the 1920s. The New London Ship and Engine Company (Nelseco) of Groton, Connecticut (a predecessor of the Electric Boat Division of General Dynamics Corporation) had commenced the manufacture of a range of diesel engines, mainly for submarine propulsion but modified for the commercial market. Nelseco had purchased two 100-foot tugboat hulls from the United States Shipping Board for completion as diesel tugs. These vessels, which were canceled hulls from the Design 1086 program and prospective sisters to *Bear* and *Burro*, were towed to Groton. There, six-cylinder Nelseco engines of 600 horsepower were installed, and the completed vessels named *Jumbo* and *Lion*. Both were sold to Cornell and placed in line-haul service on the river. Although less powerful than the steam-powered "big tugs," they proved to be economical pullers, and both lasted until nearly the end of Cornell's corporate existence. (One of the author's lasting memories of *Jumbo* and *Lion* is an audible one: the unmistakable tattoo of the Nelseco exhaust as one or the other tug battled a strong Hudson tide on a quiet summer evening.)

Once *Jumbo* and *Lion* were in service, the Coykendall brand of magic was worked on the conversion of four existing tugs to Nelseco-powered diesel vessels. First came *Charlie Lawrence*, a unremarkable steamer which, by virtue of an eighteen-foot lengthening and the installation of a six-cylinder engine in 1924, became the unforgetable *Cornell*. She was particularly memorable to her crews, who had to walk her deck upon "duck boards" to keep their feet dry. After the conversion, her freeboard (the distance from waterline to deck) was so small that, while underway, water freely flowed over the deck. She was known as "The Submarine" to many crew members. This attribute may have contributed to the vessel's loss when she foundered in Tappan Zee off Tarrytown on November 4, 1955.

Two other vessels followed in quick succession: *Frank*, named for one of Tom Coykendall's brothers, became *Cornell No. 20*, and *Eli B. Conine* emerged from her rebuilding as *Cornell No. 41*. The conversion of *No. 41* may have been a blessing, for the Nelseco engine replaced a complicated complicated and possibly unique four-cylinder steeple-compound engine (two cranks, with a high- and low-pressure cylinder on each crank, tandem fashion). Cornell had inherited this mechanical headache when *Eli B. Conine* was acquired from Rose Brick Company in 1907.

The last conversion was the one which made real sense. *J. H. Williams*, one of a pair built in 1904 by T. S. Marvel Shipbuilding Company, was given a Nelseco engine in 1929 and renamed *Cornell No. 21*. One is inclined to wonder why her sister, *Wm. E. Cleary*, was not converted to diesel, along with the slightly smaller 1900-built vessels, *J. G. Rose* and *G. W. Decker*, and Burlee's *W. N. Bavier*. Timing—and money—may have been the reason. Two years after *No. 21* left the shops, the full impact of the Great Depression hit the nation, and the Hudson Valley, New York City (Cornell's major market), and the steamboat company itself were all but prostrated by its effects. Things would never be the same on the river, and *Cleary, Rose, Decker,* and *Bavier* remained steamers.

At its peak, the dieselization program was envisioned to include several other tugs which might have formed a part of the company's short-lived presence on the New York State Barge Canal System. It is known that both *John D. Schoonmaker* and *H. D. Mould* were to have been re-powered with Nelseco engines similar to those installed in the four small diesel tugs. It is conceivable that the program might have included the above-mentioned steel-hulled vessels as well as still other wooden tugs.

During the pinnacle of Tom Coykendall's creative period in the 1920s, he investigated two innovative propulsion ideas. First came a low-pressure diesel-hydraulic arrangement proposed for the tug *Charlie Lawrence*. A Nelseco diesel engine was to drive a hydraulic pump, which in turn powered a hydraulic motor connected to the propeller shafting. The principal advantage of such a system, at least in the mind of Tom Coykendall, might have been that he could have placed the major system components so as to maintain satisfactory trim on the vessel. There might also have been less of a tendency for vibration in the engine-shafting-propeller train. One serious disadvantage was that of weight, and excessive machinery weight, worse in the hydraulic plant, was a problem through the rest of the tug's life, manifested in the extremely low freeboard of the vessel. Perhaps this factor caused Coykendall to abandon the scheme.

Of greater historical importance during this period was his interest in using the steam turbine as a tugboat power plant. The Westinghouse Electric and Manufacturing Company approached Cornell with a proposal to furnish a small turbine and reduction gear for this purpose. Although the concept was considered for a short time, no further action was taken. In retrospect, it may have been fortunate that the turbine idea was abandoned. Westinghouse was eventually able to persuade Great Lakes Dredge and Dock Company to install an 850-horsepower turbine in the tug *Harry B. Williams* in 1931, but *Williams* with her modern power plant was apparently not a resounding success.

Another event which occurred during the late 1920s was the purchase of the tug *Montauk*. The one feature which differentiated this boat from the rest of the Cornell steam tugs was her oil-burning boiler. Since a short-lived experiment burning oil on the sidewheeler *General McDonald* in the early days of the twentieth century, coal had been the only fuel used on the steamers. *Montauk* and her oil burners saw limited use while owned by the company, and she was disposed of for scrap in June 1935 after about seven years in the fleet. Coal remained king on Rondout Creek until *Edwin Terry*—the very last of the steamers—left the fleet early in 1958.

Tom Coykendall died in August 1934 at the age of sixty-seven. His declining years were marked by poor health and personal problems, but it is possible that the real cause of his death was professional disappointment that his innovative career had failed to stem the downward spiral of the Cornell Steamboat Company's fortunes during the early days of the Great Depression. After entering the 1930s on an optimistic note (a common response to the initial downturn in business in the United States), the company's business plummeted as the decade of the 1930s wore on.

In 1930, the tugs were generally all busy, with few to be found in the Creek during the towing season. Two or three years later, idle towboats were to be seen moored at the shops and across the Creek in Sleightsburgh, their boilers cold and their engines stilled. One after another, these coal-burning workhorses dropped their fires and never again felt the pull of a hawser on their after bitts. But for a resurgence of activity during World War II, it was to be nearly the end of the line for this company—and for this industry—which for over a century had carried on a tradition started by Thomas Cornell.

Cornell's namesake, Thomas Cornell Coykendall, may have seen this in 1934. We, who look at his achievements from the perspective of the better part of a century later, are much the richer for the career of this accomplished engineer. During a stroll through the shops, stilled and silent just before their abandonment, one could almost hear an echo of Tom Coykendall's voice as he expounded his most recent innovation. Many were brilliant; a few led to a cul-de-sac, but the fertile mind of this forgotten engineering wizard of Rondout kept the Cornell Steamboat Company as close to the forefront of towing industry technology as was possible during its peak years.

William duBarry Thomas

Appendix B

The Art of Towing on the Hudson

For those who were not witness to the towing of barges and other vessels on the Hudson River as practiced for over a century by the Cornell Steamboat Company, it is difficult to imagine three acres of barges loaded with crushed stone, brick, and other commodities, all being propelled downriver by two tugboats—a large line-haul tug along with another smaller tug in attendance as a helper. The safe and timely arrival of this cargo at the New York City stakeboat was in the hands of one skilled man, the captain of the line-haul tug.

Visualize a flotilla of, say, thirty-two barges, each measuring around 110 feet in length with a beam of thirty-five feet, arriving at New York. Each barge might carry a thousand tons of crushed stone or an equivalent amount of brick. The barges are lashed firmly together, four wide and eight long, so as to make as near to solid a mass as possible. There was a bit of give and take in the flotilla; it was not possible to "make up the tow," to use boatmen's term, rigidly because of the natural elasticity of the manila lines which were used. (Later, synthetic lines, such as nylon or polypropylene, might be used, but the properties of these materials were, if anything, even stretchier than manila.)

The line-haul tug pulled this flotilla astern, at the end of a long hawser (the boatmen would say "on the hawser"), which was connected to the forward corners of the flotilla by means of a bridle to provide the tow with some degree of directional stability. If a single hawser was connected to the center of the flotilla, there would be a tendency for the assembled barges to oscillate from side to side ("yawing" describes this motion). The danger this would be to the barges, the tug and other river traffic, is easy to visualize. (There have been instances, not necessarily seen on the Hudson, of a towed vessel yawing so violently that she moved to a position almost abeam of the towboat. In a few worst cases, the eccentric pull of the hawser has been sufficient to capsize the towing vessel.)

Our notional tow, which extends a quarter of a mile from the bow of the tug to the stern of the last barges, would arrive at a location known as "The Market," on the Manhattan side of the North River, as the Hudson is called in New York Harbor, between Piers 78 and 80 (West 39th to 40th Streets). The flotilla would be securely moored there for distribution around the harbor and beyond. Arrival of the tow at The Market was the one event of the trip which called for line-haul tug and helper to work together with the coordination of trapeze artists. To watch these two tugs as they shepherded their flock from the wide expanse of the river into The Market was in itself a thrill; to observe this maneuver during a strong wind and unfavorable tide was even more so.

Further movement of the barges within the harbor was not the job of the line-haul and helper tugs, which, after refueling and loading stores and food as necessary (towboat men always referred to their food as "grub"), would put the northbound tow on the hawser and make their way back up the river. The barges were picked up at The Market by New York's harbor tugs operated by any of a multitude of well-known towing lines—companies like Tice, Dalzell, Reichert, Newtown Creek, McAllister, Downer, Moran and many others.

Northbound tows were assembled at the Cornell stakeboat. The stakeboat was a floating mooring point, usually a barge in the latter days, but earlier it might have been the hull of a worn-out tug or ferry. Cornell used all of these over the years, including one vessel—*James Kent*—which dated from nearly the very beginning of steam navigation on the river. Cornell's stakeboat was moored in the North River on the New Jersey side to keep the moored barges well out of the traffic lanes. Typically, the stakeboat was under the command of a captain whose task it was to assemble the northbound tow in a manner that would permit the empty barges to be dropped off en route without disrupting the integrity of the flotilla. In other words, the first barges off would usually be placed outside and near the after end of the flotilla.

Let us accompany our thirty-two barge tow from Albany to New York. The barges go straight through, but the tugs that leave the upriver port are not the same ones that will drop off the flotilla at the New York stakeboat. Cornell operates through-tows in two segments, and the upriver tugs will exchange tows with the northbound tugs, usually in the vicinity of Poughkeepsie. The exact location of the exchange depends upon the state of the tide, the weight of the respective tows, and the power of the tugs assigned to the two segments.

When the tow starts from the upper river, it is under the care of the diesel tug *Jumbo,* with *Cornell No. 20* as a helper, and the flotilla contains a modest six barges from Albany. As the tow proceeds downstream, barges are added—a pair of brick barges from Sutton & Suderley at Coeymans; then, perhaps, two Dwyer or Wright & Cobb covered barges of bagged cement from the string of cement plants below Catskill. En route, the tow passes the northbound upriver tow shepherded by *Lion* and *John D. Schoonmaker,* which contains empties for the brick yards and cement plants as well as a handful of canal boats headed to Buffalo for grain. After saluting our northbound fleet mates, we pick up three more brick barges from the Hutton, Staples, and Terry yards near East Kingston. From here to below Poughkeepsie, it is a straight run, there being little industry on this part of the river, unless the helper tug calls at Rondout for a Cornell tug "deadheading"—without power and in need of a tow—to New York for dry docking.

Below Poughkeepsie, *Geo. W. Washburn,* the line tug, and *G. W. Decker,* the helper, take charge of the tow. New York Trap Rock Corporation, a major shipper on the river, contributes twelve barges of various grades of crushed stone at its extensive Clinton Point quarry, plus two empty barges headed to Newburgh for repairs. In Newburgh Bay, the Dennings Point brick yard at Beacon adds still another barge load of Trap Rock product, and the two empty barges from Clinton Point are dropped off at Trap Rock's Hudson River Shipyards, just south of the city of Newburgh. The crews of both *Washburn* and *Decker* might reflect that both their vessels had been built at the T. S. Marvel shipyard, a half mile north of the Hudson River plant.

Now the two tugs and their charges get ready for some real steamboating through the magnificent Hudson Highlands, entered at the south end of Newburgh Bay under the forbidding brow of Storm King. They then pass West Point with Magazine Point opposite, making the sweeping turns to port, then starboard, as the tow passes through the appropriately named World's End. The twenty-six barges follow the arc of the tugs' wakes, but dangerous eddies can be encountered here, and the safe passage of the tow is a job well done. Then comes a short, straight run past Highland Falls, under the Bear Mountain Bridge. After another long turn to starboard, past Dunderberg Mountain and Jones Point, *Washburn* and her charges reach the upper end of Haverstraw Bay. Here we meet and pass the northbound tow of empties pulled by the mighty *Perseverance,* with *Edwin Terry* as helper. The Tomkins Cove quarry of Trap Rock adds five more barges to our tow, and a single barge from the De Noyelles brick yard at Haverstraw makes up the last of the thirty-two. From this point on, with no other changes to be made in the flotilla, it will be a non-stop run to the stakeboat. Our 30,000-ton cargo of building materials will eventually contribute to the construction miracle that is New York City. *Washburn* and *Decker* will lay over for the night and start north with another tow of empty barges the following day.

The mission of the helper tug is best described by its name. As the tow proceeds, either up the river or down, the helper tug such as *G. W. Decker* will leave the tow as necessary to drop off or pick up barges at individual customers' wharves. For this to be done on the fly, the line-haul tug will usually slow down sufficiently to make the process of casting off or making fast these barges a safe and speedy operation. A barge having been added to or removed from the tow, the helper then will make fast to the big tug, adding her horsepower to move the sizable amount of real estate at the after end of the hawser. Alternatively, if another move is shortly needed, the helper will make fast alongside the tow itself and put her throttle in "full ahead." As the tow rounds West Point, the helper might be called upon to help keep things under control, depending upon the state of the tide.

Fog has always been the curse of river men. When *Washburn* and *Decker* passed through the Highlands, the weather was ideal—very little wind, the tide at its most favorable, and crystal-clear visibility. It is not always that way. In those pre-radar days (neither *Washburn* nor *Decker* ran late enough to be so equipped), it was frequently necessary to lay to until conditions improved. If that were not done, or the fog descended suddenly upon the tow as she was about to transit World's End, it was the sheer skill of the captain and pilot that got them through safely. This was akin to flying blind, but without instruments and with solid land not far away to port and starboard.

Despite the hazards of the passage, day after day, year after year, these transits of the nearly 150 miles of Hudson River between Albany and New York were surprisingly free from casualty. The fact that *Washburn* and *Decker* had 30,000 tons of barge and cargo almost constantly bearing down on them—tugs on the hawser can pull, but don't have brakes—is testament enough to the skill of the men on the Cornell tugs.

William duBarry Thomas

Appendix C
Instructions to Captains
A Cornell Steamboat Company Memo Early in the Twentieth Century

Captains are held responsible as follows:

1. For seeing that a full crew as requested by boat's papers is on board at all times.

2. For correct making of time sheets and their prompt delivery to the office at the end of each day.

3. For seeing that custom house papers are in order and in the proper place on the steamer, and for notification to the office when such papers are about to expire.

4. For the correct keeping of logs and their prompt delivery to the office. Daily harbor log must contain on its front the name of every boat towed with all information as called for. On the back of the log must be a continuous account of the movements of the tug for the full 24 hours and also notations of all coal and other supplies received. Full details should be entered as to any assistance rendered other steamers. River and canal logs must contain on the front the full list of the tow with all information called for, and on the back the complete record of the movement of the tow as called for.

5. For the prompt report of all damages to the tugs or to other steamers and barges with full details as called for on the blank.

6. For the proper authorization to the cook for purchase of grub supplies on credit so as not to overrun the board allowance and for the proper expenditure of grub money when supplies are purchased for cash.

7. For the ordering of rope, fenders and other supplies and for the return of unused stock.

Appendix D

Geo. W. Washburn, "King of the Hudson"

For more than half a century, the Cornell Steamboat Company, headquartered on the Rondout Creek, was the most dominant force in towing on the Hudson River. From Cornell's incorporation in 1880, when it succeeded the business of Major Thomas Cornell, through the start of the Great Depression of the 1930s, many would-be competitors sought to gain a foothold in this profitable business. Among those who attempted to scuttle the Cornell colossus were the Austin, Washburn, Schuyler, Beverwyck, and Ronan towing lines, as well as the powerful American and Knickerbocker ice companies. All eventually found themselves a part of the Rondout company's extensive holdings, with their vessels wearing the distinctive buff and black stack colors of the Cornell fleet.

Early in 1889, the Cornell fleet was made up of about thirty vessels—ten modern propellers built during the 1880s, and equal numbers of superannuated side-wheel steamers and elderly propeller tugs. Two of the newer vessels, *Edwin Terry* and *Ira M. Hedges*, were iron-hulled tugs built by John H. Dialogue & Sons at Camden, New Jersey, for the Washburn Steamboat Company in 1883 and acquired by Cornell the following year. All the others had wooden hulls, including their most recent vessel, *John D. Schoonmaker*, built at Rondout in 1888. Additional powerful tugs were needed to handle the increasing numbers of barges, canal boats, and sailing vessels that made up their tows to and from ports along the river from Haverstraw to Albany. The company proceeded with plans to built new tugs of iron or steel.

The waterfront gossip of the day, as reported by *The Nautical Gazette*, asked the question uppermost in the minds of those along the river:

> The Cornell Steamboat Company has about decided to build two new tugs next spring. Who will get the contracts?

In the autumn of 1888, Cornell had sent its side-wheel towboat *George A. Hoyt* to Newburgh to be hauled on the marine railway at the Marvel yard for badly needed repairs. *George A. Hoyt*, the last side-wheel towboat built as such for service on the Hudson, was then only in her seventeenth year, having been constructed at New Baltimore in 1873. When she was hauled, her hull was found to be so deteriorated that she was condemned, relaunched, and laid up at the Newburgh shipyard. In July of 1889, Cornell sold this worn-out vessel to Thomas S. Marvel and placed an order with the firm for one of the two tugs about which *The Nautical Gazette* had speculated. Construction of the second would have to wait two years. *George A. Hoyt* was subsequently dismantled at Newburgh.

Bearing the yard's Hull 33, the newly ordered tug was later to carry the name *Geo. W. Washburn*, honoring the Saugerties brick manufacturer whose fleet of tugs, owned by the short-lived Washburn Steamboat Company, had been acquired by Major Cornell five years before. Washburn became a director of the Cornell firm after the 1884 sale of his fleet. *Geo. W. Washburn* was the first of seven tugs that would be built by Thomas S. Marvel for the Cornell Steamboat Company over a period of fifteen years.

The Marvel firm's original quotation for the construction of the vessel, submitted to Cornell in June of 1889, offered three types of boilers: return tube with brick furnaces, marine leg or Scotch. The price for for the vessel equipped with return tube boilers was $59,000; with marine leg boilers, $59,500; and with Scotch boilers, $60,000. The contract was executed on the basis of fitting marine leg boilers, but several negotiated changes from the original specification set the final contract price at $60,000. The returned cost of the vessel to T. S. Marvel & Company was $48,963.56.

Geo. W. Washburn was an iron-hulled vessel of 298 gross and 149 net tons, and measured 123.0 feet by 26.0 feet by 13.8 feet. Her hull was clearly the largest of any tug that had been built at Newburgh up to that time—exceeding in all three dimensions the massive *John H. Cordts*, previously the largest. The new tug's two steel marine-leg boilers, which measured 8 feet in diameter and 15 feet long and delivered steam at a pressure of 120 pounds per square inch, were built by P. Delany & Company at a cost of $9,500. She was fitted with a compound engine from the Marvel shops, having cylinders measuring 24 and 48 inches in diameter with a piston stroke of 36 inches. This engine was slightly smaller

A rare view of the launching of *Geo. W. Washburn* at T. S. Marvel and Company's yard at Newburgh on March 8, 1890. Unlike most vessels, *Washburn* was christened by a male. Sidney Barritt, the twelve-year old son of Captain Newby S. Barritt, of Rondout, was the sponsor. Captain Barritt had supervised the construction of the vessel for Cornell. (William duBarry Thomas Collection)

than that built for *John H. Cordts* by Ward, Stanton & Company in 1883; the cavernous cylinders of that vessel's engine were 28 and 52 inches in diameter with a stroke of 40 inches. (*John H. Cordts* had been built for the Washburn Steamboat Company, but within two years became a member of the Cornell fleet.)

Geo. W. Washburn's engine was described by Howard Eaton, one of her latter-day engineers, as being "long legged." The connecting rods were longer than average, which permitted the crosshead bearings and crank-pin bearings to transmit power from piston to connecting rod to crankshaft with less than average radial motion. This reduced the lateral forces acting on the bearings, which, in turn, reduced bearing wear. The engine was a joy to behold and a greater joy to operate and maintain.

The tug's keel was laid in the autumn of 1889, and work on the hull continued through the winter. She was launched into the Hudson at 1:27 on the afternoon of Saturday, March 8, 1890, having been christened in the age old manner—using a bottle of Mumm's Extra Dry—by Master Sidney Barritt, the twelve-year old son of Captain Newby S. Barritt of Rondout. Barritt, a tugboat captain and sometime owner, was Cornell's superintendent in charge of construction of the vessel. He is best remembered as the owner and master of *Jonty Jenks*, a 50-foot tug that was under his command in the 1870s and early 1880s. Barritt had, in the words of a reporter of the Newburgh *Daily Journal*, "been in the city every other day or two during the building of the boat."

Newburgh's three newspapers reported the events of the day. The Newburgh *Daily News* stated matter-of-factly that "she slid gracefully into the water and her stern parted the thin ice." The Newburgh *Daily Register*'s reporter on the spot was a little more emotional:

> Just as the Washburn left her position on the stays [sic] the Fishkill-on-Hudson, the James T. Brett, and the Field all appeared, it seemed as if by magic, and presented a most beautiful sight.

The "Field" was *George Field*, a Newburgh tug that retrieved the newly launched vessel and towed her back to the shipyard wharf. But it was the scribe from the Newburgh *Daily Journal* who ran off with the prize for Victorian prose that day:

> When the signal for the launch was given, a few blows against the retaining skid were heard by those in the immediate vicinity, and then the vessel began its graceful descent down the ways into the water. Slowly, steadily, and without a tremor the metal structure left the bed which it has occupied for so

many weeks and entered the element wherein it will find a busy existence in the future.

The new vessel had a handsome profile, with a single well-proportioned stack atop a varnished wood deck house. *Geo. W. Washburn* was completed in August of 1890 and enrolled at Albany on the 14th of that month. She was immediately placed in service on the river, commencing a career that was to last nearly sixty years.

About 1920, she was extensively rebuilt. Her two leg boilers, then operating at a pressure much below that for which they were built, had reached the end of their economic life and were replaced with a pair of surplus water-tube boilers purchased from the United States Shipping Board. At about this time, Cornell had purchased the unfinished tugboat hull *Perseverance* from the Shipping Board, along with a triple-expansion engine and two Scotch boilers. These were installed in the incomplete vessel, which was christened with the name assigned by the Shipping Board—*Perseverance*. Her most striking feature was her pair of tall fore-and-aft stacks. When *Geo. W. Washburn* was reboilered, she was given a similar pair of stacks, proportionally not as tall as those of the much larger *Perseverance*, and, in the eyes of many, much more handsome.

Although the Great Depression of the 1930s led to a decrease in the towing business on the river, *Geo. W. Washburn* and her fleet mates continued to run. The business boom of World War II brought a badly needed second breath to the river. The Cornell fleet was relatively busy, and the company prospered for the most part during the war years. Sometime after the end of hostilities and the resultant slackening of business, the big steam tugs were laid up, their places taken by smaller and more economical diesel tugs like *Jumbo* and *Lion*.

In July of 1949, *Geo. W. Washburn* was towed away from the Cornell Steamboat Company's Rondout shops, bound for a New York scrap yard. She had been sold to John Witte, of Rossville, Staten Island, at whose yard—the final resting place of many New York vessels that had come to the ends of their economic lives—she was unceremoniously cut up for scrap. Her old running mates, *Perseverance* and *Stirling Tomkins*, would follow her before the year ended, leaving the Hudson River without a large steam tugboat for the first time since the early 1800s.

Geo. W. Washburn was a special towboat, one of those few vessels that combined great power with an unusually handsome appearance. She was thought by many to have been one of the finest tugs ever built. Her hull lines, typical of those of a Marvel-built tug, were incomparable. They seemed to be paradoxical as well: full enough for a work boat, but at the same time nearly as fine as those of a yacht.

Although many more powerful tugs were built, few could match *Geo. W. Washburn* when power, ease of handling, handsomeness of hull, speed, workmanship, and stateliness were all considered. These separate attributes of the vessel combined to make a magnificent whole. Even her near sister, *Edwin H. Mead*, which emerged from the shipyard of Thomas S. Marvel two years later and was built from nearly the same mold, was completely overshadowed by this regal tug. The steamboat *Mary Powell* was frequently called the "Queen of the Hudson." If she was, then *Geo. W. Washburn* certainly deserves the title "King."

William duBarry Thomas

Appendix E
Fleet List

Thomas Cornell
Thomas W. Cornell and Company
Cornell Steamboat Company
Rhinebeck and Kingston Ferry Company

This fleet list shows vessels owned in whole or in part by Thomas Cornell, Thomas W. Cornell and Company, the Cornell Steamboat Company and the Rhinebeck and Kingston Ferry Company

The side-wheel passenger steamboats are shown first, followed by that unique member of the Cornell fleet, *City of Kingston*, a screw-propeller passenger steamer. Then come the side-wheel towboats. Next, we explore the propeller tugs— from the modest high-pressure boats of the 1860s to state-of-the-art push-towboat *Rockland County* a century later. Finally, the Rhinebeck and Kingston ferries and a few spurious vessels which have crept into the Cornell legend quite erroneously. Not shown are the many vessels which were operated by the company under charter over the years, unless they were later purchased.

The abbreviations used are as follows: O/N = Official Number; GT = Gross Tonnage; NT = Net Tonnage; N/A = Not Applicable. The length, beam and depth shown for vessels extant after 1885 (are statutory dimensions taken from the annual List of Merchant Vessels. These dimensions do not necessarily correspond to moulded dimensions, but were determined according to the tonnage admeasurement rules.

The compiler wishes to point out a caveat when observing the tonnages shown below. The rules for tonnage admeasurement changed significantly during the latter half of the nineteenth century, and, as a result, the tonnages shown for some of the vessels may have varied over their lives. This is especially true with the side-wheel steamboats, where their tonnages may also have been altered as a result of passenger vessels having been converted into towboats. In addition, net tonnage was not incorporated into the tonnage rules until 1882, so that vessels which had ceased to exist by that year are shown with one tonnage only. In general, tonnage admeasurement was (and continues to be) based upon an arcane set of rules. Arguably, the determination of tonnage is politically motivated and bears little resemblance to real-world needs.

Finally, a note about the completeness and accuracy of this fleet list. A fleet list is always a work in progress, and the compiler has attempted to present the information below as accurately as possible. Additions and corrections will always be welcomed by e-mail at purple@catskill.net and will be posted on the website of Purple Mountain Press at www.catskill.net/purple/cornell.htm

SIDE-WHEEL STEAMBOATS

MANHATTAN

O/N 16663 447 GT
Dimensions not known Wooden Hull
Beam Engine

1847: Built as passenger steamboat by Devine Burtis, Brooklyn, NY, for service between Albany and New York. 1855: Purchased by Thomas Cornell for service as night boat between Rondout and New York. 1863: (Mar) Replaced by new steamboat *Thomas Cornell*, and reportedly sold to Anthony Rybold, Delaware City, DE, to run on Patuxent River. During Civil War ran between Philadelphia and Cape May, and was chartered to Federal government on several occasions. c1865: Sold for service between Mobile, AL, and New Orleans, LA. 1965 (May 13) Damaged by fire at New Orleans; later rebuilt. 1869: Abandoned after vessel sank in Mobile Bay. Raised and returned to Delaware River. Subsequently dismantled at Wilmington, DE.

MARY POWELL

O/N 16982 819-87/95 GT
267' x 34'-6" x 9'-2" (as built) Wooden Hull
Beam Engine 62" (later 72")' x 144"

1861: Built by Michael J. Allison, Jersey City, NJ, for Absalom L. Anderson et al, Rondout, NY. 1862: Lengthened to 288.' Tonnage now 889-78/95 GT. 1865: Readmeasured under new rules; 983 GT (from 1883, also 877 NT). 1865 (17 Oct):

Purchased by Thomas Cornell, Rondout, NY. Same day half interest sold to Daniel Drew. 1867 (26 Feb): Thomas Cornell again sole owner. 1869 (12 Jul): Sold to Alfred Van Santvoord and J. McB. Davidson. 1872 (Jul): Sold to Absalom L. Anderson. 1875: New cylinder 72" diameter. 1883 (29 Jan): Purchased by Thomas Cornell. 1885 (May): Sold to Mary Powell Steamboat Co. 1917 (5 Sep): Last trip. Laid up in Rondout Creek. 1919 (19 Nov): Sold to Newburgh Iron & Metal Co. 1920 (17 Apr): Sold to John A. Fischer, Rondout, NY. Dismantled in Rondout Creek.

NORTH AMERICA

O/N (N/A)   499-33/95 GT
222'-0" x 25'-6" x 9'-0"   Wooden Hull
Beam Engine   48" x 132"

1840: Built as passenger steamboat by Devine Burtis, Brooklyn, NY, for Isaac Newton et al. Later owned by William B. Dodge, then sold to William Hunt, then back to William B. Dodge. 1851: Purchased by Thomas Cornell from William B. Dodge. 1852: Sold to Charles Anderson et al, New York, NY. 1863 (Jul): Sold to United States Army Quartermasters Dept. 1863 (8 Oct): Burned at Algiers, LA. (The persons shown represent only a few who owned this vessel, which changed hands frequently before and after Thomas Cornell's ownership.)

RIP VAN WINKLE

O/N 21450   465 GT
240'-0" x 26-8" x 8'-8"   Wooden Hull
Beam Engine   54" x 120"

1845: Built as passenger steamboat by George Collyer, New York, NY, for the Schuyler Line of Albany, of which H. Morton, was the managing owner. 1851: Sold to Daniel Drew, of New York. 1852: Acquired by Absalom Anderson, Nathan Anderson and William F. Romer, of Rondout. 1871: Purchased by Thomas Cornell from Ovid J. Simmons, Saugerties, NY. 1872 (16 Apr): Collided with bridge abutment at Albany, NY, shearing off starboard wheel and shaft, and heavily damaging the engine. Vessel subsequently dismantled. (The persons shown above represent only a few who owned or managed this vessel before Thomas Cornell's ownership.)

THOMAS CORNELL

O/N 24756   1024 GT
310' x 34' x 10'   Wooden Hull
Beam Engine   72" x 144"   600 NHP

1863: Built as passenger steamboat by Elisha S. Whitlock, Greenpoint, NY, for Thomas Cornell for service between Rondout and New York. Launched on 20 January 1863 and trials on 15 September. 1882 (27 Mar): Ran aground on Danskammer Point, above Roseton, NY, in fog while bound from Rondout to New York. Later towed to Rondout, machinery removed and hull cut in half and converted to two coal barges.

WILLIAM COOK

O/N 26577   982 GT   173 NT
265'-0" x 30'-0" x 11'-0"   Wooden Hull
Beam Engine   56" x 144"

1865 (Oct): Built as passenger steamboat at Hoboken, NJ, for Camden & Amboy Railroad for service between New York and Long Branch, NJ. 1872: Laid up. 1874: Purchased by Thomas Cornell. 1877: Placed on express milk route between Rondout and New York. Vessel popularly known as "The Milkmaid" during this period. 1881: Place in excursion service at New York. 1884: Abandoned.

PROPELLER STEAMBOAT

CITY OF KINGSTON

O/N 126214   1117 GT   816 NT
240.0' x 33.5' x 12.5'   Iron Hull
Compound Engine   30"-56" x 36"   1400 HP

1884 (May): Built by Harlan & Hollingsworth Co., Wilmington, DE, for Cornell Steamboat Co. for service between Rondout and New York. Launched 11 March. First trip from New York to Rondout on 31 May. 1889 (Sep): Sold to Puget Sound and Alaska Steamship Co. Fitted for voyage to West Coast at T. S. Marvel & Co., Newburgh, NY. 1889 (18 Nov): Sailed from New York. 1890 (early Jan): Passed through Strait of Magellan. On 17 Feb arrived at Port Townsend, WA. Ran between Tacoma, WA, and Bellingham, WA, making intermediate landings; later between Tacoma and Victoria, BC. 1899 (23 Apr): Sank after collision at 0430 hrs. with British steamship *Glenogle* off Brown's Point, near Tacoma, while inbound to that port.

SIDE-WHEEL TOWBOATS

A. B. VALENTINE

O/N 1937   308 GT   191 NT
205.0' x 25.0' x 9.0'   Wooden Hull
Beam Engine: 48" x 120"

1869: Rebuilt from towboat *Santa Claus* (q.v.) by James S. Dean, Red Hook (Brooklyn), NY, for Thomas Cornell. Launched on 31 March. Hull, with engine, towed to Rondout for installation of boilers and joiner work. 1901: Sold to J. H. Gregory, Perth Amboy, NJ, and dismantled. Left Rondout for Perth Amboy on 17 December of that year. (Named for Thomas Cornell's longtime representative at New York.)

ALIDA

O/N 866   608 GT   Later: 528 GT (as towboat)
249'-5" x 28'-6" x 9'-9" (as built)   Wooden Hull
Beam Engine   56" (later 62") x 144"

1847: Built as passenger steamboat by William H. Brown, New York, NY. 1848 (Apr): Lengthened to 272'-0" x 29'-0" x 10'-0" prior to this date. 1855: Sold to Alfred Van Santvoord. Late 1860s: Converted to towboat. Sold to Robinson & Betts, Troy, NY. 1875: Purchased by Thomas Cornell from Robinson & Betts. Last ran in December of that year. 1880: Sold to Daniel Bigler for scrap. 1883: Dismantled at Port Ewen, NY.

AMERICA

O/N 1704   441 GT   Later: 407 GT   235 NT
220.0' x 30.0' x 9.0'   Wooden Hull
Beam Engine   76" x 132"

1852: Built as towboat at Brooklyn, NY, for Samuel Schuyler, Albany, NY. 1890: Sold to Beverwyck Towing Line. 1894 (Aug): Purchased by Cornell Steamboat Co. from Beverwyck Towing Line. 1902: Sold to J. H. Gregory, Perth Amboy, NJ, for scrap. (*America* was the third large side-wheeler built as a towboat.)

AUSTIN

O/N 1707   380 GT   257 NT
197.0' x 31.3' x 8.3'   Wooden Hull
Beam Engine   60" x 120"   400 HP

1853: Built as towboat at Hoboken, NJ, for Albany & Canal Towing Line (Jeremiah Austin), Albany, NY. 1876: Purchased by Thomas Cornell. 1898: Last year of service. 1899 (Summer): Sold to J. H. Gregory, Perth Amboy, NJ, for scrap. (*Austin* was the fourth large side-wheeler built as a towboat.)

BALTIC

O/N 2640   372 GT   Later: 287 GT (as towboat)
170' (other dimensions not known)   Wooden Hull
Beam Engine   48" x 120"   375 HP

1849: Built as passenger steamboat at Greenpoint, NY for service between Greenport, NY, and Saybrook, CT. c 1852: Sold to Samuel Schuyler, Albany, NY, and converted to towboat. 1869: Acquired by Thomas Cornell from Samuel Schuyler in exchange for towboat *Cayuga*. 1876 (19 Jul): Burned at Van Wies Point, below Albany, NY. Wreck raised, towed to Rondout, where engine and boilers were removed and hull dismantled.

C. VANDERBILT

O/N 4856   689 GT   481 NT
300.0' x 36.0' x 9.0'   Wooden Hull
Beam Engine   72" x 144"

1847: Built as passenger steamboat at New York, NY, for Cornelius Vanderbilt for service on Long Island Sound. 1857: To Hudson River as Troy night boat. 1873: Sold to Robinson, Leonard & Betts and converted to towboat. 1875: Sold to Samuel Schuyler, Albany, NY. 1879 (5 Jun): Engine heavily damaged while off Nyack, NY. Rebuilt. 1890: Sold to Beverwyck Towing Line. 1894 (Aug): Purchased by Cornell Steamboat Co. from Beverwyck Towing Line. Apparently never used by Cornell. 1896: Dismantled at Rondout, NY.

CAYUGA

O/N 4901   471 GT   Later: 398 GT
210.0' x 28.5' x 9.0'   Wooden Hull
Beam Engine   62" x 132"

1849: Built as towboat at New York, NY, probably for Alfred Van Santvoord. Engine built by Henry R. Dunham & Co., New York. 1869: Purchased by Thomas Cornell from Alfred Van Santvoord. Then acquired by Samuel Schuyler from Thomas Cornell in exchange for towboat *Baltic*. 1886 (Autumn): Engine heavily damaged. Vessel laid up. c1887: Dismantled and hull converted to coal barge. (*Cayuga* was the second large side-wheeler built as a towboat.)

CERES

O/N 4875   124 GT   78 NT
107.0' x 23.6' x 6.9'   Wooden Hull
Beam Engine   30" x 72"

1856: Built as towboat by Benjamin Terry, Keyport, NJ. Engine built by Berryman & Storms, Jersey City, NJ. 1861 (Sep): Sold to United States Navy and became USS *Ceres*. Armed merchant vessel (one 32-pounder, one 30-pounder) in Virginia and North Carolina waters. 1864 (May): Took part in sinking and later salvage of Confederate ram CSS *Albemarle*. 1865 (Oct): Purchased by Thomas Cornell. 1887: Dismantled at Rondout.

EMERALD

O/N (N/A)   245-92/95 GT
132'-2" x 23'-0" x 8'-7"   Wooden Hull
Crosshead Engine

1825: Built as passenger steamer by Lawrence & Sneden, New York, NY, for Thomas Gibbons and Cornelius Vanderbilt. Shortly afterwards, burned at New Brunswick, NJ, Rebuilt. 1834: Lengthened by about 24.' New dimensions and tonnage: 156.6' x 23.6' x 8.7' and 307-90/95 tons. 1835: Sold to People's Line. 1837: Sold to Jacob H. Tremper. c1850s: Purchased by Thomas Cornell Later converted to towboat. 1857: Said to have been abandoned. (The history of *Emerald* has been the subject of much misinformation and inconsistency over the years.)

FRANCIS H. CARTER

O/N 9822   114 GT
Dimensions not known   Wooden Hull
Beam Engine

c1850: Built as *Onondaga* on Onondaga Lake at Brewerton, NY. Brought to Hudson River and in 1860 rebuilt as *Francis H. Carter* at Rondout, NY for Thomas Cornell. 1861 (Aug): Damaged by fire and scuttled at New York. Raised and rebuilt. 1862: First documented. 1885: Abandoned. (Name *Frank Carter* appeared on wheelboxes. Allegedly, the vessel was erroneously called *Francis H. Carter* instead of *Frances A. Carter*.)

GENERAL McDONALD

O/N 10979   541 GT   424 NT
222.0' x 29.7' x 9.7'   Wooden Hull
Beam Engine   68" x 132"

1851: Built as passenger steamboat at Baltimore, MD. Ran from Baltimore to Frenchtown, MD. Later ran from Philadelphia to Cape May, followed by service at New York. 1855: Sold to Albany and Canal Towing Line (Jeremiah Austin), Albany NY, and converted to towboat. 1876: Purchased by Thomas Cornell from Austin. 1905: Sold to J. H. Gregory, Perth Amboy, NJ, and dismantled. (*General McDonald* was the subject of the Cornell Steamboat Company's experimentation with oil fuel around 1901.)

GEORGE A. HOYT

O/N 85287   298 GT   204 NT
165.2' x 30.5' x 9.4'   Wooden Hull
Beam Engine

1873: Built as towboat at New Baltimore, NY for Thomas Cornell. 1888 (Autumn): Hauled on marine railway at T. S. Marvel & Co., Newburgh, NY. Hull found to badly deteriorated. 1889 (Jul): Sold to T. S. Marvel & Co. and broken up at Newburgh. (*George A. Hoyt* was the seventh and last side-wheel towboat on the Hudson River expressly built for that purpose.)

HERALD

O/N 11936   394 GT
215.0' x 25.0' x 10.0' (after 1849)   Wooden Hull
Beam Engine   40" x 132"

1842: Built by Brown & Collyer, Baltimore, MD, as passenger steamboat *Medora* for Baltimore Steam Packet Co. (Old Bay Line). Boiler exploded at start of trial trip on 14 April. Twenty-six persons killed, including president of company. Vessel sunk but raised and hull rebuilt as *Herald* for Old Bay Line. 1849: Lengthened about 31 feet. 1862: Purchased by Thomas Cornell and converted to towboat. Tonnage then 329. 1863 (5 Dec): Rescued many persons from burning steamboat *Isaac Newton* opposite Fort Lee, NJ. 1880: Retired from service. Later dismantled. (Some sources state that *Herald* was dismantled in 1881, but document were not surrendered until 1885.)

HIGHLANDER

O/N (N/A)   313 GT
160' x 24' x 8'   Wooden Hull
Beam Engine   41" x 120"

1835: Built as passenger steamboat by Lawrence & Sneeden, New York, NY, for Thomas Powell et al, Newburgh, NY, for service between Newburgh and New York. Later ran as excursion steamer and between Rondout and New York. c1851: Purchased by Thomas Cornell and converted to towboat. 1852: Sold to Stephen Flanagan & Company, Philadelphia, for use as a towboat. 1866: Dismantled and engine used in new iron-hulled towboat *William H. Aspinwall*, built at Philadelphia.

JACOB LEONARD

O/N 75401   105 GT   55 NT
125.0' x 40.3' x 6.3'   Wooden Hull
Beam Engine   34" x 96"

1872: Built as towboat at New Baltimore, NY, for Robinson & Betts (Troy Towing Line), Troy, NY. 1874: Sold to Samuel Schuyler, Albany, NY. 1890: Sold to Beverwyck Towing Line, Albany, NY. 1894 (Aug): Purchased by Cornell Steamboat Co. from Beverwyck Towing Line. 1895: Dismantled. (Beam shown above is from official records but is erroneous. Actual moulded beam was 28'-3". Possibly never ran for Cornell Steamboat Co.)

JAMES KENT

O/N (N/A)   364 GT
135' x 31'   Wooden Hull
Engine Type and Dimensions unknown

Although *James Kent* was owed by Thomas Cornell as a stake boat at Weehawken, NJ, long after her active career had ended, she is included here because of her historical significance. Built in 1823 by Blossom, Smith & Dimon, New York, NY, as the last vessel for Robert Fulton and Chancellor Livingston before the February 1824 United States Supreme Court decision (Gibbons vs. Ogden)that ended Fulton's monopoly. Engine built by James P. Allaire. 1828: Ran between New York and Hartford, CT. 1842: Abandoned and later converted to a coal barge for the Delaware & Hudson Coal Co. c1860: Purchased by Thomas Cornell and converted to stake boat. 1895: Dismantled.

JAMES MADISON

O/N 75039   324 GT
170' (about) Other dimensions not known   Wooden Hull
Beam Engine   40" x 120" (probably)

1836: Built as passenger steamboat by J. Vaughan, Philadelphia, PA, for Benjamin Carpenter for service between Newburgh and New York. 1845: Ran between Albany and New York. 1846: Renamed *Oneida*. 1848: Renamed *James Madison*. 1850: Purchased by Thomas Cornell and converted to towboat. 1852 (28 Jul): Rescued survivors from burning of steamboat *Henry Clay*. 1872: Parts of engine to new towboat *Geo. A. Hoyt* (q.v.) Vessel sold to George Bigler, of Port Ewen, NY, and broken up.

JOHN F. RODMAN

O/N (N/A)   41 GT
73'-7" x 14' x 4'-4"   Wooden Hull

Beam Engine

1849: Built as towboat at Nyack, NY, probably for Jeremiah A. Houghtaling (3/12), Thomas Cornell (5/12) and Peter Dubois (4/12), Esopus, NY. 1850 (Dec): Charles A. Traver (3/12), Thomas Cornell (5/12) and Peter Dubois (4/12), Kingston, NY. 1853 (Mar): John C. Bard, Caldwell's Landing, NY. 1856 (Apr): Edward Van Wart and John C. Bard. 1857 (May): John C. Bard and James Conklin. 1857 (Sep): John C. Bard. 1865 (May): A. C. Hall and W. Applegarth, Baltimore, MD. 1865 (Dec): A. C. Hall, W. Applegarth and W. C. Johnson. 1867: Abandoned.

JOHN MARSHALL

O/N 75043   449 GT
200' x 26' x 8'   Wooden Hull
Beam Engine   50" x 132"

1844: Built as passenger steamboat at Baltimore for service on Chesapeake Bay. Later ran between Boston and Portland, ME, then back to Chesapeake Bay. 1856: Sold to owners at Albany. Converted to towboat. 1863: Purchased by Thomas Cornell. 1867 (Dec): Engine room accident resulted in scalding of two crew members. 1882 (Spring): Retired from service. 1887: Sold, dismantled and hull converted to barge.

MADISON COUNTY

O/N 17925   124 GT
Dimensions not known   Wooden Hull
Beam Engine

1851: Built as passenger steamboat on Onondaga Lake at Brewerton, NY c1859: Brought to Hudson River and rebuilt as towboat at Rondout, NY, for Thomas Cornell. 1875: Dismantled.

MAURICE WURTS

O/N 17006   95 GT   Later: 180 GT
94'-7" in length   Wooden Hull
Beam Engine

1851: Built as double-ended towboat at New York, NY, for Delaware & Hudson Canal Co. c1852: Rebuilt as single-ender with conventional bow. Date uncertain: Purchased by Thomas Cornell. 1876: Abandoned.

MOHEGAN

O/N (N/A)   399 GT
180'-9" x 25'-0" x 9'-2"   Wooden Hull
Beam Engine

1839: Built as passenger steamboat at New York, NY, for Long Island Sound service. 1847: Sold to William B. Dodge et al. 1850: Purchased by Thomas Cornell and converted to towboat. 1856: Abandoned.

MOUNT WASHINGTON

O/N 17009   359 GT   Later: 194 GT
190'-0" x 24'-0" x 7'-0"   Wooden Hull
Beam Engine

1846: Built at Philadelphia as passenger steamboat *Mount Vernon* for Washington and Fredericksburg Steamboat Co. 1861 (Apr): Sold to U. S. Army Quartermaster Dept. Later USS *Mount Vernon*, then USS *Mount Washington*. 1865: Sold to Joseph and Henry Pratt, Troy, NY. Redocumented as *Mount Washington* and converted to towboat. 1870: Sold to Robinson & Betts, Troy, NY. 1875: Purchased by Thomas Cornell from Robinson & Betts. 1880: Abandoned. 1881: Sold to George Bigler and dismantled at Port Ewen, NY.

NEW YORK

O/N 18657   524 GT   Later: 383 GT (as towboat)
230' x 23'   Wooden Hull
Crosshead Engine   52" x 120"   350 HP

1836: Built as passenger steamboat by Lawrence & Sneden, New York, NY, for New York and New Haven Steamboat Co. for service between those points. 1839: Sold to Cornelius Vanderbilt. c1856: Sold to Alfred Van Santvoord and converted to towboat. 1869: Purchased by Thomas Cornell from Alfred Van Santvoord. 1875: Retired and sold to Levi Bacharach, Rondout, NY, and dismantled near Kingston Point.

NIAGARA

O/N 18577   510 GT   352 NT
265'-0" x 28'-6" x 9'-3"   Wooden Hull
Beam Engine   60" (later 65")' x 132"

1844: Built as passenger steamboat by George Collyer, New York, NY, for Troy Line. 1848: Sold to Housatonic Railroad for service between Bridgeport and New York. 1854: Returned to Hudson River and later converted to towboat for Samuel Schuyler. 1890: Sold to Beverwyck Towing Line. 1894 (Aug): Purchased by Cornell Steamboat Co. from Beverwyck Towing Line. 1898: Dismantled.

NORWICH

O/N 18578   255 GT   127 NT
160.0' x 25.0' x 8.6'   Wooden Hull
Crosshead Engine   40" x 120"   450 HP

1836: Built as passenger steamboat by Lawrence & Sneden, New York, NY, for New London & Norwich Steamboat Co., for service between Norwich, CT, and New York. 1841 (Jul to Dec): Chartered to Baltimore Steam Packet Co. to run between Baltimore and Norfolk, then returned to Long Island Sound. 1842: Sold to James Cunningham, New York, NY for service between Rondout and New York. 1843 (28 Dec): Sold to Isaac Newton and Daniel Drew; same day sold to William B. Dodge and John S. Moore, Rondout, NY 1848 (Aug): Purchased by Thomas W. Cornell & Co. from William B. Dodge. 1851: Henceforth devoted almost exclusively to towing. 1877 (24 Jun): Collided with steamboat *St. John* near Coxsackie, NY. 1882 (26 Nov): Engine badly damaged by failure of crosshead near Piermont, NY. 1906 (16 Dec): Burned and sank while laid up in Rondout Creek. 1909 (30 Aug): Damaged by fire at Cornell shops, Rondout Creek. Repaired in time to participate in Hudson-Fulton Celebration as "Oldest Steamboat in the World." 1917 (19 Mar): Sank in Rondout Creek. Later raised. Last year of active service. 1923 (Nov): Sold to Michael Tucker and dismantled at Port Ewen, NY. (*Norwich* was the last side-wheel towboat in existence on the Hudson River.)

OSWEGO

O/N 19035   329 GT   211 NT
212.0' x 28.0' x 8.0'   Wooden Hull
Beam Engine   52" x 132"   700 HP

1848: Built as towboat by Capes & Burtis, Brooklyn, NY, for Alfred Van Santvoord. 1869 (Jan): Purchased by Thomas Cornell from Alfred Van Santvoord. 1918 (Sep): Last ran. Laid up in Rondout Creek. 1921: Dismantled above Kingston Point. (*Oswego* was the first large side-wheeler built as a towboat.)

P. C. SCHULTZ

O/N 19905   158 GT   103 NT
123.9' x 22.0' x 8.7'   Wooden Hull
Beam Engine   32" x 84"   80 HP

1863: Built as towboat by Benjamin Terry, Keyport, NJ, for Peter C. Schultz. Later sold to A. C. Cheney (Cheney Towing Line), Albany, NY. 1892 (Apr): Purchased by Cornell Steamboat Co. from Cheney Towing Line. 1900: Dismantled.

PITTSTON

O/N 19910   94 GT   58 NT
108.0' x 20.0' x 6.0'   Wooden Hull
Beam Engine   32" x 96"

1852: Built as towboat by Eckford Webb, Greenpoint, NY (some sources say New York, NY) for Pennsylvania Coal Co. 1868: Purchased by Thomas Cornell. 1909 (Sep): Sold for scrap.

SANDY

O/N 115175   45 GT   22 NT
91.0' x 19.5' x 5.8'   Wooden Hull
Beam Engine

1870: Rebuilt from towboat *Sarah E. Brown* (q.v.) at Rondout, NY, for Thomas Cornell for service around Rondout Creek. 1893 (about): Dismantled after having sunk during March 1893 freshet in the Rondout Creek. (Named for "Sandy" Forsyth, longtime captain of Cornell steamboats.)

SANTA CLAUS

O/N 23689   358-48/95 GT
181'-5" x 24'-3" x 8'-5"   Wooden Hull
Beam Engine   42" (later 48")' x 120"

1845: Built as passenger steamboat by William and Thomas Collyer, New York, NY, for E. Fitch & Co., Wilbur, NY. 1847: Lengthened. New dimensions 209' x 24.6' x 8.3'. 1853: Purchased by Thomas Cornell from E. Fitch & Co. 1855: Converted to towboat. 1868: Abandoned. During the winter of 1868-69 rebuilt as towboat *A. B. Valentine* (q.v.)

SARAH E. BROWN

O/N 23259   82 GT
91.0' x 19.5' x 5.8'   Wooden Hull
Beam Engine

1852: Built as towboat at Astoria, NY. Date uncertain: Purchased by Thomas Cornell. 1870: Rebuilt as towboat *Sandy* (q.v.) at Rondout, NY. (Reportedly had initials "S. E. B." on her wheelboxes rather than her full name, which led to vessel being referred to informally by local boatmen as "Suckers, Eels and Bullheads.")

SILAS O. PIERCE

O/N 22806   129 GT   78 NT
159.0' x 28.0' x 4.0'   Wooden Hull
Beam Engine   34" x 84"

1863: Built as towboat by Morton & Edmonds, Athens, NY, for Thomas A. Briggs. Chartered to the Federal Government during Civil War. First vessel to pass through Dutch Gap on James River, VA. Carried Jefferson Davis and family to Fortress Monroe at end of hostilities. 1865: Sold to Albany and Canal Towing Line (Jeremiah Austin), Albany, NY. 1876: Purchased by Thomas Cornell. 1911 (Autumn): Dismantled at Rondout.

SYRACUSE

O/N 23692   608 GT   459 NT
218.0' x 33.0' x 9.0'   Wooden Hull
Beam Engine   72" x 144"

1857: Built as towboat at Hoboken, NJ, for Albany & Canal Towing Line (Jeremiah Austin), Albany, NY. 1876: Sold to Samuel Schuyler, Albany, NY. 1890: Sold to Beverwyck Towing Line. 1894 (Aug): Purchased by Cornell Steamboat Co. from Beverwyck Towing Line. 1898: Sold to J. H. Gregory, Perth Amboy, NY, and dismantled. (*Syracuse* was the sixth large side-wheeler built as a towboat.)

TELEGRAPH

O/N (N/A)   243 GT
Dimensions not known   Wooden Hull
Beam Engine

1836: Built as passenger steamboat at New York, NY. 1847: Sold to Thomas W. Cornell & Co. for service between Rondout and New York. Later ran from Newburgh to Albany and Troy, then utilized as towboat. 1870 (28 Jun): Collided with steamboat *Drew* and sank off four miles south of Catskill, NY.

WALTER B. CRANE

O/N 80001   72 GT   44 NT
88.0' x 20.0' x 5.0'   Wooden Hull
Beam Engine   60 HP

1853: Built as towboat at Hoboken, NJ, for Thomas Cornell and Peter Dubois, for service in Rondout Creek. 1863: (Mar) Thomas Cornell purchased Dubois' interest in the vessel. 1887: Sank at Port Ewen, NY, and subsequently abandoned. Engine removed; boiler marked location of resting place for many years.

WASHINGTON

O/N (N/A)   258 GT
139'-10" X 22'-10" X 8'-9"   Wooden Hull
Crosshead Engine   36" x 102"

1833: Built as passenger steamboat by Lawrence & Sneden, New York, NY. c.1836: Lengthened to 162' x 22'-10" x 8'-9". 311 GT. 1854: Purchased by Thomas Cornell from Daily Line and converted to towboat. 1859 (Dec): Converted to barge. Disposition not known.

PROPELLER TUGS

Thomas Cornell acquired his first propeller tug, *H. P. Farrington*, in 1862. She was followed by others built or purchased through 1872. Between 1881 and 1883, four modern tugs were built, and in 1890 the age of iron and steel commenced in the fleet. with the construction of *Geo. W. Washburn*.

Major additions were made to the fleet with the purchase of competitors' vessels in 1892, 1894, 1901, 1903 and 1913. Further highlights include the dieselization program of the 1920s and the revitalization of the fleet in the 1950s.

A. C. CHENEY

O/N 105710   186 GT   93 NT
116.0' x 26.8' x 10.1'   Wooden Hull
Single Cylinder Engine   32" x 42"   450 HP

1877: Built by Bulman & Brown, Newburgh, NY, for Cheney Towing Line. 1892 (Apr): Purchased by Cornell Steamboat Co. from Cheney Towing Line. 1910 Condemned by steamboat inspectors. (Nov.): Abandoned.

ADRIATIC

O/N 786   41 GT   20 NT
60.1' x 16.7' x 7.0'   Iron Hull
Single Cylinder Engine

1860 (Apr): Built Harlan & Hollingsworth Co., Wilmington DE (Hull 66) for Stephen and James M. Flanagan, Philadelphia, PA. (Many minor changes of ownership through 1877, with Flanagan Brothers interest decreasing, and that of E. E. Conklin increasing. Vessel moved from Philadelphia to New York in 1865). 1877 (Oct): Owen and Horace Dennett, and E. E. Conklin, New York, NY. (Same day owner altered to Hudson River Towing Co.) 1880 (Aug): Sold to Cheney Towing Line, New York, NY. 1892 (Apr): Purchased by Cornell Steamboat Co. from Cheney Towing Line. 1896 (Nov): Sold to Charles McNally, Saugerties, NY Renamed *H. L. Finger*. 1902 (Aug): Sold to Thomas A. Quigley and Michael K. Neville, Brooklyn, NY. 1903 (Apr): Renamed *Gladys*. 1905 (May): Sold to George M. Musier, Alsen, NY 1913 (Dec): Abandoned.

ALICIA A. WASHBURN

O/N 105942   207 GT   160 NT
136.6' x 29.8' x 9.5'   Wooden Hull
Single Cylinder Engine, Condensing   200 HP

1880: Built as a combination tug and deck lighter by Ward, Stanton & Co., Newburgh, NY, for Washburn Steamboat Co., Saugerties, NY 1884: Purchased by Cornell Steamboat Co. from Washburn Steamboat Co. Never documented under ownership of Cornell Steamboat Co. and possibly never operated by them. 1884 (Oct): Sold to Samuel Holmes, then to "Florida parties." Traded in Gulf of Mexico. 1886 (9 Jan): Burned and sank in Gulf of Mexico while on voyage from Mobile to New York with cargo of cotton. (Vessel could carry deck load of 300 tons of brick in addition to towing barges.)

BEAR

O/N 219483   181 GT   32 NT
95.5' x 24.7' x 12.2'   Wooden Hull
Compound Engine   18"-38" x 26"   450 HP

1920: Built by Leathem & Smith T. & W. Co, Sturgeon Bay, WI, for United States Shipping Board (Design 1086). Purchased by Cornell Steamboat Co. from United States Shipping Board. Rarely used, if at all, after 1930s. 1949: Abandoned. Scuttled at Port Ewen, NY. Sister vessel: *Burro*.

BETTY

O/N 239971   138 GT   66 NT
75.9' x 23.0' x 10.8'   Steel Hull
4-cyl National Diesel Engine   600 HP

1940: Built as *H. F. DeBardeleben* (Hull 107) by Equitable Equipment Co., Madisonville, LA, for DeBardeleben Coal Co., New Orleans, LA. Later Coyle Lines, Inc. 1957: Purchased from Ship Service, Inc. Renamed *Betty*. 1958: Transferred to Lenroc Towing Corp. 1959: Sold to Olson Towboat Co., Eureka, CA. Renamed *Virginia Phillips*. 1969: Sold to Oscar C. Niemeth, Lafayette, CA. Renamed *Blue Eagle*. 1970: Sold to Shellmaker, Inc., San Francisco, CA. 1972: Sold to C.I.C. Leasing Corp., Los Angeles, CA. 1974: Sold to Carson Porter, Morro Bay, CA.

BISMARCK

O/N 3398   124 GT   62 NT
94.6' x 22.2' x 10.0'   Wooden Hull
Compound Engine   20"-36" x 26"   425 HP

1888: Built at Philadelphia, PA, for Ross & Howell, Bangor, ME. 1902: Sold to James T. Morse, Boston, MA. 1907: Transferred to Knickerbocker Steam Towage Co., Bangor, ME. 1913 (Aug): Purchased by Cornell Steamboat Co. from Knickerbocker Steam Towage Co. 1914 (Nov): Sold to Peter Cahill (Cahill Towing Line), New York. 1927 (Apr): Dismantled.

BRITANNIA

O/N 3105   317 GT   200 NT
100.0' x 21.0' x 9.5'   Wooden Hull
Compound Engine   16"-38" x 28"   325 HP

1879: Built by Ward, Stanton & C0., Newburgh, NY for Frederick Luckenbach and Jacob F. Genthner. 1898: Sold to British owners for service at Bermuda. 1906: Redocumented as American vessel by Joseph B. Morrell, New York, NY. 1908: Sold to Knickerbocker Steam Towage Co., Bangor, ME. Later served on Hudson River. 1913 (Aug): Purchased by Cornell Steamboat Co. from Knickerbocker Steam Towage Co. 1917 (Feb): Sold to Eastern Transportation Co., Baltimore, MD. 1931 (Feb): Abandoned.

BURRO

O/N 219565   179 GT   30 NT
95.5' x 24.7' x 12.2'   Wooden Hull

Compound Engine   18"-38" x 26"   450 HP

1920: Built for United States Shipping Board (Design 1086) by Leathem & Smith Towing & Wrecking Co, Sturgeon Bay, WI. 1920: Purchased by Cornell Steamboat Co. from United States Shipping Board. 1925 (c25 Mar): Sold to E. E. Barrett & Co., New York, NY and renamed *Geo. N. Barrett*. 1949: Sold to Moran Towing & Transportation Co., New York, NY. 1954 (Jul): Dismantled. Sister vessel: *Bear*. (The early departure of *Burro*, a new vessel, from the Cornell fleet might at first be attributed to the realization by the company that she would be surplus to their needs. Two other factors may have contributed to her sale: First, her purchase, along with *Bear*, might have put an unforseen financial strain on the company in the face of the level of traffic experienced on the river during the post-WWI period, and, less likely, the Design 1086 tugs, eminently satisfactory as docking tugs, may have been less so in line-haul river towing.)

C. D. MILLS

O/N 5661   33 GT   16 NT
66.0' x 15.0' x 6.8'   Wooden Hull
Single Cylinder Engine

1864: Built at East Albany, NY 1864: Purchased by Thomas Cornell from John Dillon et al. 1904 (Nov): Dismantled

C. W. MORSE

O/N 126574   509 GT   254 NT
154.4' x 30.0' x 17.6'   Wooden Hull
Compound Engine   32"-55" x 36"   1050 HP

1889 (Aug): Built at Philadelphia, PA, for The Morse Transportation Co., Bath, ME. 1899 (Aug): Transferred to Knickerbocker Steam Towage Co. 1903 (Feb): Purchased by Cornell Steamboat Co. from Knickerbocker Steam Towage Co. 1912 (Mar): Sold to McAllister Bros., New York, NY. 1916 (17 Jul): Sold to Sugar Products Shipping Co., Inc., New York, NY. Same day, vessel cleared New York for Africa via San Juan and never heard from again. Presumed to have foundered. Registry document surrendered at New York on 14 Sep 1916.

CAMELIA

O/N 4867   128 GT   64 NT
113.0' x 19.0' x 10.3'   Wooden Hull
Single Cylinder Engine   30" x 30"

1862: Built as *Governor* at Buffalo, NY for Rufus C. Palmer et al, Buffalo, NY. 1863 (17 Sep): Sold to United States Navy. Renamed USS *Camelia*. 1865 (15 Aug): Sold at auction to John Potts, New York, NY. Date uncertain: Sold to Cheney Towing Line, New York, NY. 1892 (Apr): Purchased by Cornell Steamboat Co. from Cheney Towing Line. 1905: Abandoned

CHARLIE LAWRENCE
[later *Cornell* (II)]

O/N 125314   48 GT   24 NT
74.0' x 17.3' x 7.2'   Wooden Hull
Single Cylinder Engine   18" x 18"

1874 (Dec): Built as *Charlie Lawrence* at Philadelphia, PA, for Isaac Albertson, Philadelphia. 1878 (Dec): Sold to David and James Baird, and James P. Stetson, all of Camden, NJ. 1880 (Feb): Sold to Francis C. Cates, Boston, MA, thence to a partnership of 23 person of Boston, MA, including B. C. Morse and George H. Morse. 1881 (Aug): Sold to Abraham Rich (Kennebec Steam Towage Co.), Gardiner, ME. 1911 (Mar): Sold to Knickerbocker Steam Towage Co., New York. 1913: Purchased by Cornell Steamboat Co. from Knickerbocker Steam Towage Co. 1924: Re-engined with 6-cylinder Nelseco diesel engine and lengthened. Renamed from *Charlie Lawrence*. 1955 (4 Nov): Foundered off Tarrytown, NY. (Originally a quite conventional steam tug, the vessel became an unusually long and narrow one as a result of the nearly 18 feet added to her length. See *Cornell* [II] for further comment.)

CHRISTIANA

O/N 4326   105 GT   52 NT
107.0' x 20.0' x 8.6'   Wooden Hull
Single Cylinder Engine

1864: Built at Wilmington, DE, then sold to United States Navy before documentation. Renamed USS *Amaranthus*. 1865 (Sep): Sold at auction. Date uncertain: Sold to Cheney Towing Line. 1892 (Apr): Purchased by Cornell Steamboat Co. from Cheney Towing Line. 1900: Abandoned.

COE F. YOUNG

O/N 125135   65 GT   33 NT
74.3' x 19.0' x 8.6'   Wooden Hull
Single Cyl. Engine, Condensing   24" x 24"   220 HP

1872: Built by Morgan Everson, Sleightsburgh, NY, for Thomas Cornell. 1938: Abandoned. (Vessel was laid up at Sunflower Dock, Rondout Creek, and later sank there. She remained there until mid-1950s, when machinery and other iron was removed by scrap merchants.) Sister vessel: *Thomas Dickson*.

COLUMBIA

O/N 4880   89 GT   52 NT
112.1' x 18.4' x 7.5'   Wooden Hull
Single Cylinder Engine

1863: Built by William Cramp & Sons, Philadelphia, PA, for George H. Power, Hudson, NY. 1863 (Dec): First documented. 1870 (May): Purchased by Thomas Cornell from George H Power. 1902 (Sep): Abandoned. (Built as *Greenwood* but apparently first documented as *Columbia* when rebuilt following a disastrous boiler explosion on 15 June 1863, while she was on her first trip. Only one man, the captain, survived of eight crew members aboard. The explosion also resulted in the deaths of five members of a family living on a canal boat under tow alongside at the time. They were aboard the tug when the accident occurred.)

CONQUEROR

O/N 4893   176 GT   91 NT
123.0' x 21.0' x 10.1'   Wooden Hull
Single Cylinder Engine   30" x 30"

1862: Built as *Dictator* at Buffalo, NY for McCready & Co., Buffalo, NY. 1863 (22 Sep): Sold to United States Navy. Renamed USS *Sweet Brier*. 1865 (25 Oct): Sold at auction to D. T. Rowland, New York, NY. 1866 (Dec): Redocumented as

Conqueror. Date uncertain: Sold to Cheney Towing Line, New York, NY. 1892 (Apr): Purchased by Cornell Steamboat Co. from Cheney Towing Line. 1900: Abandoned.

CORNELL [I]

O/N 200400 435 GT 296 NT
149.7' x 28.1' x 15.2' Steel Hull
Compound Engine 20"-53" x 36" 1400 HP

1902: Hull built by Townsend & Downey, Shooters Island, NY, for Cornell Steamboat Co. Engine built and installed at Cornell shops, Rondout, NY. Boilers (2) built at Buffalo, NY, and installed at Rondout. 1917: Sold to Standard Oil Co. of Louisiana, New Orleans, LA. Renamed *Istrouma*. Later owned by Esso Standard Oil Co. 1956: Dismantled.

CORNELL [II]
[ex-*Charlie Lawrence*]

O/N 125314 79 GT 53 NT
91.5' x 17.9' x 7.3' Wooden Hull
6-cylinder Nelseco Diesel Engine 330 HP

1874: Built as *Charlie Lawrence* at Philadelphia, PA. 1913 (Aug): Purchased by Cornell Steamboat Co. from Knickerbocker Steam Towage Co. 1923: Lengthening and conversion to diesel-hydraulic propulsion proposed but not carried out. 1924: Lengthened and re-engined with conventional diesel propulsion. Renamed from *Charlie Lawrence*. 1955 (4 Nov): Foundered off Tarrytown, NY. (Vessel was known to crew members as "The Submarine." Low freeboard that resulted after re-engining and lengthening reportedly caused a chronic overflow of water onto main deck. Portable duck-boards allowed crew to keep their feet dry. It is surmised that low freeboard and advanced age may have contributed to the vessel's loss.)

CORNELL NO. 20
[ex-*Frank*]

O/N 120938 68 GT 46 NT
75.6' x 17.8' x 7.6' Wooden Hull
4-cylinder Nelseco Diesel Engine 240 HP

1893: Built as *Frank* by J. McCausland, Rondout, NY, for Cornell Steamboat Company. Named for Frank Coykendall. 1925: Re-engined with diesel engine and renamed *Cornell No. 20*. 1955: Sold. Renamed *Glen II*. Foundered off Manasquan Inlet, NJ, while en route to new home port.

CORNELL NO. 21
[ex-*J. H. Williams*]

O/N 201196 101 GT 69 NT
75.6' x 19.5' x 11.0' Steel Hull
4-cylinder Nelseco Diesel Engine 240 HP

1904: Hull built by T. S. Marvel & Co., Newburgh, NY (Hull 154) for Cornell Steamboat Co. Engine, boiler and joiner work installed at Rondout. 1929 (Oct): Re-engined with diesel engine and renamed *Cornell No. 21*. c1950: Fitted with new "modern" stack. 1958: Transferred to Lenroc Towing Corp. 1959 (Jul): Sold to Reichert Towing Line, New York, NY. Renamed *Blackjack 21*. 1966 (Jun): Dismantled. Sister vessel: *Wm. E. Cleary*.

CORNELL NO. 41
[ex-*Eli B. Conine*]

O/N 136782 124 GT 84 NT
85.7' x 21.0' x 10.4' Wooden Hull
6-cylinder Nelseco Diesel Engine 330 HP

1900: Built as *Eli B. Conine* by Jackson & Sharp, Wilmington, DE, for Capt. Eli B. Conine, reportedly for service on the Harlem Transfer. Date Undetermined: Sold to Rose Brick Co., Roseton, NY. 1907: Purchased by Cornell Steamboat Co. from Rose Brick Co. 1908 (Apr): Erroneously reported to have been renamed *Charles Mulford*. 1925: Re-engined and rebuilt at Cornell Shops, Rondout, NY. Renamed *Cornell No. 41*. 1958: Transferred to Lenroc Towing Corp. Later sold to Rossville Salvage Co. (John Witte) for scrap.

DELTA

O/N 6568 31 GT 23 NT
61.2' x 13.3' x 6.3' Wooden Hull
Single Cylinder Engine 16" x 16" 225 HP

1863: Built as *Linda* at Philadelphia, PA. 1864 (3 Jun): Sold to U. S. Navy. (27 Nov) Renamed USS *Delta*. Also known as *Tug No. 4*. Used as torpedo tug in James River, later in North Carolina waters. 1865 (5 Sep): Sold at New York, NY. (2 Oct) Redocumented as *Delta*. 1875: Home port Machias, ME. Later acquired by Ross & Howell, Bangor, ME. 1902 (Feb): Sold to Knickerbocker Steam Towage Co (C. W. Morse). 1913 (9 Jul): Purchased by Cornell Steamboat Co. from Knickerbocker Steam Towage Co. 1914: Sold to Weehawken Dry Dock Co., Weehawken, NJ 1924: Abandoned. (Probably never used by Cornell.)

DR. DAVID KENNEDY

O/N 157011 16 GT 10 NT
46.1' x 13.1' x 4.3' Wooden Hull
Single Cylinder Engine 12" x 12" 73 HP

1880 Built at Rondout, NY, for Henry Krows and Charles Bishop, Rondout, NY. 1883: Purchased by Thomas Cornell from Henry Krows and Charles Bishop. 1938 (Jan): Abandoned. Vessel hauled out, dismantled and left to deteriorate at Sleightsburgh, NY. Still there in early 1950s. (Named for the well-known Rondout doctor who marketed "Dr. Kennedy's Favorite Remedy," a Victorian nostrum of local fame. Bottles bearing the imprint of this elixir are widely sought after.)

E. C. BAKER

O/N 136052 153 GT 76 NT
102.0' x 21.6' x 9.0' Iron Hull
Compound Engine 20"-40" x 26" 550 HP

1889 (Jul): Built by Neafie & Levy, Philadelphia, PA, for Henry Burleigh & Bro., Whitehall, NY., later same year sold to Lake Champlain Towing Co., Whitehall, NY. 1901 (Jul): Purchased by Cornell Steamboat Co. from Lake Champlain Towing Co. 1917 (Apr): Sold to Thomas J Scully, South Amboy, NJ. Renamed *Thomas J. Scully*. 1917 (Jun): Sold to Joseph H. Moran, New York, NY. 1918 (Feb): Sold back to Thomas J. Scully. 1918 (Apr): Sold to Neptune Line, Inc., New York, NY. 1921:

Renamed *Revere*. 1925: Sold to Olsen Water & Towing Co., Inc. 1954: Dismantled.

E. D. HALEY

O/N 205790   55 GT   37 NT
70.0' x 17.6' x 7.6'   Wooden Hull
Single Cylinder Engine 18" x 18"   150 HP

1908: Built at Belfast, ME, for Knickerbocker Steam Towage Co, Bangor, ME. 1913 (Aug): Purchased by Cornell Steamboat Co. from Knickerbocker Steam Towage Co. 1914 (Aug): Sold to Ross Towboat Co, Boston, MA. 1916: Sold to Pareis Bros.Towing Co, Jersey City, NJ. 1926: Sold to Westervelt Towing Line, Inc., New York, NY. 1945: Dismantled.

E. H. MEAD
[ex-*Ruth*]

O/N 8918   62 GT   38 NT
79.5' x 17.5' x 8.0'   Wooden Hull
Single Cylinder Engine

1862: Built as *Ruth* (q.v.)(O/N 21856) at Rondout, NY for J. B. Pardee and Silas Saxton. 1863: (Nov) Purchased by Thomas Cornell. 1872: Abandoned. 1873 (Apr): Rebuilt by Morgan Everson, Sleightsburgh, NY, from hull of vessel and renamed *E. H. Mead*. 1890 (Mar): Dismantled. (It is possible that the engine and boiler of *Ruth* were incorporated into *E. H. Mead*, but no positive evidence of this survives.)

E. L. LEVY

O/N 135980   142 GT   71 NT
104.5' x 21.5' x 8.6'   Iron Hull
Compound Engine 20"-36" x 26"   550 HP

1888 (May): Built by Neafie & Levy, Philadelphia, PA, for Peter Dionne, Whitehall, NY. 1889: Sold to Lake Champlain Towing Co., Whitehall, NY. 1901 (Jul): Purchased by Cornell Steamboat Co. from Lake Champlain Towing Co. 1917 (Apr): Sold to Thomas J Scully, South Amboy, NJ. Renamed *Mary F. Scully*. 1917 (Jun): Sold to Joseph H. Moran, New York, NY. 1918 (Feb): Sold back to Thomas J. Scully. 1918 (Apr): Sold to Neptune Line, Inc., New York, NY. 1921: Renamed *Chelsea*. 1925: Sold to Moran Towing & Transportation Co., Inc. Renamed *Marion Moran*. 1948 (Feb): Sold to Martin J. Kehoe Towing Co., Inc. Renamed *Marion Kehoe*. 1948 (Sep): Dismantled by Sarnelli Salvage Scrap in Gowanus Canal, Brooklyn, NY.

EDWIN H. MEAD

O/N 136322   248 GT   124 NT
122.4' x 26.0' x 12.0'   Iron Hull
Compound Engine 22"-44" x 32"   750 HP

1892: Built by T. S. Marvel & Co., Newburgh, NY, (Hull 55) for Cornell Steamboat Co. 1894 (23 Oct): Collided with ferry *Westfield* off Governors Island, New York. 1940: Dismantled. (*Edwin H. Mead*, built as a slightly smaller but similar running mate for *Geo. W. Washburn*, was never able to equal the performance— and mystique— of her near sister.)

EDWIN TERRY

O/N 135671   90 GT   45 NT
84.5' x 19.4' x 10.2'   Iron Hull
Compound Engine 16"-32" x 24"

1883 (May): Built by John H. Dialogue & Son, Camden, NJ, for Washburn Steamboat Co. 1884: Purchased by Cornell Steamboat Co. from Washburn Steamboat Co. 1958 (Jan): Sold to Carroll Towing Corp., New York, NY. Renamed *Anna Carroll*. 1958 (Apr): Dismantled.

ELI B. CONINE
[later *Cornell No. 41*]

O/N 136782   117 GT   80 NT
85.7' x 21.0' x 10.4'   Wooden Hull
4-Cyl. Steeple Compound Engine
    13"-24"-22"-26" x 26"   650 HP

1900: Built by Jackson & Sharp, Wilmington, DE, for Capt. Eli B. Conine, reportedly for service on the Harlem Transfer. Date Undetermined: Sold to Rose Brick Co., Roseton, NY. 1907: Purchased by Cornell Steamboat Co. from Rose Brick Co. 1908 (Apr): Erroneously reported to have been renamed *Charles Mulford*. 1925: Re-engined with 6-cyl. Nelseco diesel engine and rebuilt at Cornell shops, Rondout, NY. Renamed *Cornell No. 41*. 1958: Sold to Rossville Salvage Co. (John Witte) for scrap.

ELLEN M. RONAN

O/N 135696   73 GT   36 NT
79.4' x 19.7' x 8.6'   Wooden Hull
Compound Engine 15"-25" x 22"   240 HP

1883: Built at Athens, NY, for Patrick Ronan (Ronan Towing Line). 1887: Transferred to Estate of Patrick Ronan. 1897: Sold to Charles W. Morse (Consolidated Towing Line). 1901: Purchased by Cornell Steamboat Co. from Charles W Morse. 1926: (18 Dec) Sunk in East River. Raised and returned to service. 1949: Dismantled and remains of hull placed ashore at Sleightsburgh, NY.

EMPIRE

O/N 136093   41 GT   20 NT
67.2' x 16.0' x 6.9'   Wooden Hull
Single Cylinder Engine 17" x 20"

1889: Built by W. D. Ford, Athens, NY, for James Laverty et al, Brooklyn, NY. 1893 (Feb): Sold to Henry Heissenbuttel, Brooklyn, NY. 1893 (Apr): Sold to McAllister Bros., Brooklyn, NY. 1894 (Jan): Sold to William B. Barnett (Barnett Brothers), New York, NY. 1901 (May): Purchased by Cornell Steamboat Co. from William B Barnett. 1947 (Jan): Abandoned. (Vessel was laid up at Sunflower Dock, Rondout Creek, and later sank there. She remained there until mid-1950s, when machinery and other iron was removed by scrap merchants.)

ENGELS

O/N 127347   34 GT   23 NT
58.0' x 15.6' x 6.5'   Wooden Hull
Single Cylinder Engine 14" x 16"   200 HP

1899 (Oct): Built as *C. Rissberger* at Athens, NY, for William P. Smith, Rensselaer, NY. Sold later that year to Charles F. Engels,

Haverstraw, NY. Renamed *Engels.* 1909 (May): Purchased by Cornell Steamboat Co. from Charles F. Engels. 1920 (Jan): Sold to O'Brien Bros. Towing Co., Inc., New York, NY. Renamed *Thos. F. O'Brien.* 1925: Renamed *Harold F. O'Brien.* 1929 (Aug): Renamed *O'Brien No. 1.* 1929 (Dec): Sold to Bowerd Towing Co., Kearny, NJ. Renamed *Mary R. Bowers.* 1936: Sold to Fred B. Dalzell & Co., New York, NY. 1937 (Nov): Dismantled.

EUGENIA

O/N 115110   15 GT   7 NT
43.0' x 12.0' x 5.0'   Wooden Hull
Single Cylinder Engine   10" x 10"

1865: Apparently built as *Saratoga* (O/N 22270, 8.09 Tons, 39.6' x 11.0' x 3.2) y Charles S. Bidwell, Buffalo, NY, for A. T. Kingman, Buffalo, NY. 1867: Sold to J. S. Van Riper, Buffalo, NY. 1870 (Jun): Left district. 1872: First extant document as O/N 115110, 10.11 GT, 6.08 NT, 43.0' x 10.0' x 4.0, owner shown as George W. Chamberlain, Greenbush, NY. 1877: Sold to Alonzo B. Chamberlain, Greenbush, NY. 1881: Sold to Maria J. Glassford et al, Albany, NY. 1883: Sold to Henry R. Conger and Amasa Drew, Burlington, VT. 1887: Sold to James M. Clute, Schodack Landing, NY. 1888: Sold to William H. Smith and Robert H. Van Zandt, New Baltimore, NY. 1889: Transferred to Robert H. Van Zandt, New Baltimore, NY. 1890: Transferred to Robert H. Van Zandt and Ulster Davis, Greenbush, NY. 1894: Transferred to Ulster Davis and Estate of Robert H. Van Zandt, Greenbush, NY. Rebuilt at Albany, NY, to dimensions and tonnages stated above. 1903 (May): Sold to Albany Towing Co., Albany, NY. 1905: Purchased by Cornell Steamboat Co. from Albany Towing Co. 1920 (Apr): First documented under ownership of Cornell Steamboat Co. 1934: Probable last year of operation. 1943 (Jun): Dismantled. Vessel hauled out and deteriorated at Sleightsburgh, NY. Still there in early 1950s. (The early history of this vessel is clouded in uncertainty. There is no conclusive proof that O/N 22270 and O/N 115110 were the same vessel, but both were built in Buffalo in 1865 and both left the district at about the same time. After the first O/N 115110 license was issued, O/N 22270 disappears from the records. It is concluded that a rebuilding of the vessel took place after her arrival in the Albany area. The difference between the two in dimensions and tonnage may be attributable both to this and to different interpretations of the arcane tonnage rules as seen by the Customs admeasurers at Buffalo and Albany.)

F. LAVERGNE

O/N 9821   34 GT   17 NT
68.0' x 16.6' x 6.6'   Wooden Hull
Single Cylinder Engine   50 HP

1869: Built at Rondout, NY. c1882: Sold to Washburn Steamboat Co., Saugerties, NY. 1884: Purchased by Cornell Steamboat Co. from Washburn Steamboat Co. 1901: Dismantled. Boiler installed in new tug *Rob.*

FRANK
[later *Cornell No. 20*]

O/N 120938   61 GT   30 NT
75.6' x 17.8' x 7.6'   Wooden Hull
Single Cylinder Engine   18" x 18"   155 HP

1893: Built by J. McCausland, Rondout, NY, for Cornell Steamboat Company. 1925: Re-engined with 4-cylinder Nelseco diesel engine. Renamed *Cornell No. 20.* 1955: Sold. Renamed *Glen II.* Foundered off Manasquan Inlet, NJ, while en route to new home port. (Named for Frank Coykendall.)

G. C. ADAMS

O/N 85568   80 GT   40 NT
83.6' x 20.0' x 7.0'   Wooden Hull
Single Cyl. Engine, Condensing   26½" x 26"   300 HP

1878: Built by John J. Lawlor, Jersey City, NJ for Samuel Schuyler. 1891: Sold to Estate of Patrick Ronan, Albany, NY. 1894 (Nov): Sold to Charles W. Morse (Consolidated Towing Line). 1901 (May): Purchased by Cornell Steamboat Co. from Charles W Morse. 1910: Rebuilt by C. Hiltebrant Dry Dock Co., South Rondout, NY. 1938 (Jul): Dismantled. Scuttled at Port Ewen, NY.

G. W. DECKER

O/N 86548   77 GT   52 NT
68.1' x 19.6' x 8.0'   Steel Hull
Compound Engine   13"-29" x 18"   210 HP

1900: Built by T. S. Marvel & Co., Newburgh, NY (Hull 123) for Cornell Steamboat Co. 1949 (Jul): Abandoned. Scuttled at Port Ewen, NY. Sister vessel: *J. G. Rose.*

GENERAL SHERIDAN

O/N 10978   53 GT
Dimensions Not Known   Wooden Hull
Single Cylinder Engine

1865: Buit by Morgan Everson, Sleightsburgh, NY, for John Dillon and Morgan Everson. Year undetermined: Purchased by Thomas Cornell. 1880: Abandoned.

GEO. C. VAN TUYL, JR.

O/N 86519   21 GT   14 NT
45.0' x 13.9' x 5.6'   Wooden Hull
Single Cylinder Engine   10" x 12"

1900: Built by Paul Leroux, Albany, NY, for Ulster Davis, Rensselaer, NY. 1903: Sold to Albany Towing Co. 1905: Purchased by Cornell Steamboat Co. from Albany Towing Co. 1922 (Dec): Sold to John P Randerson, Albany, NY. 1936 (May): Abandoned.

GEO. N. SOUTHWICK
[ex-*M. B. Harlow*]

O/N 92264   57 GT   28 NT
69.0' x 17.6' x 7.0'   Wooden Hull
Single Cylinder Engine   16" x 18"   164 HP

1891: Built at Alexandria, VA, for W. R. Taylor, A. Dean and Patrick Gorman, Alexandria, VA. 1895: Sold to John L. Roper Lumber Co., Norfolk, VA. 1902: Sold to Richard Pearsall and Camille Delaporte, New York, NY. 1903: Sold to Albany Towing Co. 1905: Purchased by Cornell Steamboat Co. from Albany Towing Co. 1908 (Jun): Renamed *Geo. N. Southwick.* 1921 (Apr): First documented under ownership of Cornell

Steamboat Co. 1943 (May): Dismantled. Scuttled at Port Ewen, NY.

GEO. W. WASHBURN

O/N 86105   298 GT   149 NT
123.0' x 26.0' x 13.8'   Iron Hull
Compound Engine   24"-48" x 36"   800 HP

1890 (Aug): Built by T. S. Marvel & Co., Newburgh, NY, (Hull 33) for Cornell Steamboat Co. Launched on 8 March. 1921: Rebuilt and reboilered by Cornell shops, Rondout, NY. Water-tube boilers fitted at this time to replace original leg boilers. 1949 (Aug): Dismantled at Witte yard, Rossville, Staten Island, NY (As built, vessel had single stack. As reboilered in 1921, vessel was fitted with two fore-and-aft stacks. Vessel was considered by many to be one of the handsomest tugs ever built.)

GEORGE B. HANCE
[ex-*R. G. Davis*]

O/N 110918   23 GT   11 NT
52.4' x 14.6' x 6.0'   Wooden Hull
Single Cylinder Engine   12" x 14"

1891 (Jul): Built as *R. G. Davis* at Athens, NY, for George Field, Newburgh, NY. 1893 (Apr): Alfred Walker and Mrs. Mary S. Horton, Newburgh, NY. 1894 (Jun): Jeremiah H. Horton and Alfred Walker, Newburgh, NY. 1895 Aug): A. Stanley Wood and Alfred Walker, Newburgh, NY. 1904 (Oct): A. Stanley Wood, Newburgh, NY. 1906 (Apr): Purchased by Cornell Steamboat Co. from A. Stanley Wood. 1920 (May): Renamed *George B. Hance*. 1934: Probable last year of operation. 1942 (Feb): Abandoned. (Disposition not known.)

GEORGE D. COOLEY

O/N 86587   34 GT   23 NT
54.4' x 15.3' x 6.0'   Wooden Hull
Single Cylinder Engine   225 HP

1901: Built at Kingston, NY, for George D. Cooley et al, Troy, NY. 1912: Purchased by Cornell Steamboat Co. from George D. Cooley but documented under ownership first of Ulster Davis, then Albany Towing Co. 1914 (Apr): Sold to United States Army Corps of Engineers. Renamed *Colonel Thayer*. c1930: Sold to I. M. Ludington Sons, Rochester, NY. Redocumented as *George D. Cooley*. c1935: Sold to Henry Kilcorse, Buffalo, NY. c1938: Forfeited for unknown reason. Subsequent career, if any, not known.

GEORGE FIELD

O/N 85748   29 GT   14 NT
55.8' x 15.0' x 6.2'   Wooden Hull
Single Cylinder Engine   14" x 15"

1882: Built at Buffalo, NY, for Coleman, Field & Horton, Newburgh, NY. Named for Capt. George Field, a partner in the owning firm, 1895 (Aug): Sold to A. Stanley Wood, Newburgh, NY. 1906: Purchased by Cornell Steamboat Co. from A. Stanley Wood. 1924 (Nov): Sold to Steamtug George Field, Inc., New York, NY. 1938 (Nov): Dismantled.

GEORGE W. PRATT

O/N 10977   41 GT   20 NT
76.5' x 17.5' x 6.8'   Wooden Hull
Single Cylinder Engine   22½" x 20"   300 HP

1863: Built by Jacob Fox, South Rondout, NY, for Thomas Cornell. 1939 (Jan): Abandoned. (Vessel was laid up at Sunflower Dock, Rondout Creek, and later sank there. She remained there until mid-1950s, when machinery and other iron was removed by scrap merchants.)

H. D. MOULD

O/N 96335   49 GT   33 NT
67.0' x 18.0' x 7.0'   Wooden Hull
Single Cylinder Engine   15½" x 17"   130 HP

1896: Built by W. D. Ford, Athens, NY, for Foster-Scott Ice Co. 1904: Purchased by Cornell Steamboat Co. from Foster-Scott Ice Co. 1926 (Apr): Installation of 240-horsepower Nelseco diesel engine proposed, but conversion was never carried out. 1943: Abandoned. Scuttled at Port Ewen, NY

H. P. FARRINGTON

O/N 9820   83 GT
75' x 17' x 7'   Wooden Hull
Single Cylinder Engine

1862: Built by Jacob Fox, South Rondout, NY, for Thomas Cornell. 1882 (23 Jan.): Destroyed by boiler explosion at Haverstraw, NY. Three crew members lost their lives. (Named for Harvey P. Farrington, a long-time associate of Thomas Cornell.)

H. T. CASWELL

O/N 95729   32 GT   17 NT
62.0' x 16.0' x 6.0'   Wooden Hull
Single Cylinder Engine   17" x 20"

1882 (Nov): Built at Kingston Point, NY, for Washburn Steamboat Co., Saugerties, NY. 1884: Purchased by Cornell Steamboat Co. from Washburn Steamboat Co   1891 (Sep): First documented under ownership of Cornell Steamboat Co. 1902 (Sep): Abandoned and broken up. Engine installed in new tug *Rob*.

HARRY

O/N 96187   49 GT   32 NT
73.5' x 17.8' x 7.8'   Wooden Hull
Single Cylinder Engine   18" x 18"

1892 (Aug): Built by J. McCausland, Rondout, NY, for Cornell Steamboat Company. 1940 (Mar): Abandoned. Hull later hauled out on marine railway at Sleightsburgh, where it deteriorated slowly. Still there in 1950, but removed in early 1950s. (Named for Harry S. Coykendall.)

HAVERSTRAW

O/N 203366   234 GT   159 NT
98.0' x 25.0' x 12.0'   Steel Hull
Compound Engine   18"-36" x 26"   500 HP

1906: Ordered from John H. Dialogue & Son, Camden, NJ, by New York Trap Rock Co. Purchased by Cornell Steamboat Co. from New York Trap Rock Co., and then sold to Lehigh Valley Transportation Co. before completion. Renamed *Aurora*. Later owned by Lehigh Valley Railroad Co. 1954: Sold to Carroll Towing Co., Inc., New York, NY. Renamed *Sally Carroll*. 1958: Dismantled. (Never ran for Cornell Steamboat Co.)

HERCULES

O/N 95443   119 GT   59 NT
111.4' x 22.8' x 10.6'   Wooden Hull
Compound Engine   19"-32" x 24"   350 HP

1876: Built as a pilot boat by Wood, Dialogue & Co., Camden, NJ, for James A. Wright. 1879: Sold to Thomas S. Sandford, New York, NY 1882 (May): Sold to partnership of Kingston and Saugerties brick manufacturers (George W., John T. and Richard C. Washburn; William M. Barnes; Edwin and Albert Terry; John H. Cordts and William Hutton). 1883 (May): Transferred to Washburn Steamboat Co. 1884: Purchased by Cornell Steamboat Co. from Washburn Steamboat Co. 1931: Last in operation. 1940 (Dec): Dismantled. Scuttled at Port Ewen, NY.

HONEYSUCKLE

O/N 11490   138 GT   69 NT
126.0' x 20.4' x 10.2'   Wooden Hull
Single Cylinder Engine   30" x 30"

1862: Built as *W. G. Fargo* at Buffalo, NY for Frank Perew, Buffalo, NY. 1863 (14 Aug): Sold to United States Navy. Renamed USS *Honeysuckle*. 1865 (15 Aug): Sold at auction. Redocumented as merchant vessel *Honeysuckle*. Date uncertain: Sold to Cheney Towing Line, New York, NY. 1892 (Apr): Purchased by Cornell Steamboat Co. from Cheney Towing Line. 1899: Abandoned.

ICE KING

O/N 85484   138 GT   69 NT
111.5' x 22.5' x 10.2'   Wooden Hull
Single Cyl. Engine, Condensing   32" x 32"   500 HP

1877: Built as *Greyhound* at Philadelphia, PA, for Frederick C. Pendleton and John H. Black, New Orleans, LA. 1885: Sold to C. W. Morse & Co., New York, NY. Renamed *Ice King*. Same year transferred to Knickerbocker Steam Towage Co., Bath ME. Later ran on Hudson River. 1903 (Jul): Purchased by Cornell Steamboat Co. from Knickerbocker Steam Towage Co. 1913 (26 Dec): Stranded 1½ miles from Sandy Hook, NJ

IMPERIAL

O/N 200905   160 GT   119 NT
107.5' x 21.6' x 11.0'   Wooden Hull
Compound Engine   15"-30" x 22"   500 HP

1904: Built by Thomas McCosker, Baltimore, MD, for James Clark Co., Baltimore, MD. 1910: Sold to Knickerbocker Steam Towage Co., Bath, ME. 1913 (Jul): Purchased by Cornell Steamboat Co. from Knickerbocker Steam Towage Co. 1916 (Oct): Sold to Peter Cahill (Cahill Towing Line), New York, NY. 1925: Sold to Card Towing Line, New York, NY. 1932: Readmeasured, 153 GT, 104 NT. 1936: Sold to Lee Transit Corp., New York, NY. Renamed *Grace Ann Lee*. 1944 (Feb): Dismantled. Sister vessel: *Princess*.

IRA M. HEDGES

O/N 100323   76 GT   38 NT
76.6' x 18.0' x 9.2'   Iron Hull
Compound Engine   14"-28" x 24"

1883: Built by John H. Dialogue & Son, Camden, NJ, for Washburn Steamboat Co. 1884: Purchased by Cornell Steamboat Co. from Washburn Steamboat Co. 1926 (Apr): Dismantled. (A slightly smaller version of *Edwin Terry*. The reason for the relatively early demise of this staunchly-built iron-hulled vessel remains a mystery.)

ISAAC M. NORTH

O/N 12289   62 GT   32 NT
83.0' x 19.0' x 6.0'   Wooden Hull
Single Cylinder Engine   24" x 24"

1862: Built as *Addie Douglas* at Philadelphia, PA, for J. Allardice (Alderdice?), Philadelphia, PA. 1863 (Oct): Sold to United States Navy. Renamed USS *Poppy*. 1865 (30 Nov): Sold at auction to William Farrington, 1866: Purchased by Thomas Cornell. Renamed *Isaac M. North*. 1893: Abandoned. (Named for Isaac M. North (1839-1914), for many years an associate of Thomas Cornell.)

J. ARNOLD

O/N 77097   23 GT   11 NT
51.2' x 14.5' x 6.0'   Wooden Hull
Single Cylinder Engine   13" x 14"

1893: Built at Albany, NY, for James H. Scott, Bath-on-the-Hudson, NY. 1902: Transferred to James H. Scott and Ulster Davis. 1903: Sold to Albany Towing Co, Albany, NY. 1905: Purchased by Cornell Steamboat Co. from Albany Towing Co. 1920: First documented by Cornell Steamboat Co. 1934: Probable last year of operation. 1940 (Mar): Dismantled. Hull sank and deteriorated at Sleightsburgh, NY. Still there in early 1950s.

J. C. HARTT

O/N 76417   222 GT   111 NT
115.7' x 27.0' x 11.1'   Wooden Hull
Compound Engine   24"-42" x 36"   750 HP

1883: Built by Neafie & Levy, Philadelphia, PA, for Cornell Steamboat Co. 1887 (29 Sep): Collided with steamer *City of Brockton* off Sandy Hook while bound for yacht races at Scotland Lightship. 1937: Last operated. 1949: Abandoned. Scuttled at Port Ewen, NY.

J. G. ROSE

O/N 77448   77 GT   52 NT
68.1' x 19.6' x 8.0'   Steel Hull
Compound Engine   13"-29" x 18"   276 HP

1900 : Built by T. S. Marvel & Co., Newburgh, NY, (Hull 122) for Cornell Steamboat Co. 1950 (Aug): Sold to McAllister

Bros., New York, NY. Never documented by McAllister. Sister vessel: *G. W. Decker*.

J. H. WILLIAMS
[later *Cornell No. 21*]

O/N 201196 90 GT 61 NT
75.6' x 19.5' x 11.0' Steel Hull
Single Cylinder Engine 16½' x 20 250 HP

1904: Hull built by T. S. Marvel & Co., Newburgh, NY (Hull 154) for Cornell Steamboat Co. (Sep): Installation of engine, boiler and joiner work completed at Rondout. 1929: Re-engined with 4-cylinder Nelseco diesel engine. (9 Oct): Renamed *Cornell No. 21*. 1951: Sold to Reichert Towing Line, New York, NY Renamed *Blackjack 21*. 1966 (Jun): Dismantled. Sister vessel: *Wm. E. Cleary*.

JAMES H. SCOTT

O/N 77261 20 GT 13 NT
42.0' x 14.0' x 5.7' Wooden Hull
Single Cylinder Engine 12½" x 14 80 HP

1897: Built at Albany, NY, for James H. Scott (?). c1903: Acquired by Albany Towing Co. 1905: Purchased by Cornell Steamboat Co. from Albany Towing Co. c1920: First documented under ownership of Cornell Steamboat Co. 1941: Abandoned. Hull sank and deteriorated at Sleightsburgh, NY. Still there in early 1950s.

JOHN D. SCHOONMAKER

O/N 76751 56 GT 38 NT
82.5' x 17.9' x 7.0' Wooden Hull
Single Cyl. Engine, Condensing

1888 (Sep): Built by J. McCau... Rondout, NY for Cornell Steamboat Co. Launched, 23 Ju... 1926 (Apr): Installation of 240-horsepower Nelseco diesel engine proposed, but never carried out. 1951 (Sep): Sold to Downer Towing Corp., New York, NY. Home port, Newark, NJ. Renamed *Downer V*. 1954 (May): Dismantled.

JOHN H. CORDTS

O/N 76424 194 GT 97 NT
114.5' x 25.0' x 10.5' Wooden Hull
Compound Engine 28"-52" x 40" 850 HP

1883: Built by Ward, Stanton & Co, Newburgh, NY, for Washburn Steamboat Co., Saugerties, NY. 1884: Purchased by Cornell Steamboat Co. from Washburn Steamboat Co. 1901: Reboilered. 1907 (3 Nov): Heavily damaged by fire at Rondout. 1908 (Jun): Returned to service. 1926 (Apr): Abandoned. (As built, had two side-by-side stacks in style of builder. When reboilered in 1901, had one stack.)

JOHN T. WELCH

O/N 77371 59 GT 40 NT
63.9' x 18.9' x 7.2' Wooden Hull
Single Cylinder Engine 16" x 20"

1899 (Aug): Built at Tottenville, NY, for Richard J. Foster and Augustus C. Sprague (Foster-Scott Ice Co.) 1903 (Jan): Purchased by Cornell Steamboat Co. from Foster-Scott Ice Co. 1920 (Jun): Sold to O'Brien Bros. Towing Co., Inc., New York, NY. Renamed *O'Brien*. 1924 (25 Mar): Sunk in collision with tug *Diamond S*. off Pier 36, North River. Raised and declared total loss. 1925: Sold to Newark & New York Towboat Co., Newark, NJ, and rebuilt. Renamed *Kearny*. 1927 (Apr): Abandoned after having sunk at unstated location.

JULIA A. BRAINARD

O/N 75400 15 GT 15 NT
54.5' x 12.2' x 6.0' Wooden Hull
Single Cylinder Engine 15" x 15"

1872 (May): Built at Albany, NY, for E. Brainard, Albany, NY. 1890: Acquired by Hudson River Bridge Co. for service as bridge tender at Poughkeepsie, NY. 1905 (Jul): Purchased by Cornell Steamboat Co. from Hudson River Bridge Co. 1920 (Mar): Abandoned. (Note that gross and net tonnages are identical. It is surmised that this was as a result of a clerical error, never corrected, when the measurement of net tonnage was introduced in 1882.)

JUMBO

O/N 223541 217 GT 55 NT
95.9' x 25.0' x 13.8' Wooden Hull
6-cyl Nelseco Diesel Engine 600 HP

1918: Hull built by John W. Sullivan Co., New York, NY, for United States Shipping Board (Design 1086). Originally to have been a steam tug. Contract cancelled and unfinished hull later sold to New London Ship & Engine Co. (Nelseco), New London, CT. Completed as diesel tug. 1924: Purchased by Cornell Steamboat Co. from New London Ship & Engine Co. 1958: (Feb) Transferred to Lenroc Towing Corp. (May) Sold to Rossville Salvage Co. (John Witte) for scrap. (Hull identical to *Lion*, *Bear* and *Burro*.)

KNICKERBOCKER

O/N 14292 123 GT 61 NT
103.2' x 23.9' x 9.4' Wooden Hull
Single Cylinder Engine 32" x 32" 130 HP

1873 (Sep): Built at Philadelphia, PA, for Knickerbocker Steam Towage Co., Gardiner, ME. 1898 (Oct): Apparently sold to McDonald Dredging Co., New York, NY, 1899 (Jun): Returned to Knickerbocker Steam Towage Co., Bath, ME. 1903 (Jul): Purchased by Cornell Steamboat Co. from Knickerbocker Steam Towage Co. 1917 (Oct): Sold to United States Government. 1920 (Feb): Redocumented under ownership of Independent Tow Boat Co., Wilmington, DE. 1933 (Jan): Abandoned and vessel scrapped.

LION

O/N 224394 218 GT 56 NT
95.9' x 25.0' x 13.8' Wooden Hull
6-cyl Nelseco Diesel Engine 600 HP

1920: Vessel's hull built by unknown builder for United States Shipping Board (Design 1086). Originally to have been a steam tug. Contract cancelled and unfinished hull later sold to New London Ship & Engine Co. (Nelseco), New London, CT, 1925: Completed as diesel tug and purchased by Cornell Steamboat

Co. from New London Ship & Engine Co   1957: Sold to Rossville Salvage Co (John Witte) for scrap. (Hull identical to *Jumbo*, *Bear* and *Burro*. Official records state that vessel was built at New London, CT, in 1924 by New London Ship & Engine Co. Her hull was probably built elsewhere and the vessel completed at New London.)

M. B. HARLOW
[later *Geo. N. Southwick*]

O/N 92264   57 GT   28 NT
69.0' x 17.6' x 7.0'   Wooden Hull
Single Cylinder Engine   16" x 18"   164 HP

1891: Built at Alexandria, VA, for W. R. Taylor, A. Dean and Patrick Gorman, Alexandria, VA. 1895: Sold to John L. Roper Lumber Co., Norfolk, VA. 1902: Sold to Richard Pearsall and Camille Delaporte, New York, NY. 1903: Sold to Albany Towing Co. 1905: Purchased by Cornell Steamboat Co. from Albany Towing Co. 1908 (Jun): Renamed *Geo. N. Southwick*. 1921 (Apr): First documented under ownership of Cornell Steamboat Co. 1943 (May): Dismantled. Scuttled at Port Ewen, NY.

MABEL

O/N 92525   50 GT   26 NT
61.2' x 18.0' x 7.0'   Wooden Hull
Single Cylinder Engine   16" x 18"

1893: Built at Athens, NY, for Parker C. Ronan, Albany, NY. c1901-03: Purchased by Cornell Steamboat Co. 1916 (Aug): Sold to Jersey City Stock Yards Co. Renamed *Veribest*. 1920 (Feb): Sold to Overseas Shipping Co., Inc., New York. 1926 (Feb): Sold to American & Cuban Steamship Line, Inc., New York. 1930 (Jul): Sold to Daniel Roe Towing & Transportation Co., Inc., New York. 1933 (Jan): Sold to Steamtug S. & H. No. 1, Inc. (Sound and Harbor Towboat Co.), New York. Renamed *S. & H. No. 1*. 1941 (Nov): Dismantled.

MARY A. CORNELL

O/N 249560   275 GT   187 NT
117.5' x 28.0' x 13.5'   Wooden Hull
8-Cylinder Enterprise Diesel Engine   1200 HP

1944: Built as *LT-374* by Barber Marine Yards, Inc., Seattle, WA, for United States Army. 194?: Purchased by Robert B. Wathen, Baltimore, MD. Renamed *Jack*. 1952: Purchased by Cornell Steamboat Co. from Robert B. Wathen. Renamed *Mary A. Cornell*. 1958: Transferred to Lenroc Towing Corp. 1959: Sold to Olson Towboat Co. Renamed *Elizabeth Olson*. Later career not recorded.

MONTAUK

O/N 92645   121 GT   51 NT
96.6' x 22.0' x 10.0'   Wooden Hull
Compound Engine   17"-36" x 26"   500 HP

1895: Built by Jackson & Sharp, Wilmington, DE, for Long Island Rail Road, New York, NY. 1927: Sold to George Atkins (broker). 1928: Purchased by Cornell Steamboat Co. from George Atkins. 1935 (Jun): Abandoned. (Only oil-burning steam tug owned by Cornell Steamboat Co.)

NEWBURGH

O/N 203367   234 GT   159 NT
98.0' x 25.0' x 12.0'   Wooden Hull
Compound Engine   18"-36" x 26"   500 HP

1906: Ordered from John H. Dialogue & Son, Camden, NJ, by New York Trap Rock Co. Purchased by Cornell Steamboat Co. from New York Trap Rock Co., and then sold to Suderman & Dolson, Galveston, TX, before completion. Renamed *Mariner*. 1908 (Jan): Sold to Isthmian Canal Commission. (Never ran for Cornell Steamboat Co.)

OSCEOLA

O/N 155096   182 GT   95 NT
117.0' x 29.0' x 9.0' (see note below)   Wooden Hull
Compound Engine   24"-42" x 36"

1884: Built by Ward, Stanton & Co., Newburgh, NY, for Patrick Ronan (Ronan Towing Line). 1887: Transferred to Estate of Patrick Ronan. 1897: Sold to Charles W. Morse (Consolidated Towing Line). 1901: Purchased by Cornell Steamboat Co. from Charles W Morse. Rebuilt and reboilered at Cornell Shops, Rondout, NY. 1931 (Jan): Abandoned. Scuttled at Port Ewen, NY late in previous year. (Machinery and upperworks installed in hull of *Watchman* (q.v.) in 1930, but that vessel never completed. As built, *Osceola* had two side-by-side stacks in style of builder. After being reboilered, had one stack. Despite the apparent difference in statutory dimensions, vessel was a sister of *Pocahontas*. The beam of *Osceola* as shown above and in official records was incorrect, apparently as a result of an admeasurer's error which was neither detected nor corrected. Her correct beam was around 26.4 feet.)

P. C. RONAN

O/N 150700   29 GT   14 NT
52.0' x 16.0' x 5.6'   Wooden Hull
Single Cylinder Engine   12" x 14"

1895 (Jun): Built at Albany, NY, for Joel W. Hitchcock, Greenbush, NY. 1897: Sold to Horatio D. Mould et al, Brooklyn, NY. 1899: Sold to Richard J. Foster, New York, NY, and Augustus C. Sprague, Bath, ME. 1903 (Jan): Purchased by Cornell Steamboat Co. from Richard J Foster and Augustus C. Sprague. 1923 (Sep): Sold to The American Construction Co, Cleveland, OH. 1927: Sold to John E. Matton & Son, Waterford, NY. 1928: Re-engined with 120 HP diesel engine. 1943 (Mar): Sold to R. C. Huffman Construction Co., Buffalo, NY. 1950: Abandoned at Tampa, FL. (*P. C. Ronan* had a diverse 55-year career without change of name. She was named for Parker C. Ronan, a close relative of the Ronan Towing Line's Patrick Ronan.)

PAUL LE ROUX

O/N 150958   44 GT   30 NT
72.0' x 17.4' x 7.5'   Wooden Hull
Single Cylinder Engine   14" x 16"

1902 (Dec): Built by Paul Le Roux, Albany, NY, for Peter S. Le Roux, Albany, NY. 1903 (Jun): Sold to Albany Towing Co. 1905: Purchased by Cornell Steamboat Co. from Albany Towing Co. but remained under Albany Towing Co. ownership. 1912 (Jan): Sold to George D. Cooley, Troy, NY. 1917 ((May):

Sold to Hawley Miller, New Baltimore, NY and John P. Randerson, Albany, NY. Vessel rebuilt at New Baltimore. 1918 (Mar): Sold to Olsen Water & Towing Co., New York, NY. 1921 (Jan): Sold to Richard J. Barrett, Hoboken, NJ. (Apr) Renamed *Wm. Bowman*. 1923 (Feb): Sold to George P. Finnegan and Arthur W. Funnegan, Brooklyn, NY. 1932 (Nov): Owned by Arthur W. Finnegan. 1940 (Dec): Sold to Bay Scow Towing & Transportation Co., (Stephen F. Blackler), Brooklyn, NY. 1941 (Dec): Last renewal of license. 1955 (15 Feb): Out of documentation.. Document endorsed "Whereabouts of owner and vessel unknown." (It is likely that this vessel was dismantled when her inspection certificate expired and the required surrender of her last document was simply ignored.)

PERRY

O/N 20172   107 GT   53 NT
99.4' x 21.9' x 5.0'   Wooden Hull
Single Cylinder Engine

1863: Built at Philadelphia, PA. (24 Dec) Sold to U. S. Army Quartermasters Corps. 1866: Redocumented. 1875: At New Orleans, LA. Later acquired by Knickerbocker Steam Towage Co. 1913 (9 Jul): Purchased by Cornell Steamboat Co. from Knickerbocker Steam Towage Co. 1914: Sold to owners in Bath, ME. 1921: Abandoned. (May never have been brought to Hudson River by Knickerbocker.)

PERSEVERANCE

O/N 221698   385 GT   261 NT
142.0' x 31.6' x 14.4'   Wooden Hull
Triple-Expansion Engine   17"-25"-43" x 30"   1000 HP

1919: Hull built by Crowninshield Shipbuilding Co., Somerset (not Fall River, as reported in official records), MA, for United States Shipping Board (Design 1055). 1921: Purchased incomplete, but with engine installed, by Cornell Steamboat Co. from United States Shipping Board. Completed at Cornell shops, Rondout, NY. 1948 (Nov): Last under steam. !949: Sold to J. Kerzman & Sons for scrap. (15 Dec) Left Rondout under tow for Cornwall, NY. 1953 (Mar): Last enrollment document surrendered, endorsed "Out of Documentation." (Although the Shipping Board's Design 1055 tugs were built with one stack, when *Perseverance* was completed at Rondout, she was fitted with two stacks— one for each of her two Scotch boilers.)

POCAHONTAS

O/N 150326   177 GT   94 NT
118.0' x 26.4' x 9.3'   Wooden Hull
Compound Engine   24"-42" x 36"

1884: Built by Ward, Stanton & Co., Newburgh, NY, for Patrick Ronan (Ronan Towing Line). 1887: Transferred to Estate of Patrick Ronan. 1897: Sold to Charles W. Morse (Consolidated Towing Line). !901: Purchased by Cornell Steamboat Co. from Charles W. Morse. Rebuilt and reboilered at Cornell Shops, Rondout, NY. 1939: (Apr) Made last trip. 1940: Abandoned. (1 May) Scuttled at Port Ewen, NY. (Despite differences in statutory dimensions, vessel was nearly identical to *Osceola*. As built, had two side-by-side stacks in style of builder. After being reboilered, had one stack.)

PRIMROSE

O/N 150963   58 GT   40 NT
70.5' x 19.3' x 8.0'   Wooden Hull
Single Cyl. Engine, Condensing   16" x 20"

1902: Built by Ford Brothers, Athens, NY for Foster-Scott Ice Co. 1904: Purchased by Cornell Steamboat Co. from Richard J Foster (Foster-Scott Ice Co.) 1944 (Mar): Abandoned. (Vessel was laid up at Sunflower Dock, Rondout Creek, and later sank there. She remained there until mid-1950s, when machinery and other iron was removed by scrap merchants.)

PRINCESS

O/N 203445   151 GT   103 NT
107.0' x 22.2' x 10.7'   Wooden Hull
Compound Engine   15"-30" x 22"   500 HP

1906: Built by Thomas McCosker, Baltimore, MD, for James Clark Co., Baltimore, MD. 1910: Sold to Knickerbocker Steam Towage Co., Bath, ME. 1913 (Jul): Purchased by Cornell Steamboat Co. from Knickerbocker Steam Towage Co. 1916 (Oct): Sold to Peter Cahill (Cahill Towing Line), New York, NY. 1924 (Jan): Sunk in collision with steamship *El Valle* off Pier 49, NR, New York. One life lost. Vessel raised. 1928 (18 Mar): Foundered off New Jersey coast near Barnegat Light. Crew Rescued. Vessel subsequently abandoned. (Official records may show abandonment of *Princess* because owners originally proposed salvage but later deemed such action economically unfeasible.) Sister vessel: *Imperial*.

PROMETHEUS

O/N 19607   296 GT   164 NT
145.0' x 31.0' x 10.7'   Wooden Hull
Single Cylinder Engine   36" x 30"   150 HP

1862 (Nov): Built as passenger and freight steamer (664 GT) by Thomas J. Wetmore (?), Norwich (listed as New London), CT for Thomas and Pliny Nickerson et al, Boston, MA. 1867: Stephen T. and Edmund A. Souder et al, Philadelphia, PA. 1870 (Apr): Jacob T. Alburger & Co. et al, Philadelphia, PA. 1870 (May): George T. Clyde, Philadelphia, PA. 1872 (Oct): Salem & New York Express Steam Ship Corp., Salem, MA. 1872 (Dec): Hudson River Towing Co, New York, NY. Converted to tug and reboilered. Readmeasured as shown above. 1880 (Aug): Sold to Cheney Towing Line, New York, NY. 1892 (Apr): Purchased by Cornell Steamboat Co. from Cheney Towing Line. 1894 (Jun): Dismantled with intent to rebuild as stake boat. Later broken up. (Probably never ran as tug for Cornell Steamboat Co.)

R. G. DAVIS

[later *George B. Hance*]

O/N 110918   23 GT   11 NT
52.4' x 14.6' x 6.0'   Wooden Hull
Single Cylinder Engine   12" x 14"

1891 (Jul): Built at Athens, NY, for George Field, Newburgh, NY. 1893 (Apr): Sold to Alfred Walker and Mrs. Mary S. Horton, Newburgh, NY. 1894 (Jun): Jeremiah H. Horton and Alfred Walker, Newburgh, NY. 1895 Aug): A. Stanley Wood and Alfred Walker, Newburgh, NY. 1904 (Oct): A. Stanley Wood, Newburgh, NY. 1906 (Apr): Purchased by Cornell

Steamboat Co. from A. Stanley Wood. 1920 (May): Renamed *George B. Hance*. 1934: Probable last year of operation. 1942 (Feb): Abandoned. (Details of disposal of this vessel and *Wm. H. Baldwin* are not known.)

R. G. TOWNSEND

O/N 110549   83 GT   41 NT
81.6' x 20.5' x 8.5'   Wooden Hull
Compound Engine 17"-30" x 24

1882 (Sep): Built at Philadelphia, PA, for Cornell Steamboat Co. 1905 (2 Mar): Sunk near Nyack, NY, while breaking ice. Raised and repaired. 1951 (Dec): Out of Documentation and sold to McAllister Bros., New York, NY. Later dismantled.

R. J. FOSTER

O/N 200183   45 GT   31 NT
70.0' x 16.6' x 7.0'   Wooden Hull
Single Cylinder Engine   14½" x 18"   124 HP

1903: Built at New Baltimore, NY, for Foster-Scott Ice Co. 1904: Purchased by Cornell Steamboat Co. from Richard J Foster (Foster-Scott Ice Co.) 1948 (Aug): Dismantled. Scuttled at Port Ewen, NY.

RALPH ROSS

O/N 2197   193 GT   82 NT
97.0' x 24.5' x 8.5'   Wooden Hull
Single Cylinder Engine   200 HP

1870: Built at Philadelphia, PA, probably for Ross & Howell, Bangor, ME. 1902 (Feb): Sold to Knickerbocker Steam Towage Co (C. W. Morse). 1913: Purchased by Cornell Steamboat Co. from Knickerbocker Steam Towage Co. 1917 (Feb): Dismantled and hull converted to stake boat. 1930: Scuttled at Port Ewen, NY.

ROB

O/N 111421   47 GT   32 NT
74.8' x 18.2' x 7.5'   Wooden Hull
Single Cylinder Engine   17" x 20"   125 HP

1902: Built by John J. Baisden, Sleightsburgh, NY, for Cornell Steamboat Company, using the engine from *H. T. Caswell* and the boiler from *F. Lavergne*. Named for Robert Coykendall. 1941: Sold to McMahon Towing Inc, Lyndhurst, NJ. Fitted with 300-horsepower diesel engine. c1957: Sold to Independent Petroleum Transportation Service, Inc., Rockville Centre, NY. 1963: Dismantled. (Named for Robert Bayard Coykendall.)

ROBERT A. SCOTT

O/N 201011   50 GT   34 NT
75.0' x 18.8' x 8.0'   Wooden Hull
Single Cylinder Engine   16" x 20"   250 HP

1904: Built at New Baltimore, NY, for Hawley Miller and C. P. Woodward, New Baltimore, NY. 1905 (Jun): Purchased by Cornell Steamboat Co. from Hawley Miller and C. P. Woodward. 1917 (Mar): Sold to Joseph A Ryan, Brooklyn, NY. 1921: Transferred to Steamtug Robert A. Scott, Inc. (Joseph H. Ryan). 1938 (Jul): Dismantled.

ROCKLAND COUNTY

O/N 280864   274 GT   186 NT
95.4' x 30.1' x 10.2'   Steel Hull
Twin Screw, 2 Fairbanks-Morse Diesel Engines   1800 HP

1960 (Apr): Built by Dravo Corp., Wilmington, DE, for Cornell Steamboat Co. 1960: Sold to Red Star Towing & Transportation Co. Later transferred to Red Star subsidiary, Ocean Prince, Inc. Still in service.

ROCKTOW

O/N 237773   99 GT   67 NT
76.7' x 21.0' x 9.3'   Steel Hull
7-cyl Fairbanks-Morse Diesel Engine   800 HP

1938: Built as *Cardinal* by Ira S. Bushey & Son, Brooklyn, NY, for Motor Tug Cardinal, Inc. (Bushey). 1944: Sold to Fred B. Dalzell & Co. (Tice Towing Line) Renamed *Magnetic*. 1950: Purchased by Cornell Steamboat Co. from Fred B. Dalzell & Co. Renamed *Rocktow*. 1959: Sold to Carroll Towing Corp., New York, NY. Renamed *Carroll Brothers*. 1964: Sold to R.T.C. No. Three Corp. (Reinauer Oil Transport Corp.) Renamed *Laurie Ann Reinauer*. <1968: Sold, later reportedly lost.

ROYS J. CRAM

O/N 110520   19 GT   9 NT
50.0' x 12.0' x 7.0'   Wooden Hull
Single Cylinder Engine

1882: Built at East Saginaw, MI, for Carkin, Stickney & Cram Co., East Saginaw, MI. 1900: Sold to H. T. Wickes, Saginaw, MI. 1902: Sold to J. J. Madden, Troy, NY. 1903: Sold to Albany Towing Co. 1905: Purchased by Cornell Steamboat Co. from Albany Towing Co., bur never documented by Cornell. 1905 (8 Jul): Burned at New Baltimore, NY (This minuscule vessel was arguably the most obscure tug in the Cornell fleet during the Twentieth Century. No image of the vessel during her three-year stay at Albany is known to exist.)

RUTH

[later *E. H. Mead*]

O/N 21856   89 GT
79.5' x 17.5' x 8.0'   Wooden Hull
Single Cylinder Engine

1862: Built at Rondout, NY, for J. B. Pardee and Silas Saxton. Home port, New York. 1863: (Nov) Purchased by Thomas Cornell. 1872: Abandoned. 1873: (Apr): Rebuilt by Morgan Everson, Sleightsburgh, NY, from hull of vessel. Renamed *E. H. Mead* (q.v.) and new official number (8918) awarded as new vessel. 1890 (Mar): Dismantled.

S. L. CROSBY

O/N 115925   103 GT   51 NT
90.8' x 22.5' x 9.0'   Wooden Hull
Compound Engine 20"-34" x 36"   350 HP

1883: Built at Philadelphia, PA, for Cornell Steamboat Co. 1891 (28 Aug): Collided with steamer *W. C. Redfield* and sunk near Cranstons, below West Point. Raised and repaired at Athens. c1935: Probable last year of operation. 1944: Abandoned. 1944 (Apr): Scuttled at Port Ewen, NY.

SAMMY CORNELL

O/N 23875   30 GT   18 NT
64.0' x 14.0' x 7.0'   Wooden Hull
Single Cylinder Engine   18" x 18"

1867: Built by Morgan Everson, Sleightsburgh, NY, for Thomas Cornell. 1891: Dismantled. Part of engine to new tug *Harry*. Hull sold and broken up in New Baltimore, NY. (Documented as *Samuel Cornell*, but universally referred to as "Sammy." The vessel's pilot house nameboard, which is in a private collection, displays the name "Sammy Cornell.")

SARANAC

O/N 116105   56 GT   28 NT
69.0' x 18.8' x 7.4'   Wooden Hull
Single Cylinder Engine   20" x 22"

1886: Built by Peter Magee, Athens, NY, for Patrick Ronan (Ronan Towing Line), Albany, NY. 1887: Transferred to Estate of Patrick Ronan. 1897 (Nov): Sold to Charles W. Morse (Consolidated Towing Line). 1901 (May): Purchased by Cornell Steamboat Co. from Charles W Morse. 1941 (Mar): Dismantled. Scuttled at Port Ewen, NY.

SAXON

O/N 22789   179 GT   91 NT
138.0' x 25.0' x 8.6'   Wooden Hull
Single Cylinder Engine   36" x 30"

1861: Built as passenger and freight steamer (413 GT) at Brewer, ME. 1881: Reboilered and converted to tug. Probably sold to Cheney Towing Line, New York, NY at about this time. 1892 (Apr): Purchased by Cornell Steamboat Co. from Cheney Towing Line. Abandoned shortly after purchase. Never ran for Cornell Steamboat Co.

SENATOR RICE

O/N 117218   98 GT   66 NT
90.1' x 20.2' x 10.0'   Wooden Hull
Compound Engine   15"-34" x 26"

1902: Built by J. McCausland, Rondout, NY, for Jacob and Charles Rice, Kingston, NY, and Thomas Quigley and W. J. Nevels, Brooklyn, NY. Launched on 1 November. 1907 (Oct): Purchased by Cornell Steamboat Co. from Jacob Rice et al. 1946 (Jun): Dismantled.

STIRLING TOMKINS

O/N 217615   357 GT   197 NT
126.0' x 29.9' x 13.7'   Wooden Hull
Triple-Expansion Engine   18"-28"-45" x 30"   1000 HP

1919 (Apr): Built as *Artisan* by M. M. Davis & Son, Solomons, MD. for United States Shipping Board (Design 1061). 1920 (Sep): Sold to Cahill Towing Line, New York, NY. 1930 (Jun): Purchased by Cornell Steamboat Co. from Cahill Towing Line. (11 Jun): Renamed *Stirling Tomkins*. 1948 (Jun): Last under steam. 1949: Sold to J. Kerzman & Sons for scrap. (15 Dec): Left Rondout under tow for Cornwall, NY. 1954 (Mar): Last enrollment document surrendered, endorsed "Out of Documentation." (Named for President of New York Trap Rock Corporation.)

TERROR

O/N 24045   69 GT   34 NT
88.5' x 20.8' x 7.5'   Wooden Hull
Single Cylinder Engine   30" x 30"   350 HP

1854 (Jun): Built at Philadelphia, PA, for Hugh Ross, Bangor, ME. 1872: Sold to Eastern Transportation Line, New York, NY. 1879: Sold to Cheney Towing Line, New York, NY. 1892 (Apr): Purchased by Cornell Steamboat Co. from Cheney Towing Line. 1910: Condemned by steamboat inspectors. 1911 (Mar): Abandoned. Hull reportedly taken to Kingston Point for disposal. (Thirty-eight years of age when acquired by Cornell, *Terror* remained in operation for nearly two more decades!)

THOMAS CHUBB

O/N 145485   34 GT   19 NT
59.0' x 15.4' x 6.6'   Wooden Hull
Single Cylinder Engine   15" x 13"

1888 (May): Built by W. D. Ford, Athens, NY, for Emma F. Hayner, Greenbush, NY. 1903 (Jun): Purchased by Albany Towing Co. 1905: Purchased by Cornell Steamboat Co. from Albany Towing Co. but never documented under Cornell ownership. 1908 (2 Sep): Burned at Race Course Island, Hudson River. (Had a carved wooden fish— perhaps a chub?— atop pilot house.)

THOMAS CORNELL

O/N 249587   275 GT   187 NT
117.5' x 28.0' x 13.5'   Wooden Hull
8-Cylinder Enterprise Diesel Engine   1200 HP

1944: Built as *LT-494* by Minneford Yacht Yard, City Island, NY, for United States Army. 1946: Sold to Card Towing Line, New York, NY. Renamed *Harry Card*. 1948: Sold to McAllister Bros., Inc., then chartered to Cornell Steamboat Co. 1950: Purchased by Cornell Steamboat Co. from McAllister Bros. Inc. Renamed *Thomas Cornell*. 1958: Transferred to Lenroc Towing Corp. 1959: Sold to Olson Towboat Co., Eureka, CA. Renamed *Jean Nelson*. 1970: Sold to Mexican owners. Later career not known.

THOMAS DICKSON

O/N 24950   67 GT   40 NT
74.8' x 19.0' x 8.6'   Wooden Hull
Single Cyl. Engine, Condensing   24" x 24"   220 HP

1872: Built by Morgan Everson, Sleightsburgh, NY, for Thomas Cornell. 1927 (Sep): Abandoned. Hull sunk at East Kingston, NY. Sister vessel, *Coe F. Young*.

THOMAS P. FOWLER

O/N 145641   160 GT   80 NT
97.5' x 24.0' x 11.0'   Steel Hull
Compound Engine   400 HP

1893: Built by T. S. Marvel & Co., Newburgh, NY (Hull 61) for Cornell Steamboat Co. 1898 (23 Apr): Sold to United States Navy at start of Spanish-American War. Renamed USS *Mohawk*. 1942: Name cancelled, redesignated *YT-17*, later *YTL-17*. 1947: Sold to W. S. Sanders, Norfolk, VA. Documented as *Mohawk*. 1948: Sold to Stone Towing Line, Wilmington, NC. 1963:

Dismantled. (The third of the three modern tugs—*Washburn, Mead* and *Fowler*—built in the early 1890s, she was in appearance a smaller version of the *Mead*.)

TRITON

O/N 145568   259 GT   129 NT
114.5' x 26.5' x 14.5'   Wooden Hull
Triple-Expansion Engine 15½"-24"-40" x 30" 700 HP

1890: Built at Boston, MA, for Frederick Luckenbach, New York, NY. 1894 (Nov): Sold to Knickerbocker Steam Towage Co. 1903 (Feb): Purchased by Cornell Steamboat Co. from Knickerbocker Steam Towage Co 1907 (Dec): Sold to Lamberts Point Tow Boat Co. Norfolk, VA. 1915: Rebuilt at Berkley, VA. 1917 (Oct): Sold to Potter Transportation Co., Inc., New York, NY. 1918 (Sep): Transferred to Potter Steamship Co., Inc., New York, NY. 1919 (Aug): Sold to Atlantic Coast Transportation Co., New York, NY. 1929 (Mar): Sold to Durham Navigation Corp., New York, NY. 1932 (Jan): Abandoned.

VICTORIA

O/N 95532   77 GT   38 NT
82.1' x 17.5' x 8.8'   Wooden Hull
Compound Engine   15"-30" x 22"

1878: Built as *Hercules* by Wood, Dialogue & Co., Camden, NJ, for David Tillson, Rockland, ME. 1881: Sold to F. B. Sprague et al, Boston, MA. 1884: Sold to Baker, Whiteley & Co., Baltimore, MD. Renamed *Victoria*. 1886: Sold to Patrick Ronan (Ronan Towing Line). 1887: Transferred to Estate of Patrick Ronan. 1897: Sold to Charles W. Morse, New York, NY (Consolidated Towing Line). 1901 (May): Purchased by Cornell Steamboat Co. from Charles W Morse. c1934: Probable last year of operation. 1944 (May): Abandoned. Scuttled at Port Ewen, NY.

VOLUNTEER

O/N 161578   64 GT   32 NT
72.0' x 18.8' x 8.5'   Wooden Hull
Single Cylinder Engine   20" x 18"

1888: Built at Bordentown, NJ, for Benjamin W. Robinson, Philadelphia, PA. 1890: Sold to John Reese, Philadelphia, PA. 1891: Sold to Annette M. Church, New Bedford, MA. 1897: Sold to Andrew Ferris, Port Chester, NY. 1904: Sold to James F. Dwyer, Kingston, NY, 1908: Sold to Curtis Blaisdell Co., New York, NY. 1912 (Apr): Purchased by Cornell Steamboat Co. from Curtis Blaisdell Co. 1914 (Apr): Sold to Reuben B. Drew et al, Brooklyn, NY. 1916: Sold to Olsen Water & Towing Co., Inc., Brooklyn, NY. Renamed *Marie Olsen*. 1939 (Sep): Abandoned.

W. A. KIRK

O/N 202660   61 GT   41 NT
65.6' x 19.0' x 8.0'   Wooden Hull
Single Cylinder Engine   17" x 20"   300 HP

1905: Built as *Walter B. Pollack* at New Baltimore, NY, for James H. Williams, Albany, NY. 1909: Sold to Egerton Towing Line, New York, NY. 1926: Sold to New York Towing & Transportation Co., New York, NY. Renamed *W. A. Kirk*. 1927: Purchased by Cornell Steamboat Co. from New York Towing & Transportation Co. Never documented under ownership of Cornell Steamboat Co. 1939 (Feb): Dismantled. 1942: Scuttled at Port Ewen, NY.

W. B. McCULLOCH

O/N 150816   18 GT   13 NT
46.3' x 14.0' x 5.5'   Wooden Hull
Single Cylinder Engine   12½" x 14"

1899: Built as *P. McCabe, Jr.* at Athens, NY, for William P. Smith, Rensselaer, NY. 1901: Sold to Thomas Ward et al, Watervliet, NY. 1903: Sold to Albany Towing Co., Albany, NY. 1904: Renamed W. B. McCulloch. 1905: Purchased by Cornell Steamboat Co. from Albany Towing Co. 1920: First documented under ownership of Cornell Steamboat Co. 1943 (Jun): Abandoned. Vessel hauled out, dismantled and left to deteriorate at Sleightsburgh, NY. Still there in early 1950s but demolished soon thereafter.

W. E. STREET

O/N 80846   104 GT   52 NT
92.0' x 22.0' x 9.3'   Wooden Hull
Compound Engine

1881 (Oct): Built by Neafie & Levy Ship & Engine Building. Co., Philadelphia, PA, for Cornell Steamboat Co. 1909 (Aug): Abandoned. (Engine was to have been used in new vessel ordered from T. S. Marvel Shipbuilding Co., of Newburgh. New vessel cancelled and never completed. See that vessel's entry following that of *York River*.)

W. N. BAVIER

O/N 81790   110 GT   75 NT
82.4' x 21.5' x 11.4'   Steel Hull
Compound Engine   12"-27" x 21"   300 HP

1901: Hull built by Burlee Dry Dock Co., Port Richmond, NY. Engine built and installed by Cornell Steamboat Company at Rondout. 1945: Abandoned. (Although a relatively modern steel-hulled vessel, *W. N. Bavier* appears to have seen little, if any, service after the mid-1930s.)

WATCHMAN

O/N (N/A)   Tonnages never determined.
126.0' x 29.9' x 13.7'   Wooden Hull
Original engine to have been triple-expansion, identical to that of *Stirling Tomkins*.

1919: Hull built by M. M. Davis & Son, Solomons, MD for United States Shipping Board (Design 1061). Early 1920s: Purchased as unfinished hull by Cornell Steamboat Co. from United States Shipping Board. c1930: Machinery and upperworks from tug *Osceola* transferred to *Watchman*. Resulting vessel never completed, but remained laid up in Rondout Creek 1949: Abandoned. Scuttled at Port Ewen, NY.

WILSON P. FOSS

O/N 81663   58 GT   39 NT
64.2' x 18.0' x 8.1'   Wooden Hull

Single Cylinder Engine   16" x 20"   178 HP

1899 (Nov): Built by William Mathison, Brooklyn, NY, for Jacob E. Conklin and Wilson P. Foss, Haverstraw, NY. 1900 (Jun): Purchased by Cornell Steamboat Co. from Jacob E. Conklin and Wilson P. Foss. 1949 (Mar): Dismantled. Hull remained partially sunk at Sleightsburgh, NY.

WM. E. CLEARY

O/N 201197   90 GT   61 NT
75.6' x 19.5' x 11.0'   Steel Hull
Single Cyl. Engine, Condensing   16" x 20"   250 HP

1904: Hull built by T. S. Marvel & Co., Newburgh, NY (Hull 155), for Cornell Steamboat Co. (Sep): Installation of engine, boiler and joiner work completed at Rondout. 1949 (Apr): Dismantled. Sister vessel, *J. H. Williams*.

WM. H. BALDWIN

O/N 81744   38 GT   26 NT
54.0' x 16.8' x 6.8'   Wooden Hull
Single Cylinder Engine   13" x 16"

1901 (Apr): Built at New Baltimore, NY, for William T. Pratt, Watervliet (later Brooklyn), NY. 1907 (Mar): Sold to Knickerbocker Steam Towage Co, Bath, ME. 1913 (Aug): Purchased by Cornell Steamboat Co. from Knickerbocker Steam Towage Co. 1934: Probable last year of operation. 1942 (Feb): Abandoned. (Details of disposal of this vessel are not known.)

WM. S. EARL

O/N 80149   24 GT   12 NT
55.0' x 14.8' x 5.8'   Wooden Hull
Single Cylinder Engine   16½" x 15"   120 HP

1859: Built at Philadelphia, PA, probably by Neafie & Levy. 1881 (1 Dec): Damaged by fire at Greenbush, NY, while owned by Henry Bedell. c1882: Sold to Washburn Steamboat Co., Saugerties, NY. 1884: Purchased by Cornell Steamboat Co. from Washburn Steamboat Co. 1903 (13 Dec): Badly damaged by fire at Rondout and rebuilt. 1936 (30 May): Again damaged by fire at Rondout and rebuilt. 1947: Last time steam was raised. 1949 (20 Jul): Abandoned. Scuttled at Port Ewen, NY, at the advanced age of ninety years. (Having risen like a phoenix from the ashes of three serious fires, *Wm. S. Earl* was the sentimental favorite of Edward Coykendall. Hence her long life. If there ever was a fitting candidate for preservation, it was *Wm. S. Earl*, but, alas, this was not to be.)

WOODBRIDGE

O/N 85164   21 GT   10 NT
49.3' x 14.0' x 6.0'   Wooden Hull
Single Cylinder Engine   64 HP

1870: Built as *Georgianna* at New Brunswick, NJ, for George W. Fouratt and Charles Parison, South Amboy, NJ/ 1881: Sold to Easton & Amboy Railroad Co., South Amboy, NJ. 1900: Renamed *Woodbridge*. 1904: Transferred to Lehigh Valley Transportation Co., South Amboy, NJ. 1910: Sold to Edward G. Murray, New York, NY. 1911: Sold to Knickerbocker Steam Towage Co. 1913 (Aug): Purchased by Cornell Steamboat Co. from Knickerbocker Steam Towage Co. 1920 (Mar): Abandoned. (Last renewal of license was dated 20 August 1919, which indicates that vessel may have been used during the period from 1913 to 1919.)

WRESTLER

O/N 81244   198 GT   99 NT
115.0' x 25.5' x 13.2'   Wooden Hull
Compound Engine (?)

1889 (Nov): Built by The Atlantic Works, Boston, MA, for the New Bedford Steam Coasting Co., New Bedford, MA. 1897: Sold to William C. Appleton and Asa Haley, Managing Owners, Boston, MA. 1899: Sold to Red Star Towing & Wrecking Co., Boston, MA. 1903: Sold to Long Island Rail Road Co., Richmond Hill, NY. 1919 {Oct): Dismantled. Hull later purchased by Cornell Steamboat Co. for reconstruction and installation of engine. Rebuilding later abandoned. 1930: Hull scuttled at Port Ewen, NY.

YORK RIVER

O/N 27530   64 GT
Dimensions not known   Wooden Hull
Single Cylinder Engine

Before 1860: Built at Philadelphia, PA (see note below). 1861: Sold to Confederate States Navy. Renamed CSS *Teaser*. Vessel armed with one 32-pounder and one 9-pounder rifle. 1862 (8-9 Mar): Played minor role in battle between USS *Monitor* and CSS *Virginia*. 1862 (4 Jul): Captured in the James River near Drewry's Bluff by the United Sates Navy gunboat *Maratanza* 1865 (Jul): Sold and documented at Georgetown, DC, as *York River*. Later purchased by Thomas Cornell. 1873 (Summer?): Damaged by fire at New York. 1873 (Oct): Engine and boiler removed at Rondout and converted by Morgan Everson, Sleightsburg, NY, to barge for Washington Ice Co. (It is possible, but not yet proven, that this vessel was built as the tug *Wide Awake* at Philadelphia in 1855.)

Unnamed [T. S. Marvel Hull 192]

Official Number and Tonnages Not Assigned
95'-0" x 23'-0" x 11'-6"   Steel Hull
Engine from *W. E. Street* (q.v.) was to have been installed.

1907: Ordered by Cornell Steamboat Co. from T. S. Marvel Shipbuilding Co., Newburgh, NY (Hull 192). According to Harry A. Marvel, keel laid and steelwork erection commenced. Work stopped after a few frames had been erected, and the vessel was dismantled on the building ways. (From the dimensions, it is assumed that this unnamed vessel would have been similar to *Thomas P. Fowler* (q.v.), the third of the three pioneering iron and steel hulled tugs in the Cornell fleet.)

RHINEBECK-KINGSTON FERRIES

The listing below includes all steam ferries known to have been the property of the private owners of the Rondout-to-Rhinecliff ferry, prior to resumption of service by the New York State Bridge Authority in 1946 with the diesel ferry *George Clinton*.

Thomas Cornell or the Coykendall family were involved in the ownership or management of all vessels shown except the first steam vessel to operate on the route, *Knickerbocker*.

KINGSTON

O/N 125614 401 GT 272 NT
142.8' x 30.0' x 10.4' Iron Hull
Two 6-cyl Diesel Engines 500 HP

1877: Built as beam-engined steam ferry *Columbia* (Hull 162) by Harlan & Hollingsworth Co., Wilmington, DE, for West Jersey Ferry Co. Operated between Philadelphia and Camden, NJ. Late 1920s: Converted to twin-screw (double-ended) diesel-propelled ferry for Long Island Sound Ferries Corp., New York. Renamed *New Rochelle*. 1930 (May): Purchased by Rhinebeck & Kingston Ferry Co. Renamed *Kingston*. 1943: Sold to Harris County, TX. 1944: Out of documentation. (Sixth ferry between Rondout and Rhinebeck.)

KNICKERBOCKER

O/N (N/A)
Dimensions Unknown Wooden Hull
Beam Engine (probable)

1845: First operated on Rhinebeck-Kingston ferry. 1853 (Jun): Sold to owners at Catskill, NY, for service between Catskill and Oak Hill. (First ferry between Rondout and Rhinebeck. Little is known of this apparently undocumented vessel, except that she was a small side-wheeler. Her date and place of build are unknown.)

LARK

O/N 14935 156 GT
93'-0" x 24'-0" x 8'-0" Wooden Hull
Beam Engine 28" x 72"

1860: Built by Webb & Bell (Eckford Webb), Brooklyn, NY, for Rhinebeck & Kingston Ferry Co. Arrived at Rondout on 15 July. 1905: Abandoned. (Fourth ferry between Rondout and Rhinebeck.)

ORIOLE

O/N 19095 124 GT
Dimensions not known Wooden Hull
Beam Engine

1862: Built at Sleightsburgh, NY, for Rhinebeck & Kingston Ferry Co. 1893: Abandoned. (Third ferry between Rondout and Rhinebeck.)

RHINE

O/N (N/A) 106-93/95 GT
85'-9" x 20'-6" x 6'-9" Wooden Hull
Beam Engine 32" x 72"

1852: Built at New York, NY, for Charles H. Russell as sole owner. 1862: Abandoned. (Second ferry between Rondout and Rhinebeck.)

THOMAS W. OLCOTT

O/N 24758 289 GT
148.0' x 28.0' x 8.0' Wooden Hull
Beam Engine

1848: Built at Albany, NY. 1877: Purchased by Thomas Cornell for Kingston & Rhinebeck Ferry Co. Probably never used on company's ferry route. 1879: Converted to rail transfer ferry to carry cars for Ulster & Delaware Railroad, Wallkill Valley Railroad and Rhinebeck & Connecticut Railroad between Rondout and Rhinecliff. 1888: Abandoned.

TRANSPORT

O/N 145042 318 GT 226 NT
115.0' x 26.5' x 9.8' Iron Hull
Beam Engine 32" x 108"

1875: Built by Wm. Cramp & Sons, Philadelphia, PA, for Camden & Amboy Railroad. 1881: Purchased by Rhinebeck & Kingston Ferry Co. from Camden & Amboy. 1881 (26 Aug): First trip at Rondout. 1938 (13 Sep): Last trip as ferry. Laid up. 1941 (Aug): Converted to stakeboat for Cornell Steamboat Co. (Fifth ferry between Rondout and Rhinebeck.)

SPURIOUS VESSELS

The following section lists five vessels which have been stated by other sources over the years as having been owned by the Cornell Steamboat Company. They are included here to put to rest nearly a century of misconception relating to the Cornell fleet. In none of these instances has reliable indication of ownership by the company been found or, in two cases, has any trace of a vessel of the name been uncovered.

The principal source for these entries is the undated and widely circulated outline entitled "History of the Cornell Steamboat Company," by Captain William B. Barnett. Captain Barnett's work remains, however, a valuable document, providing a contemporary view of the company's fleet and of the tugs' captains and chief engineers.

AMBITION

O/N 83   35 GT   17 NT
61.4' x 14.5' x 6.0'   Wooden Hull
Single Cylinder Engine

1864: Built at Baltimore, MD, for Wm. R. Tomlinson and W. E. Woodall, Baltimore. (Tomlinson's name is spelled four different ways— Tomlinson, Tumlinson, Tumblinson and Tumblenson— on the five documents issues to these owners.) This vessel was owned by the Cheney Towing Line from 25 April 1881 to 1 May 1882. On the latter date she was sold to Charles Conklin, Catskill, NY (see *J. W. Conklin* below), and thereafter was owned by John J. Donahue and Jeremiah Ball, of Brooklyn, NY, and other owners in Newport, RI and Boston, MA. At the time the Cheney tugs were purchased by Cornell in 1892, *Ambition* was owned by Jonathan Close, of Boston, and was dismantled as "unfit for service" in August 1893. It is possible, but unlikely, that she was then under charter to Cheney in 1892, but the vessel was definitely not a part of the sale to Cornell.

ANNA

O/N 1705   201 GT   133 NT
146.0' Xx 25.0' x 8.2'   Wooden Hull
Beam Engine 40" x 120"   200 HP

The side-wheel towboat *Anna*, built at Albany in 1854, is included here because she was a part of the complex 1869 transaction which brought *Oswego*, *Cayuga* and *Baltic* to the Cornell fleet. Originally, Thomas Cornell wanted to purchase *Oswego*, *Cayuga* and *Anna*, from Alfred Van Santvoord, but, after some "horse-trading", Cornell received *Oswego* and *Cayuga*, but immediately exchanged the latter with Schuyler for *Baltic*. Schuyler was the buyer of *Anna* from the start.. Despite 130 years of legend, *Anna* was never owned by Thomas Cornell.

J. W. CONKLIN

Listed by Barnett as having been purchased from Cheney Towing Line. No trace of a tugboat named *J. W. Conklin*, or one of a similar name, has ever been found. (The late Donald C. Ringwald once speculated that the name "J. W. Conklin" might have been mentioned to Captain Barnett by a more-than-slightly inebriated boatman as he emerged from a lowly Rondout saloon one summer night. Coincidentally, however, E. E. Conklin was secretary of the Hudson River Towing Company, a predecessor of the Cheney Towing Line, around 1873.)

S. E. SEARS

Listed by Barnett as having been purchased from "Newburgh Line" along with *R. G. Davis* and *George Field*. No trace of a tugboat named *S. E. Sears* has ever been found. It is possible that Barnett was referring to the tug *Frank A. Sears* (also known as *F. A. Sears*), owned in Newburgh through 1882 and later in Yonkers and finally in Brooklyn, but there no evidence that she was ever owned by the Cornell Steamboat Co. The vessel burned at New York early in 1890.

THOMAS CORNELL

O/N 24365   77 GT
Dimensions not known.   Wooden Hull
Single-Cylinder Engine

A tugboat named *Thomas Cornell* was built at Rondout in 1861 by Jacob Fox, but was never owned by her namesake. She was in fact owned at one time or another by Peter C. Schultz, an associate of Thomas Cornell's, or other members of the Schultz family. The vessel was a fixture in the creek until she was converted to a barge in 1879.

W. E. CHENEY

O/N 80282   71 GT   35 NT
84.0' x 20.0' x 7.0'   Wooden Hull
Single-Cylinder Engine

Built 1865 at South Rondout, NY, and named for Warner E. Cheney. Originally documented as *Warner E. Cheney*. Although this vessel is known to have operated on the Hudson River from time to time and by name has a possible connection to the Cheney Towing Line, there is no indication that she was ever a Cornell tug.

Appendix E: Fleet List

Acknowlegments

If ever a history needed writing, the story of the Cornell Steamboat Company was one; and if ever a writer needed guidance, advice, information, cooperation, insight, correcting, and at least an elementary understanding of his subject, this writer is he. And I am grateful for all of it.

In the research for and writing of this book, so much was generously provided to me, and I give my sincere thanks to everyone. For what is right in this book, I am indebted to the following persons, and I take responsibility for the rest.

Thanks to C. W. Spangenberger, Roger W. Mabie, and William duBarry Thomas, who gave everything they had to this work for the sake of remembering and honoring the Cornell Steamboat Company and its people. Thanks also to Allynne Lange, curator of the Hudson River Maritime Museum, for her generosity, kindness, and cooperation in the research and for reading the manuscript.

Thanks to Edward Kalaidjian, another reader, and to Charles Fiero, Mrs. Charles Henderson, and Seward Osborne for insights, cooperation, and in one case a gift.

Thanks to Peter Fallon, past president of the Hudson River Maritime Museum, and to Joseph Emerson, museum director, and Robert Levitt, assistant director, as well as to the museum's dedicated staff and volunteers for their hospitality and unreserved cooperation. Thanks also to Amanda Jones of the Ulster County Historical Society, and to Steve Trueman for sharing his tugboat expertise, and to Kingston historian Edwin M. Ford for his assistance and advice. Thanks to Clark Leiching and Harry Lowe for recalling their days in Rondout Creek, and to Dr. Arthur Hazenbush, for sharing his knowledge of his grandfather, Wellington Shultis, a Cornell captain and employee of long standing.

Particular thanks to Steven Delibert, president of the Ulster and Delaware Chapter of the National Railway Historical Society, and to Russell Hallock, for their insights and corrections on railroading aspects of the text.

Thanks to artist Len Tantillo, who does so much to bring to life the maritime history and heritage of the Hudson River, and to photographer John Matthews, whose lifelong interest has brought him such a splendid collection of maritime photographs. Thanks to the staff of the Kingston Public Library and to Nancy McKechnie of Vassar College Library; also to staff members of the New York State Library in Albany; to David Hill, archivist at Columbia University, and to the staff of Columbia's Office of Public Affairs. Thanks to Karin L. Summerlin, assistant vice president for public affairs at SUNY New Paltz; Sue Greenhagen of the SUNY Morrisville library; the staffs of the Chatham, New York, Public Library, and the local history staff at the Berkshire Athenaeum, Pittsfield, Massachusetts.

Thanks, also, to Kay Spangenberger and Peggy Mabie for making those interviews seem not so much like work. And thanks to my wife, Els Murray, who goes through it all with me.

And not least, thanks to publishers, Wray and Loni Rominger of Purple Mountain Press, who were so committed to telling the Cornell story as part of their ongoing mission to present the rich maritime history of the Hudson River to the world.

Without a doubt, all of us owe a profound debt of gratitude to the late Donald C. Ringwald, eminent Hudson River maritime historian, whose meticulous, dedicated research and writing—a legacy that was published over many years—is at the foundation of this work.

It is hoped that Don Ringwald would have approved of, and enjoyed, this book.

Selected Bibliography and Sources

Adams, Arthur G. *The Hudson Through the Years.* Westwood, N.J.: Lind, 1983.

Best, Gerald M. *The Ulster and Delaware Railroad Through the Catskills.* San Marino, Calif.: Golden West Books, 1972.

Beers, F. W. *County Atlas of Ulster, New York.* New York: Walker & Jewett, 1875.

Benson, William O. with Roger W. Mabie. "On Getting ready for Spring." *Tempo, Your Sunday Freeman Magazine,* 19 March 1972.
____. "Remembering those Boat race Days at Poughkeepsie." *Tempo, Your Sunday Freeman Magazine,* 18 June 1972.
____. "'Ramsdell' and 'Washburn' have Some Fun." *Tempo, Your Sunday Freeman Magazine,* 6 August 1972.
____. "The Loss of the Diesel Tug 'Cornell.'" *Tempo, Your Sunday Freeman Magazine,* 5 November 1972.
____. "'City of Kingston' Becomes a Cape Horner." *Tempo, Your Sunday Freeman Magazine,* 26 November 1972.
____. "A Story of Two Tugs' Travail in the Winter Ice." *Tempo, Your Sunday Freeman Magazine,* 21 January 1973.
____. "The Most Impressive Tugboat of All." *Tempo, Your Sunday Freeman Magazine,* 25 March 1973.
____. "Freshets in Rondout Creek Sweep Fleet Away." *Tempo, Your Sunday Freeman Magazine,* 8 April 1973.
____. "The Incredibly Long Life of the 'Norwich.'" *Tempo, Your Sunday Freeman Magazine,* 20 May 1973.
____. "Hanging on Cornell Tows in the Fog." *Tempo, Your Sunday Freeman Magazine,* 30 December 1973.
____. "Labors (And Mishaps) of Tugboat 'Hercules.'" *The Sunday Freeman* 23 January 1977.
____. "September 30, 1918—Big Day on the Rondout." *The Sunday Freeman,* 14 August 1977.
____. "Coaling Up at Rondout." *The Sunday Freeman,* n.d.
____. "A Hudson River Sleighride." *Sunday Freeman,* n.d.
____. "Christmas on the 'Crosby.'" *Tempo, Your Sunday Freeman Magazine,* n.d.
____. "All Right, Cap . . . All Gone." *Tempo, Your Sunday Freeman Magazine,* n.d.
____. "How to Become an Ice Breaker." *Tempo, Your Sunday Freeman Magazine,* n.d.

Clearwater, Alphonso T. *The History of Ulster County, New York.* Kingston, N.Y.: W. J. Van Deusen, 1907.

Delibert, Steven. "The Hundred-Year Dynasty of Cornell & Coykendall." *The Rip Van Winkle Flyer;* Fall and Winter, 1999.

D'Onofrio, Sam, Ed. "Push Type Towboat Christened 'Rockland County' in Haverstraw—Designed for Hudson River Conditions." *Screenings—N.Y. Trap Rock Corporation Monthly Magazine;* July, 1960; 3-9.

Editors. *Proceedings of the Ulster County Historical Society, 1947 to 1953.* Marbletown, N.Y.: Ulster County Historical Society, 1954.

Editors. "Sparks of Fire from a Paddle Wheel." *Nautical Gazette,* 20 February 1886.

Editors. "Rondout Lighthouse," *The Pilot's Log,* 1999; 5-6; The Hudson River Maritime Museum, Kingston, N.Y.

Editors. "Coykendall Dies; Columbia Trustee." *The New York Times,* 19 November 1954.

Harding, Maria. "Hudson Brickmaking." *Kingston Daily Freeman,* 28 September 1989.

Hume, Fred R., Jr. "Sale of Oldest River Carrier Hints Changes in Methods." *The Waterways Journal,* April 19, 1958; 10.
____. "Push Style to Make Belated Debut on Hudson River." *The Waterways Journal,* May 30, 1959; 7.

Jonas, Louise. "Ferries at Kingston Have Only a Past." *Poughkeepsie Sunday New Yorker,* September 26, 1943.

Lang, Steven, and Peter H. Spectre. *On the Hawser, A*

Tugboat Album. Camden, Me.: Down East Books, 1980.

Lange, Allyne. "Hudson River Cargoes and Carriers." *The Pilot's Log,* 1999, 35-38. Article on an exhibit at the Hudson River Maritime Museum, Kingston, N.Y.

Lewis-Jones, Trevor. Ed. "Towing on an 'AC' River." *The Compass.* Socony-Vacuum Oil Co., Inc. (Vol. XXIII, No. 4) 10-12.

Lowenthal, Larry. *From the Coalfields to the Hudson—A History of the Delaware & Hudson Canal.* Fleischmanns, N.Y.: Purple Mountain Press, 1997.

Mabie, Roger W. "The Hudson River Port of Rondout." *Sea History* (Autumn, 1985): 12-15.

Murdoch, George W. Author of approximately 150 articles published in the Kingston *Daily Freeman,* Kingston, N.Y., relating the histories of Hudson River steamboats.

Osborne, Seward R. *The Saga of the "Mountain Legion": (156th N.Y. Vols.) in the Civil War.* Hightstown, N.J.: Longstreet House, 1994.

Ringwald, Donald C. *Hudson River Day Line.* Berkeley, Calif.: Howell-North Books, 1965.
_____. *The Mary Powell.* Berkeley, Calif.: Howell-North Books, 1972.
_____. *Steamboats for Rondout.* Providence: The Steamship Historical Society of America, 1981.
_____. "History of the Kingston-Rhinecliff Ferry." Kingston, N.Y.: Kingston *Daily Freeman,* January 8, 1957.
_____.and Gail Schneider. "Rondout and the Cornell Steamboat Company, 1847-1964." Catalog of an exhibition at the Hudson River Maritime Museum, Kingston, N.Y., 1983.

Schuyler, Philip N., Ed. "Cornell Steamboat Company." *The Hundred Year Book.* New York: A. S. Barnes and Company, 1942.

Steuding, Bob. *Rondout, A Hudson River Port.* Fleischmanns, N.Y.: Purple Mountain Press, 1995.

Sullivan, Joseph F. "Rondout Past and Present." Kingston, N.Y.: A series of articles in the Kingston *Daily Freeman,* 1958.

Woods, Ron. *Kingston's Magnificent City Parks.* Kingston, N.Y., 1992.

Unpublished Sources

Kent, Raymond L. "The Cornell Steamboat Company." Master's thesis, New York University, 1958.

Mastropaolo, Gerard M. "Cornell Steamboat Company Vessels, 1837-1964." August 1986.

Spangenberger, C.W. "A Report of Our Operating Needs." Written for the Cornell Steamboat Company, Kingston, N.Y., 1948.
_____. "The Cornell Steamboat Company." Lecture presented to the Hudson River Maritime Museum, Kingston, N.Y. n.d. [??]

Thomas, William duBarry. "The King of the Hudson: George W. Washburn—Hull 33—1890."
_____. "Laid Down, But Never Completed: An Unnamed Tug—Hull 192—1907."

Collections

Hudson River Maritime Museum. Estate of Thomas Cornell ledger books; the Saulpaugh Family Collection; photo archive, various archival material related to the Cornell Steamboat Company, including letter books, legal papers, and ledgers.

Roger Mabie collection, including the poem "The Breaking of the Ice Gorge," author anonymous; photographs, fleet lists, and vessel descriptions.

William duBarry Thomas collection, including photographs, fleet list, descriptions of vessels, newspaper reports related to the Cornell Steamboat Company, its vessels and personnel.

C. W. Spangenberger collection, including Cornell Steamboat Company Corporation minutes, correspondence, personnel files, fleet lists, insurance, and financial records.

Kingston Area Free Public Library. Rare book and local history section and its microfilmed newspaper accounts from the Kingston-Rondout area.

Ulster County Historical Society. Business letter books of S. D. Coykendall, 1880-82, and Thomas Cornell, 1888-90.

Index of Vessels and General Index

VESSELS

A. B. Valentine, 50-51, 57, 68, 79, 88, 91, 100, 196
A. C. Cheney, 83, 87, 200
Addie Douglas, 55
Adriatic, 87, 88, 200
Alicia A. Washburn, 69, 200
Alida, 31, 51, 58, 79, 196
Ambition, 87, 215
America, 52, 86, 91, 196
Anna, 51, 52, 215
Armenia, 31-32, 51
Artisan, 143
Austin, 58, 88, 91, 100, 196
Baltic, 29, 52, 57
Bear, 160, 185-186, 200
Belle, 86, 92
Benjamin B. Odell, 127-128
Berkshire, 46
Betty, 200
Bismarck, 120, 141, 200
Britannia, 120, 141, 185-186, 200
Burro, 185, 186, 200
C. D. Mills, 49, 67, 91, 114, 117, 134-135, 195, 201
C. Vanderbilt, 69, 91, 196
C. W. Morse, 98, 111, 121, 127, 140-141, 201
Camelia, 68, 87, 114, 201
Cayuga, 51-52, 64, 79, 196
Ceres, 48, 79, 196
Charlie Lawrence, 120, 129, 141, 145, 168, 186-187, 201
Charlotte Vanderbilt, 45
Chauncey Vibbard, 51
Christiana, 87, 91, 201
City of Brockton, 79
City of Catskill, 67-68
City of Kingston, 65, 67, 69, 71, 77, 79-81, 83, 108, 169, 180, 195
City of Seattle, 180
City of Springfield, 69
Clermont, 110, 179
Coe F. Young, 88, 91, 125, 148-149, 154-155, 184, 201
Columbia, 49, 88, 117, 201,
Conqueror, 87, 114, 201
Cornell [I] (1902), 15, 102, 111-115, 151, 181, 185, 202
Cornell [II] (Diesel), 129, 151, 167-168, 202
Cornell No. 20, 129, 151, 167, 172, 186, 202
Cornell No. 21, 130, 151, 173, 186, 202
Cornell No. 41, 13, 129, 151, 167, 172, 186, 202
Daniel Drew, 42, 51

Dean Richmond, 22
Delta, 120, 141, 202
Dr. David Kennedy, 61, 88, 91, 202
Duke, 167, 181
E. C. Baker, 90, 93, 110, 129, 132, 139-140, 202
E. D. Haley, 120, 141, 203
E. H. Mead 203
E. L. Levy, 90, 93, 110, 129, 132, 139, 140, 177
Edwin H. Mead, 91, 104, 109, 128, 172, 180, 185, 193, 203
Edwin Terry, 69, 79, 91, 110, 159, 167, 180, 182, 184, 187-188, 191, 203
Eli B. Conine, 100, 129, 186, 203
Ellen M. Ronan, 93, 139, 177, 203
Emerald, 26, 29, 35, 196
Empire, 147, 155, 203
Engels, 203
Esopus, 127-128, 143
Eugenia, 95, 104, 129, 131, 204
F. Lavergne, 68, 88, 156, 204
Francis H. Carter, 12, 197
Francis Skiddy, 31
Frank, 17, 120, 129, 186, 204
F. W. Vosburgh, 92
G. C. Adams, 139, 143, 149, 177, 204
G. W. Decker, 102, 110, 154-155, 160, 180, 185-186, 189, 204
General McDonald, 84, 187, 197
General Jackson, 20-24
General Sheridan, 204
Geo. C. Van Tuyl, Jr., 95, 104, 111, 123, 204
Geo. N. Southwick, 95, 111, 154-155, 204
Geo. W. Washburn, 15-16, 83, 88, 91, 109, 128, 143-144, 148, 150, 172, 180, 185-186, 189, 191-193, 205
George A. Hoyt, 48, 57-58, 79, 184, 191, 197
George B. Hance, 154, 170, 205
George D. Cooley, 95, 205
George Field, 192, 205
George L. Garlick, 92
George W. Pratt, 67, 91, 131, 205
Glenogle, 180
Greyhound, 116
H. D. Mould, 187, 205
H. P. Farrington, 61, 185, 205
H. T. Caswell, 69, 88, 91, 101, 205
Half Moon, 109-110
Harry, 88, 91, 120, 205
Harry B. Williams, 187
Harry Card, 153, 159, 162
Haverstraw, 205
Henry Clay, 31-32
Herald, 44, 57, 79, 197

Hercules, 69, 91, 105-106, 114-116, 110, 112, 132, 160, 172, 206
Highlander, 28-29, 32-33, 35, 39, 42, 45, 197
Homer Ramsdell, 106, 143-144, 147
Honeysuckle, 87, 91, 114, 206
"Ice King" (nickname), see *Norwich*
Ice King, 98, 110, 116-117, 140, 206
Imperial, 120, 129, 141, 185, 206
Ira M. Hedges, 69, 79, 106, 110, 167, 180, 184, 191, 206
Isaac M. North, 48, 55, 66, 68, 88, 206
Istrouma, 98, 121, 181, 185
J. Arnold, 95, 104, 206
J. C. Hartt, 16, 88, 91, 109, 120, 125, 129, 132-134, 148, 151, 154-155, 160, 184, 206
J. G. Rose, 16, 102, 109-110, 159, 162, 167, 180, 185-186, 206
J. H. Williams, 102, 110, 125, 130, 180, 185-186, 207
J. W. Conklin, 215
Jack, 166
Jacob Leonard, 86, 91, 197
James H. Flannery, 172
James H. Scott, 95, 104, 106, 207
James Kent, 38, 86, 188, 197
James Madison, 26-27, 29, 31-32, 35-36, 58, 79, 197
James W. Baldwin, 44-46, 67, 69, 108, 180
John D. Schoonmaker, 87-88, 91, 118-119, 121, 154-155, 159, 187, 189, 191, 207
John Dillon, 180
John F. Rodman, 29, 184, 197
John H. Cordts, 69, 77, 88, 91, 105-106, 109, 122, 147-148, 191, 192, 207
John P. Sleight, 53
John Marshall, 43, 68, 198
John T. Welch, 109-110, 207
Jonty Jenks, 192
Julia A. Brainard, 207
Jumbo, 16, 129, 143-144, 151, 167-168, 186, 189, 193, 207
Kingston (Ferry), 150, 172
Knickerbocker (Ferry), 214
Knickerbocker (Steamboat), 45
Knickerbocker (Tug), 98, 110, 140, 207
Lark (Ferry), 214
Lion, 16, 129, 143-144, 151, 167-168, 186, 189, 193, 207
M. Martin, 128
M. B. Harlow, 95, 104, 208
M. V. Schuyler, 179, 184
Mabel, 93, 139, 208
Madison County, 196
Magnetic, 168

219

Manhattan, 17, 31, 35-36, 42-45, 79, 108, 179, 180, 194
Mary A. Cornell, 164, 166, 208
Mary Atwater, 71
Mary Powell, 38-39, 41-47, 50-52, 67, 69, 79-80, 103, 118, 121, 123, 127-129, 149, 172, 179-180, 193-194
Maurice Wurts, 184, 198
Mazeppa, 35
Metamora, 68
Meteor, 169
Mohegan, 15, 25, 28, 35, 48, 58, 198
Montauk, 187, 208
Moran (Incomplete name), 92
Mount Washington, 79, 198
New Champion, 179
New Haven, 30
New London, 19
New York (Towboat), 52, 58, 198
New York (Day Line Steamer), 106
Newburgh (Steamboat), 106, 147
Newburgh (Tug), 208
Niagara, 86, 91, 198
Norfolk, 29
North America, 28-29, 31-33, 35, 39, 195
North River Steam Boat, 19, 109-110, 179
Norwich 24-26, 28-30, 35, 53-54, 61, 79-80, 88, 90-91, 93, 97, 103-105, 109, 112-114, 121, 123-124, 130, 134, 183, 198
Onteora, 109
Oriole (Ferry), 214
Osceola, 93, 98, 105, 109, 139, 143, 160, 172, 185, 208
"Other Side" (nickname), see *Riverside*
Oswego, 47, 51, 55, 68, 74, 88, 91, 110, 123-124, 127-128, 199
P. McCabe, Jr., 96, 104
P. C. Ronan, 208
P. C. Schultz, 68, 87, 91, 184, 199
Papa Guy, 175
Paul Le Roux, 95, 104, 208
Perry, 120, 141, 209
Perseverance, 15, 143, 147, 150, 159, 161, 180, 184-186, 189, 193, 209
Pittston, 34, 48, 68, 88, 91, 104, 184, 199
Pocahontas, 93, 98, 105, 107, 109, 115, 123, 128, 139-140, 160, 172, 177, 185, 209
Poppy, 48, 55
Primrose, 110, 154-155, 209
Princess, 120, 129, 141, 185, 209
Prometheus, 87, 209
R. G. Davis, 209
R. G. Townsend, 16, 80, 109, 125, 159, 184, 210
R. J. Foster, 154, 210
Ralph Ross, 120, 141, 210
Rhine (Ferry), 31, 34, 103, 214,
Rip Van Winkle, 35, 179, 195
Riverside, 84, 113, 180
Rob, 73, 102-103, 111-117, 120, 123-124, 146, 148-149, 180-181, 210
Robert A. Scott, 110, 210
Rochester, 21-22
Rockland County, 13-16, 172, 177, 179, 210
Rocktow, 168, 176, 182, 210
Roys J. Cram, 95, 104, 210
Ruth, 210
S. E. Sears, 215
S. L. Crosby, 86, 109, 116, 125, 134-135, 151, 160, 184, 210
Sammy Cornell, 38, 49, 51, 60-61, 68-69, 75, 114, 211
Sandy, 53, 88, 94, 199
Santa Claus, 26, 32-33, 35, 50, 57, 79, 100, 199
Sarah E. Brown, 24, 48, 53, 88, 94, 199
Saranac, 139, 154-155, 170, 211
Saratoga, 20-21, 129
Saxon, 87, 211
Senator Rice, 109, 211
Silas O. Pierce, 58, 88, 108, 199
"Skillypot" (nickname), see *Riverside*
Stirling Tomkins, 143, 150, 159, 161, 184, 193, 211
Sunnyside, 179
Swallow, 21-22
Syracuse, 84, 86, 91, 100, 199
Telegraph, 25-26, 79, 199
Terror, 83, 87, 91, 211
Thomas Chubb, 95, 104, 211
Thomas Cornell (Steamboat), 11, 44, 45, 47, 50, 179-180, 195
Thomas Cornell (1860), 215
Thomas Cornell (1950), 159, 164-166, 211
Thomas Dickson, 91, 125, 184, 211
Thomas P. Fowler, 88, 91, 185, 211
Thomas W. Olcott (Ferry), 214
Thomas Powell, 39, 42, 45
Transport (Ferry), 92-93, 113-114, 117, 150, 180, 214
Triton, 98, 140, 184, 212
Ulster County, 39
Victoria, 93, 139, 212
Victory, 20-21, 24-25
Volunteer, 212
W. A. Kirk, 212
W. B. McCulloch, 95-96, 212
W. E. Cheney, 215
W. E. Street, 88, 125, 184-185, 212
W. N. Bavier, 97, 102, 109, 149, 180, 185-186, 212
Walter B. Crane, 32, 68, 79, 180, 199
Washington, 35, 199
Watchman, 134, 160, 212
William Cook, 48, 59, 79, 195
Wilson P. Foss, 100, 114, 154-155, 160, 212
Wm A. Ballantine, 21
Wm. E. Cleary, 102, 110, 125, 148-149, 160, 180, 185, 186, 213
Wm. H. Baldwin, 120, 141, 154, 170, 213
Wm. S. Earl 69, 77, 88, 91, 131, 160, 213
Woodbridge, 120, 141, 213
Wrestler, 213
York River, 213
[Unnamed TSM Hull 192], 213

GENERAL

Abbey, David, Jr., 26, 35
Abbey, Henry, 94
Alaska Steamship Company, 80
Albany, N.Y., 11, 15, 17-174 *passim*
Albany and Canal Towing Company, 58
Albany and Susquehanna Railroad, 48
Albany *Argus*, 90, 107
Albany, Port of, 138, 155
Albany Towing Co., 95-96, 104, 106-107, 123, 185
Albany Towing Line, 54
Alexander Hamilton Award, 166
Allen, Earl, 157
Allison, Michael, 43
American Association of Masters and Pilots, 86
American Ice Company, 107-108, 139
Anderson family, 39
Anderson, Absalom L., 39-47 *passim*, 67, 69
Anderson, A. Eltinge, 69, 79
Anderson, Charles, 39
Anderson, Romer and Company's Barge and Steamboat Line, 26, 28-31
Anthony's Nose, 143
Appleton's Journal, 22
Arbuckle, John D., 100, 103
Ashokan Reservoir, 102, 128
Athens, N.Y., 111
Atlanta, Ga., 139
Auchincloss, Parker and Redpath, 156
Baisden, John J., 103, 129-130, 180
Baltimore and Ohio Railroad, 167
Banks, Nathaniel, 43, 47
Barber, H. E., 25
Barber, J. Steward, 26
Bard, James and John, 180
Barnett, William B., 110
Barrett, Andrew, 47
Barritt, Newby S., 91, 110, 192
Barritt, Sidney, 192
Barrytown, N.Y., 61
Barry, Wainwright, Thacher and Symmers, 156
Bath, Me., 98, 139
Baton Rouge, Miss., 121
Bayard, Robert M., 59
Bayonne, N.J., 132
Bear Mountain, 134
Bear Mountain Bridge, 71
Belmont, August, 109
Benson, William O., 116, 128-129, 134, 159-160, 181
Beverwyck Towing Company, 54, 86, 90-91, 182
"Binnewaters," 77
Bishop, Edward, 132-133
Bishop, Roland B., 110
Black, James, Jr., 71
Blanchard and Farnham, 91
Blaxlet, Robert, 100
Bloomington, N.Y., 116
Boatmen's Ball, 77
Boston Corners, N.Y., 56
"Breaking of the Ice Gorge, The," 114
Broadway, 72
Brodhead, John C., 54-55
Bronx Towing Line, 182
Brooklyn, N.Y., 44, 87, 100, 132, 170
Brooklyn Bridge, 54, 69

Brooklyn Navy Yard, 159
Bruce, Wallace, 11
Buffalo, N.Y., 36, 155
Buffalo Barge Towing Company, 98
Burlee, W. J., Dry Dock Co., 185
Burroughs, John, 80
"By Hudson's Tide," 94
C. Hildebrant Dry Dock Company, 122, 124, 148, 180
Cahill, Peter, 86, 141
Cahill Towing Company, 120
Callanan Road Improvement Company, 162-163
Camden, N.J., 79
Canada, 46, 130, 134
"Canal Defender," 91
Canal-Lakes Towing Corporation (Calatco), 155
Cashin, William D., 117
Catskill, N.Y., 45-46, 67
Catskill Mountain House, 61, 70
Catskill Mountains, 12, 35, 46, 48, 52, 59, 61, 70, 92, 136
Central-Hudson Steamboat Company, 106, 128, 143, 146
Champlain Canal, 130
Charleston, S.C., 42
Chase National Bank (later Chase Manhattan), 156-157, 160, 162-163, 166, 171, 175-176
Cheney, A. C., 86
Cheney Towing Line, 86-87, 91
Civil War, 11, 37, 42, 46, 55, 74, 79, 95, 104
Cleary Brothers Barge Company, 54
Clinton Point, 13, 16, 152
Cold Spring, N.Y., 71
Coleman, Field and Horton, 91
Colonial Sand and Gravel, 177
Colonial trolley line, 84, 93
Columbia Point, 31
Columbia (College) University, 70, 83, 98, 121, 126, 135, 145-146, 151-166 *passim*, 184
Columbia University Press, 135, 151
Coney Island, 26
Connelly, N.Y., 148
Consolidated Ice Company, 139-141
Consolidated Rosendale Cement Company, 69
Consolidated Steamship Lines, 139-141
Consolidated Towing Line, 93, 132, 139-141
Cook, John B., 117
Cornell & Bidwell, 20
Cornell & Gedney, 17
Cornell, Catherine Ann (Woodmansee), 21, 92-93
Cornell, Cornelia Lucy, 21, 59, 100
Cornell, Hiram Schoonmaker, 179
Cornell, Joseph, 19, 45
Cornell, Peter, 17-19, 28, 42, 179
Cornell, Thomas, 9, 11, 17-127 *passim*; 179, 183, 184, 187
Cornell, Thomas W., 17-19, 25, 27-28
Cornell, William, 35-36, 67

Cornell Steamboat Company, 9, 11, 59-177 *passim*
Cornell Towing Company, 48, 50, 54, 57-59, 86
Cornwall, N.Y., 41, 101
Coxsackie, N.Y., 23, 49
Coykendall, Catherine, 59, 82, 120, 144
Coykendall, Edward, 55, 70, 82, 93, 98, 100, 117-120, 128, 131, 133-137, 144-146, 150-156, 174, 181
Coykendall, Frank, 59, 70, 82, 117, 121, 144, 157, 160, 163, 166, 174, 176, 181, 182
Coykendall, Frederick, 57, 70, 82, 93, 98, 109-110, 116-127, 133, 135-138, 141, 144-146, 150-174 *passim*
Coykendall, George, 56, 59, 90, 93
Coykendall, Harry Shepard, 50, 70, 82-83, 120
Coykendall, Isabell (Hutton), 128, 138, 145
Coykendall, Mary Augusta (Cornell), 21, 37, 47, 57, 80, 82-83, 120, 124, 164
Coykendall, Mary Beach (Warrin), 98, 167, 174, 182
Coykendall, Robert Bayard, 59, 82, 120
Coykendall, Samuel D., 9, 11, 36-167 *passim*, 184
Coykendall, Samuel Decker, Estate of, 181
Coykendall, Thomas Cornell, 48, 70, 82-83, 88, 93, 101-102, 117, 121, 128-131, 144, 154, 168, 183-187
Cranston's Landing, 71
Crowninshield Shipbuilding Company, 161, 186
Culjak, Donald, 174
Culjak, Shirley, 174
Custer, Elizabeth, 80
Custer, George A., 80
D. P. Mapes Steam Freight and Passage Line, 24, 32
Daily Freeman, (of Rondout, later of Kingston) 54-55, 65-67, 88, 93, 101, 104, 107-108, 123, 160
Daily Leader, Kingston, 140
Dakota apartment house, 117, 166
Dalzell, Fred B., 110
Danskammer Point, 62-65, 67
Davis, Alfred, 129
Davis, Ulster, 95-96, 101, 107, 110-111
Dean Witter, 167
Dee, James, 143
Deeper Hudson Program, 12, 130
Delany, P., and Co., 191
Delaware and Hudson Canal, 11, 17-28 *passim*, 32-33, 36, 38, 49, 72, 87, 97, 146, 172, 180
Delaware and Hudson Coal Company, 91, 121
Delaware and Hudson Railway, 60
Delaware River, 11, 17, 20, 44-45
Delaware River Iron Ship and Engine Works, 125
Delaware Valley and Kingston Railroad, 98
Delhi and Middletown Railroad, 52
Dialogue, John H., 79, 125, 184, 191

Dodge, William, 24-26, 28-29
Donovan, M. J., 180
Donovan, Timothy J., 110-113
Dravo Corporation, 14-15, 177
Drew, Daniel, 19, 23-25, 45, 47
Dubois, Jacob W., 29, 47, 68, 88, 104
Dubois, Peter, 32, 179
Duffy, Thomas, 172-174
Dwyer Brothers, 180, 189
East River, 44, 128
East Strand, Rondout, 146
Eastern Steamboat Company, 139
Easton, Asa, 25
Eaton, Howard, 192
Eddyville, N.Y., 17, 20, 25, 87, 148
Edison, Thomas, 69
E. Fitch and Company, 26, 32
Eighmey, D. B., 68
Eisenhower, Dwight D., (U.S. president), 153
Ellenville, N.Y., 120
Erie Canal, 11, 19, 36, 98, 130
Erie Railroad, 28
Esopus, Town of, 33
Esopus Creek, 56, 143
Esopus Island, 53
Esopus Meadows, 105
Everson, Morgan, 16, 21, 125, 184
Fall River, Mass., 143, 161
Farmer's Loan and Trust, 55
Feeney Company (Reliance Marine Construction Co.), 180
Ferry Street, 72, 77, 136, 148, 157, 160, 163
Fiero, Charles, 157, 176, 181
First Baptist Church, Rondout, N.Y., 24, 36, 117
First National Bank of Rondout, 84
Flemming, Harry J., 156-157, 181
Flemming, T.W., 156, 163, 181
Foss, Wilson P. III, 166, 174, 177
Forsyth, "Sandy," 95
Fort Montgomery, 105
Fort Sumter, 42
Fowler, Douglas, 117
Fuller, A. R., Rev., 117
Fulton-Livingston steamboat monopoly, 38, 43
Fulton, Robert, 19, 38, 105, 109, 179
Gage, George, 117
Galveston, Tex., 127
Gaul, Andrew, 185
General Dynamics Corp., Electric Boat Division, 186
Gibbons, Lawrence, 172
Gillespie, Jennette, 92
Gilligan, J. J., 110
Glasco, N.Y., 143
Golgoski, John, 172
Gowanus Towing Co., 182
Grand Hotel, 61, 69-70, 84, 131
Grasselli chemical works, 71
Great Depression, 131, 135-138, 144, 146, 149, 154-155
Great Lakes Dredge and Dock Co., 187
Greenbush, N.Y., 31
Greenkill Park, 136

Greenpoint, N.Y. 13, 44
Greene County, N.Y., 43, 61
Groves, John J., 175
Haines Falls, N.Y., 61
Hamilton College, 151
Hamilton, Mel, 116
Hanley, Patrick, 120
Harlem River, 146, 152
Haverstraw, 43, 49, 61, 116, 177
Hayes, Irving, 111
Henderson, Charles, 171
Hennion, Albert, 61
Herrick, John, 117
Herzog, Catherine Cornell, 181
Herzog, E. Hunt, 120
Hess Oil Company, 171
Hickey, Thomas, 117
Highland, N.Y., 146
Highland Falls, N.Y., 143
Highmount, N.Y., 61
Hiltebrant, Conrad, shipyard, see C. Hiltebrant Dry Dock Company
Hobart Branch Railroad, 61
Hoboken, N.J., 32, 132, 134
Hoff, Benjamin. 127
Honesdale, N.Y., 35
Hornbeck, William B., 172
Horton, John, 33
Hotel Kaaterskill, 61, 70
Hudson, Henry, 105, 109
Hudson-Fulton Celebration, 30, 105, 109-110
Hudson Highlands, 22, 40-41, 143
Hudson, N.Y., 46
Hudson River, 9, 11, 29-35, 38, 45-46, 52, 57, 61, 73, 87, 94, 108, 111, 128-177 passim
Hudson River Bluestone Company, 117, 144
Hudson River Day Line, 46, 51, 93, 121, 123, 136, 146, 181
Hudson River Night Line, 46
Hudson River Railroad, 27, 31, 35
Hudson River Shipyards, Inc. 16, 189
Hudson River Steamboat Company, 51
Hudson River Towing Line, 86
Hughes, Governor Charles Evans, 98
Hussey, William C., 156
Hutton Brick Company, 138
Hyde Park, N.Y., 46, 77
Independent Towing Company, 100, 104
Iona Island, 143
Intercollegiate Rowing Association, 152
International Longshoreman's Union, 138
Interstate Commerce Commission, 100, 156, 162-163
Island Dock, 29, 86, 88, 124, 127-128, 145, 148-149, 159, 180
J. McCausland's Shipyard, 65-66
Jamaica Bay Towing Line, 182
Jeremiah Austin Towing Line, 58, 91
Jersey Central Power and Light, 149
Jungquist, Ivar, 88
Kalaidjian, Edward, 156, 166
Keller, Robert, 185
Kennelly, Frank, 172

Kingston, N.Y., 9, 11, 20, 28-33, 36, 47-50, 57, 60-61, 65, 77, 94, 98, 100, 102, 108, 117, 136-137, 144, 150, 156
Kingston City Library, 144
Kingston City Street Railway, 84
Kingston Club, 101
Kingston fire department, 148
Kingston Hospital, 145
Kingston Museum (The Senate House), 145, 156
Kingston Point, 31, 58, 92-94, 136, 158, 181
Kingston-Rhinecliff Bridge, 150, 171
Kingston Trolley Line, 136
Knickerbocker Ice Company, 87, 139, 141
Knickerbocker Steam Towage Company, 98, 120, 140-141
Krum Elbow, 146
Lackawanna Railroad, 110
Lake Champlain Towing Company, 139-140
Laurel House, 61, 70, 136
Leathem and Smith Towing and Wrecking Co., 185
Leiching, Clark, 13-16
Lenroc Towing Corporation, 176, 182
l'Hommedieu, 110
Lincoln, Abraham, 37, 39, 42, 44, 47
Little Falls, N.Y., 123
Livingston, Chancellor, 38
Lone Star Cement Corporation, 177
Long Island, 132
Long Island Sound, 24, 30
Lotma, Charles, 110
Lynn, John, 135, 146
Mabie, Roger W., 128, 146, 151, 159-160, 180, 181, 185
Mabie, William H., 69, 146, 180
Manitou, N.Y. 71
Mansion House hotel, 33
Mapes, David P., 23-25, 27, 179
"Market, The," 74, 132, 188
Marlborough, N.Y., 64
Marshall, John, 43
Marvel, T. S. and Company, shipyard, 79, 109, 125, 185, 191, 193
Marvel, T. S., Shipbuilding Co., 186
Mary Powell Steamboat Company, 69
Matson, A, 31-32
Matton, John E. and Son, 155
McAllister Brothers, 100, 103, 121, 140-141, 153, 162
McEntee & Dillon's Foundry, 28
McMullen, Andrew, 67
Meeker, Edward, 53
Melville, George W., 110
Metropolitan Steamship Company, 139
Mid-Hudson Bridge, 149
Miller, Jacob W., 110
Milton, N.Y., 129
Miron Building Products Co., 181
Mississippi River, 168, 175
Monahan, James, 105-106
Mohawk River, 111
Montrepose Cemetery, 156
Mooney, Michael, 24
Moran, Eugene F., 110

Moran, Julia C., 110
Moran, Michael, 86, 110, 121
Moran Towing and Transportation Company, 93, 108, 121, 132, 151, 155, 175
Morgan, J. P., Jr., 109
Morse, Charles W., 95, 139-141, 185
Murdock, George, 36, 48, 87, 179
Murdock, James, 104
Nautical Gazette, 53-54, 141
Neafie and Levy, 125, 139, 184
Newark Lime and Cement Company, 33, 45, 49
Newburgh, N.Y., 16, 26, 28, 36, 62, 88, 90-101 passim, 139, 174-175
Newburgh *Daily Journal*, 90
Newburgh *Gazette*, 86, 91
Newcomen, Thomas, 184
New Hamburg, N.Y., 27, 64
New London, Conn., 171
New London Ship and Engine Company (Nelseco), 129-130, 143, 186
New Orleans, 17, 43, 98, 120, 127, 151
New Paltz State Teacher's College, 145, 156
New Salem, N.Y., 17
Newtown Creek Towing Company, 110, 170
New York and Kingston Line, 20, 24
New York and Lake Champlain Towing Company, 90-91, 93
New York and Porto Rico Line, 139
New York Central Railroad, 110, 131
New York City, 11, 17-177 passim
New York Harbor, 15-16, 36, 38, 74, 86-87, 105, 108, 130, 132, 134, 150, 152, 154, 175-176
New York, Kingston and Syracuse Railroad, 55
New York State Barge Canal System, 13, 98, 123, 130, 132-133, 154-155, 170, 187
New York Times, 139, 169
New York Trap Rock Corporation, 12, 15, 100, 104, 132-133, 143, 153, 158, 163, 166, 168, 171-177, 181, 182, 189
New York University, 136
North, Isaac M., 66, 86, 87, 121
North River Construction Company, 61
Nyack, N.Y., 16
120th New York Volunteers ("Washington Guard"), 43
156th New York Volunteers ("Mountain Legion") 43, 47
Oneonta, N.Y., 60
Osterhoudt, John, 143
Oswego, N.Y., 48
Oswego Railroad, 47
Overslaugh sand bar, 111, 113
Paducah, Ky., 175
Panama Canal, 65, 81
Parsell, Abraham, 36
Patterson, Jeremiah, 57
Peary, Robert E., 110
"Pennsylvania" locomotive, 52
Pennsylvania Coal Company, 32-34, 104
People's Line, 45

Perkins, Catherine Murdock (Parsell), 36, 87, 104
Perth Amboy, N.J., 108
Phillips, Patrick, 117
Pier 93, 134
Pine Hill, 61
Planthaber's, 128
Plaza Hotel, 101
Pollack, W. B., 110
Ponckhockie, N.Y., 87, 123
Port Ewen, 12, 16, 33, 49, 53, 58, 66, 69, 75, 77, 79, 83, 86, 100, 105, 116, 124, 129, 143, 146, 151, 160
Port Jervis, N.Y., 11
Portland cement, 12
Poughkeepsie, N.Y., 11, 27, 29, 46, 73, 86, 98, 146, 149-150, 152
Powell, Mary Ludlow, 39
Proffitt, Henry W., 156-157, 160, 163, 166, 174-176
Prohibition, 130, 134
Providence, R.I., 128
Puerto Rico, 121, 141
Puget Sound, 65, 80
Rackham, Arthur, 135
Red Hook Island, 149
Redpath, Albert G, 156-157, 176
Red River campaign, 44
Red Star Towing and Transportation Company, 16, 177, 182
Rensselaer, N.Y., 87, 101, 111-113, 133
Relyea, Aaron, 116
Rhinebeck, N.Y., 46, 61
Rhinebeck and Connecticut Railroad, 52, 56, 59, 61
Rhinebeck and Kingston Ferry Company, 31, 103, 120, 144, 148-150
Rhinecliff, N.Y., 31, 47, 93
Rice, Jacob, 180
Robinson and Betts Troy Towing Line, 54, 58, 91
Rock-Air, Inc., 182
Rockland County, 132
Rockland Lake, 116
Romer, Tremper and Gillette, 32, 35
Romer and Tremper, 39, 44-45, 67
Ronan, Patrick, 139
Ronan Towing Line, 87, 90-93, 98, 139, 180
Rondout and Oswego railroad, 49, 52, 54-55
Rondout *Courier*, 34, 66
"Rondout in the Fifties," poem, 33
Rondout, N.Y., 11, 17-163 *passim*; 177
Rondout Creek, 12, 16-175 passim
Rondout lighthouse, 45, 48, 87-88, 104
Rondout Savings Bank, 49, 84
Rose Brick Company, 100, 186
Rosendale cement, 11, 21, 54, 97-98, 101, 130
Rosendale Consolidated Cement Company, 97, 117
Rothery, John, 117
Roxbury, N.Y., 59
Russell, Fred, 110
S. D. Coykendall Trust, 174-175
Sandy Hook, N.J., 116

Saugerties, N.Y., 64, 69, 79, 143
Schoonmaker, John, 87, 118, 180
Schuyler, Samuel, 52, 86
Schuyler Line Towboat Association, 52, 90-91
Senate House Museum, 180
Shandaken, N.Y., 52
Shultis, Edward T., 181
Sinnott, N.J., 110
Sleight Line, 32
Sleightsburgh, N.Y., 16, 49, 53, 67, 72, 103, 125, 131-130, 134, 148-149, 160
Society of Naval Architects and Marine Engineers, 110
Somerset, Mass., 143
South Rondout, 34, 49, 122, 124
Spangenberger, Clarence W. "Bill," 135-138, 150-153, 157-177, 182
Spangenberger, Lawrence, 136, 158
Sparkman and Stephens, Inc., 179
"Sparks from a Paddlewheel," 53
Springfield, Ill., 47
Spring Street, 36
Spuyten Duyvil, 87
Standard Oil Company of Louisiana, 98, 121, 136, 151, 181, 185
Staten Island, 132
Steam Forwarding and Freight Line, 21
Steuart Transportation Company, 175
Stony Clove and Catskill Mountain Railroad, 61, 70
Stony Point, 143
Storm King Mountain, 134
Sugar Products Shipping Company, 141
Sunflower Dock, 149, 155, 170
Sutton and Suderley, 189
Syracuse University, 146
Taft, William H. (U.S. president), 141
Tappan Zee, 141, 168
Tarrytown, N.Y., 133, 141, 168
Texaco, 121
Thacher, Proffitt, Prizer, Crawley and Wood, 182
Thobea, Charles, 116
Thomas, William duBarry, 159, 181
Thomas W. Cornell and Company, 25-26
Tomkins Cove, 16, 168
Tonight Show, 174
Townsend and Downey, 185
Townsend, R. G., 59, 90
Tremper, Jacob H., 108
Troy, N.Y., 26, 49, 73, 97, 103, 107, 111, 151-152
Tubby, Andrew, 172
Tucker, Michael, 124
Turecame Coastal and Harbor Transp. Co., 182
Twaalfskill County Club, 145
20th New York Militia ("Ulster Guard"), 26, 43
Ulster County, N.Y., 11, 26, 36, 39, 42, 50, 54, 81, 117, 145
Ulster County Historical Society, 145
Ulster and Delaware Railroad, 56, 60-61, 69-70, 83-84, 92-103 *passim*, 117, 120, 124, 128, 131, 136, 144, 156, 174

United States Army, 164
United States Congress, 37, 44, 48, 51
United States Naval Academy, 146
United States Navy, 128
United States Shipping Board, 127, 161, 185, 186, 193
United States Supreme Court, 38, 43, 156, 163
Urban Renewal, 72
Valentine, A. B., 50, 59, 100
Vanderbilt, Cornelius, 19
Vanderlyn, John, 145
Van Keuren, W. S., 71, 169
Van Santvoord, Alfred, 51-52
Vassar College, 84-86
Vlightberg, 49
von Beck, George, 26
Walker, Frank F., 167, 174-176
Walker, Frank (son), 167
Walker, Ursula (Coykendall), 120, 167, 174-176
Wallkill River, 87
Wallkill Valley Railroad, 55-56, 59-61
Wantage, N.J., 36
Ward, Aaron, 110
Ward, Stanton, and Company, 139, 192
Warner, Charles, 88
Warrington, Arthur, 121
Washburn Steamboat Company, 69, 79, 184, 191, 192
Washington, D.C., 42, 47, 61, 175
Waterford, N.Y., 93, 154-155
Watervliet, 160
Wathen, Robert B., 167
Watt, James, 184
Waud, Alfred A., 22
Weehawken, N.J., 36
Westchester County, N.Y., 19
West Chestnut Street, 50, 83, 101, 145
West 53rd Street, 132, 134
West Hurley, 56
Westinghouse Electric and Manufacturing Co., 187
West Point, 86
West Shore Railroad, 51, 60-61, 67, 86, 146
White Plains, N.Y., 19
White Star Line, 110
Whiteport, 122
Whitlock, Elisha S., 44
Whitman, Walt, 80
Wilbur, N.Y., 26, 28, 32, 57, 87
Wilbur, Henry, 25
Wilde, Oscar, 80
Wilkinson, Robert M., 159
Wilmington, Del., 15
Witte, John, 193
Woodmansee, Mary Catherine (Snyder), 21
World War I, 121, 143-144
World War II, 128, 149, 152, 155
Wright and Cobb Lighterage, Inc., 189
Wurts Street, 35-36
Young, Coe F., 35, 97

Biographical Notes

C. W. Spangenberger

C. W. "Bill" Spangenberger, the last president of the Cornell Steamboat Company, was employed by Cornell from 1933-63. A graduate of New York University and a native of Kingston, New York, Spangenberger started his career with Cornell as a collector, and as the years went by he was put in charge of the engineers, oilers, and firemen of the tugs, later becoming assistant to the president, Frederick Coykendall. Spangenberger subsequently became general manager and then executive vice president, named president of the Cornell Steamboat Company in 1954, upon the death of Coykendall.

Spangenberger continued as president of Cornell when it became a wholly owned subsidiary of New York Trap Rock Corporation; he also served as director of transportation of the parent corporation with responsibilities that included the deck scow fleet of some 300 scows. He was also vice president and general manager of another of Trap Rock's wholly owned subsidiaries--Rock-Air, Inc., a helicopter company that provided the company with transportation and made aerial surveys of the Hudson River. Spangenberger also became director of real estate for the Trap Rock Corporation, responsible for the sale and development of hundreds of acres around the corporation's quarries.

In 1963, Trap Rock went out of the towing business when it was acquired by Martin Marietta and Lone Star Industries, and Spangenberger soon afterward joined Associated Industries of New York State in the member-relations department. By the time he retired eleven years later, Spangenberger had been executive assistant to the president, director of member relations, and secretary of the corporation. He is a founding director of the Hudson River Maritime Museum, Kingston, New York, and has served as the museum board's vice president. With his wife, Kay, he was a founder of the Catskill Mountain 3500 Club, a hiking organization.

Roger W. Mabie

Roger W. Mabie is the grandson of a Hudson River pilot and captain, and during his college-year summers he worked on steamers of the Hudson River Day Line. A native of Port Ewen, New York, Mabie is a past president of the Steamship Historical Society of America. He holds a B.S. degree from Syracuse University and an M.B.A. from Harvard Business School.

During World War II, Mabie served in the United States Navy and was the commanding officer of a submarine chaser, a convoy escort vessel; he was on his way to take command of a destroyer transport when the war ended. He left the Navy with the rank of lieutenant commander. He also has sailed as a mate on ships of the American Export Line.

Mabie is a member and former chairman of the Board of Trustees of Ulster County Community College, a former supervisor of the Town of Esopus, and minority leader of both the Ulster County Board of Supervisors and the Ulster County Legislature. He is also a former member of the Board of Trustees of the Albany Savings Bank and numerous civic organizations.

William duBarry Thomas

William duBarry Thomas is a naval architect and maritime historian who has had a long love affair with the Hudson River. A lifelong interest in the Cornell Steamboat Company developed in the 1930s when he first saw *Geo. W. Washburn* and *Perseverance* towing on the river with huge flotillas of barges on the hawser. After graduation from Webb Institute of Naval Architecture in 1951, his career path first took him to Rondout Creek, where he was a naval architect with Island Dock, Inc., on the site of the D&H Canal Company's coal entrepôt. A later affiliation with a firm of naval architects, J. J. Henry Company, Inc., led him to worldwide assignments until 1986, after which he became a consultant in naval architecture.

He is a life member and past president of The Steamship Historical Society of America. His attraction to the river, Rondout Creek, and Cornell remains undiminished in that he is a member of the board of trustees of the Hudson River Maritime Museum in Kingston, New York. In addition, he is a Life Fellow of The Society of Naval Architects and Marine Engineers, and his great-grandfather, Thomas S. Marvel, was the builder of thirteen tugs owned by the Cornell Steamboat Company.